D0501288

Managing Sport and Leisure Facilities

JOIN US ON THE INTERNET VIA WWW, GOPHER, FTP OR EMAIL:

WWW: http://www.thomson.com
GOPHER: gopher.thomson.com
FTP: ftp.thomson.com
EMAIL: findit@kiosk.thomson.com

A service of I(T)P

OTHER TITLES FROM E & F N SPON

Leisure and Recreation Management
3rd Edition
G Torkildsen

Private and Commercial Recreation
2nd Edition
Edited by A F Epperson

Special Events
The art and science of celebration
J J Goldblatt

Arts Administration
J Pick

Recreation and Leisure
An introductory handbook
A Graefe and S R Parker

The Golf Course
Planning, design, construction and management
F W Hawtree

Grounds Maintenance
A contractor's guide to competitive tendering
P Sayers

Spon's Grounds Maintenance Contract Handbook
R M Chadwick

Spon's Landscape and External Works Price Book
Published annually
Edited by Derek Lovejoy and Partners and Davis Langdon & Everest

Fungal Diseases of Amenity Turf Grasses
3rd Edition
J Drew Smith, N Jackson and A R Woolhouse

For more information about these and other titles published by us,
please contact:
The Promotion Dept., E & FN Spon, 2–6 Boundary Row, London SE1 8HN

Managing Sport and Leisure Facilities

A guide to competitive tendering

Philip Sayers

WITHDRAWN

AUG 2 6 2020

UNBC Library

E & FN SPON

An Imprint of Chapman & Hall

London · New York · Tokyo · Melbourne · Madras

Chapman & Hall, 2–6 Boundary Row, London SE1 8HN, UK

Chapman & Hall GmbH, Pappelallee 3, 69469 Weinheim, Germany

Chapman & Hall USA, 115 Fifth Avenue, New York, NY 10003, USA

Chapman & Hall Japan, ITP-Japan, Kyowa Building, 3F, 2-2-1 Hirakawacho, Chiyoda-ku, Tokyo 102, Japan

Chapman & Hall Australia, 102 Dodds Street, South Melbourne, Victoria 3205, Australia

Chapman & Hall India, R. Seshadri, 32 Second Main Road, CIT East, Madras 600 035, India

First edition 1991
Reprinted 1997

© 1991 Philip Sayers

Typeset in 10 $^1/_2$ on 12pt Palatino by Mews Photosetting, Beckenham, Kent

Printed in Great Britain by
Athenæum Press Ltd, Gateshead, Tyne & Wear

ISBN 0 419 17350 1 USA

Apart from any fair dealing for the purposes of research or private study, or criticism or review, as permitted under the UK Copyright Designs and Patents Act, 1988, this publication may not be reproduced, stored or transmitted, in any form or by any means, without the prior permission in writing of the publishers, or in the case of reprographic reproduction only in accordance with the terms of the licences issued by the Copyright Licensing Agency in the UK, or in accordance with the terms of licences issued by the appropriate Reproduction Rights Organization outside the UK. Enquiries concerning reproduction outside the terms stated here should be sent to the publishers at the UK address printed on this page.

The publisher makes no representation, express or implied, with regard to the accuracy of the information contained in this book and cannot accept any legal responsibility or liability for any errors or omissions that may be made.

British Library Cataloguing in Publication Data

Sayers, Philip
  Managing sport and leisure facilities: A guide to
  competitive tendering.
  I. Title
  790.06

  ISBN 0-419-17350-1

Library of Congress Cataloging-in-Publication Data

Sayers, Philip.
      Managing sport and leisure facilities : a guide to
competitive
      tendering / Philip Sayers.
          p. cm.
      ISBN 0-442-31477-9
      1. Sports facilities–Great Britain–Management. 2.
Leisure
      industry–Great Britain–Management. 3. Contracts for
      work and labor–Great Britain. I. Title.
      GV433.G7S29   1991
      796.'06'80941–dc20   91-13774
                                                            CIP

Contents

Preface

The amendments to the Local Government Act, 1988, accelerated the move towards more commercial operation of public sector leisure facilities. The government believed that much greater attention was needed to ensure that leisure facilities operated at least cost and maximum value.

Gone are the days when local authorities could undertake the provision and management of leisure facilities without the fullest regard to the cost and income associated with these facilities.

These guidelines provide a step by step approach to competitive management. The book begins with the reasons why this change in emphasis has occurred, which is not solely due to government edict. It then discusses competitive tendering and how to prepare a tender, both from the point of view of a client and of a contractor. The book further concentrates on practical operational management and methods for providing the best possible service to the widest range of customers. It concludes with an assessment of quality assurance and profitable marketing systems.

The author is a practising leisure and amenity manager and a member of the Institute of Leisure and Amenity Management/Institute of Baths and Recreation Management joint working party on sports and leisure management. The author is grateful for the information and assistance given in the preparation of this book, particularly to those listed in the acknowledgements and reference section at the end.

Whilst every care has been taken in researching and preparing the book, the author offers the information for guidance only, without creating any legal liability. He would welcome any comments.

The male pronoun is used in the book. This is for ease of reading and should be taken to mean both male and female individuals.

Chapter One

Background to leisure management

The pressures in the 1990s for provision of efficient and effective leisure facilities are most easily understood when set in their historical perspective.

EARLY DEVELOPMENTS

The provision of public leisure facilities stems from the cholera-ridden years of the early Victorian period. The Victorians, alerted to their insanitary lifestyle, set about improving their environment in many ways. The municipal corporations and local authorities in particular were to provide the most significant advancements in health and hygiene. They developed a preoccupation with sanitation, it is true, but much more as well.

Public parks were provided for air and exercise (principally on Sundays) and wash-houses were built for the more important essentials of everyday living. The management of these facilities was little different from the management of factories. People did as they were told. This even extended to the absurdity of not walking on the grass. This formidable authoritative approach was to be associated with public leisure management for far too long.

Public halls were also constructed. They came to be associated with the most extravagant gesture of the times – the provision of elaborate and ornate town halls. These were a lasting tribute, perhaps, to the pride of Victorian municipalities. They were, however, hardly places for workers to frequent.

Physical recreation

During the next century, especially in the 1930s, a considerable

upsurge in the provision of recreation facilities took place. This
took many forms. Lavish cinemas provided escape from reality for
many: and a worthwhile commercial return for a few. Outside,
private tennis clubs, public outdoor swimming pools, and greater
access to the countryside were some of the principal milestones of
the era.

Fig. 1.1 Walking on the grass was not allowed.

Physical recreation outdoors took on a new meaning, with great
interest in sports and physical fitness. After much public agitation,
the industrial populations of the north eventually gained access to
the moors and mountains surrounding their towns. Strolls in the public
parks were no longer sufficient for their needs.

This new wave of interest in physical fitness found expression in
the 1930s 'Keep Fit' campaign. A minister of health at the time called
it 'the new movement for the improvement of the national physique'.
The movement culminated in the passing of the Physical Training and
Recreation Act of 1937.

This was complemented by the King George V commemoration
fund, which helped finance the provision of so many playing fields
up and down the country.

During the wartime years of the 1940s there was understandably
a reduction in leisure provision and use, with the exception perhaps
of the cinema. The great social reforms of the mid and late 40s asociated
with the Labour government of the time, quite rightly concentrated
on education, health, social security and planning.

Traditional management

This led to the situation in the 1950s where the leisure facilities in use were those of the 1930s, but aged with time.

The municipal baths and halls were still operated along traditional lines. For a small charge, they were available for all to use, or not to use, as they pleased. Management was, at best, passive; at worst, authoritarian. The management of the day provided for those who attended, they kept order, and that was all.

That was seen to be sufficient. It was unnecessary to promote services to a wider cross section of the community. The municipal swimming pools were still all too often concentrating on the provision of baths and laundry facilities, from which many had originated. Likewise the grass in parks was for 'keeping off'.

The civic leaders of the day no doubt knew all too well the need for a period of calm and stability. Moreover the civic purse had to provide for more elementary necessities. The first priority in the public sector was to repair and refurbish the basic infrastructure. Bombed sites and slums were demolished in favour of new housing; trams gave way to buses; and smog clogged cities slowly cleared as cleaner air filtered in through the imposition of the smoke control regulations.

As regards municipal leisure, the provision of public entertainments was perhaps the beginning of the change. The very act of putting on an entertainment event demanded a full house to pay for the costs associated with the production. Much publicity was in order. Management just could not be passive.

Promotions

Entertainments were not only promoted in the many halls throughout the land. They were also, surprisingly, promoted in swimming pools during the winter. Pools were drained in the autumn, filled with specially formed scaffolding, and then a temporary floor was laid on top. Thus the pool was converted into a makeshift auditorium. Many a rendition of *The Messiah* was heard in the chamber of a swimming pool hall. The acoustics had to be heard to be believed. But such experiences were soon to be swept into the archives of people's memories.

A sudden change in leisure took place in the 1950s. This time it was the private sector who led. A new kind of dancehall sprang up in every town. Being young was never to be the same again, once Bill Haley and the Comets had brought 'Rock around the

the Clock' to town. Ballroom dancing was all but swept away. The leisure revolution had begun.

Fig. 1.2 Ballroom dancing was all but swept away.

LEISURE REVOLUTIONS

The 1960s saw a leisure explosion. The five-day working week at last arrived. Money in the pocket, coupled with time to spend, it led to a wave of leisure activities. They were affluent years, and yet anxious too, in terms of world tension. Nevertheless, the thrust of leisure in the 1960s was towards the individual. Most people had the time and money to choose their own leisure pursuits.

In the early 1960s the public sector was still prepared to make only a relatively small contribution to the increasing demand for leisure. This tended to be on relatively traditional lines. New ash running tracks and new rectangular swimming pools began to appear. It was only later in the decade that some of the obsolete buildings were demolished. Sometimes one excellent new leisure facility would be provided instead of say three or four old and dilapidated swimming baths which had existed previously.

Public sector expansion

In the 1970s the increasing leisure time available led to a second major leisure revolution. This time, public authorities were more prepared to spend large capital sums in providing worthwhile facilities for local residents. The trend began with one or two multipurpose leisure centres, especially in the North East of England. Others quickly followed. The suddenness of the revolution was equalled only by the scale of provision. Multipurpose leisure centres suddenly appeared almost everywhere.

Then, just as the boom seemed to be past its peak, it received a significant boost from, of all things, local government reorganization. Many small local authorities were swept away in the local government reorganization of 1974. Keen to provide for the residents in their own particular small locality in the future, many authorities spent up all their financial reserves before they disappeared, often on additional local leisure facilities. Some authorities signed building contracts on their last day in existence. The Victorians would have readily understood this form of civic pride.

Sports halls, leisure centres, swimming pools and entertainment complexes were all added to the leisure fabric of the nation.

Some of the new local authorities were financially embarassed by this legacy. Others continued the trend. These authorities provided larger facilities nearer to the centre of the new authority. The hope was that this would help emphasize the importance of the authority, and furthermore attract a wider proportion of the local population.

New management

These complex facilities demanded a different breed of manager. Many committed and skilful people changed career, and a whole new profession of leisure management was born. The new managers in their turn were quick to attract a new range of customers into sports activities.

The leisure revolution was an outstanding public success. Spurred on by this success, more facilities were added by the year and more new managers were appointed to increase use still further.

But in the 1980s the downturn in the economy seriously affected these subsidized facilities. The buildings themselves started to need substantial capital expenditure for renewal and refurbishment. The heavy wear and tear of a decade was all too evident. Regrettably, the finance was often not available.

Such concerns did not affect the private sector. If the 1970s had belonged to the local authorities; then the private sector seemed determined to claim the winner's prize for innovation in the 1980s.

Lions at Longleat were by now tame tourist attractions. The new thrust was to provide theme parks on a grand scale. Grand scale meant high finance and high commercial risk. Some theme parks stayed the course, a few paid with inevitable bankruptcy. Inside, there was a dramatic revival in ice skating and tenpin bowling; even indoor cricket gained a toehold in the leisure market.

Despite the few bankruptcies, the private sector leisure provision of the 1980s was an outstanding success. Their radically different approach to promotional techniques was very evident. By the 1990s, this approach was to be focused on local authority leisure facilities. But for most of the earlier decade, the public sector was, quite rightly, trying hard to address social inequality.

MARKET DIFFERENTIATION

The leisure revolution of the 1970s had led to increased use by the wealthier sectors of society. Perversely, their increased use was subsidized as well. To try to balance this social trend and to address the rapidly increasing unemployment of the early 1980s, many authorities introduced a wide range of concessionary fees and charges. The unemployed and other disadvantaged groups were encouraged to use the facilities at reduced cost, and in some areas at no charge at all.

But local authorities found that charging less to the unemployed and other disadvantaged groups did not work. This fairly crude attempt at market differentiation was often insufficient to attract these minority groups. The stigma attached to attending the leisure centre at offpeak times was often worse than not going at all.

Some centres therefore actively pursued a more positive marketing policy. A very real attempt was made to identify the non-users, and to address the reasons why certain groups of people were not using the facilities.

The introduction of women-only bathing sessions provided a good example of positive marketing. Too often, public bathing had been provided for all groups of people and all age groups at all times. At last this was identified as a significant deterrent to many groups of potential customers. By providing separate sessions for specific groups, such as women, competitive swimmers, and ethnic groups, a start was made in redressing the balance. The Sports Council mounted a number of sustained campaigns to promote activities to specific social groups, such as the over-50s.

Despite these initiatives, leisure centres still tended to attract the majority of custom from the higher socio-economic groups. Ironically, those who could have afforded to pay more were enjoying paying less.

RISE OR FALL

Over the years the bureaucracy of local government had also stamped its mark on leisure management. Local government (contrary to popular belief) is excellent at innovation and change. It is not always so good at the plain administration of existing facilities. The 1980s saw local authorities' attention diverted to the all-important task of economic rejuvenation. Positive approaches to improved leisure provisions could wait.

Leisure centres were not necessarily attracting the high level of usage which the size and cost of the premises demanded. The game of squash, for example, the very heartland of many leisure centres, began to decline in popularity. Some authorities could not find the finance to change a few courts to different uses.

Worse, some leisure centres began to resemble the municipal baths from which they had sprung. A new impetus was needed to revitalize and rejuvenate not only leisure facilities, but also the benefits to the users.

Only as flumes and leisure pools were introduced was there any significant increase in usage. These proved to be the essential magnet which could attract a range of family groups to leisure centres and swimming pools.

Otherwise, too many centres began to show their age and lose their appeal. It was often difficult for local authorities to justify high capital expenditure on renewing and improving leisure centres, instead of undertaking a range of other, more compelling, actions with their limited financial resources.

THE POLITICAL DIMENSION

With economy and efficiency becoming the theme tune for the 1980s, a few local authorities set about subjecting their direct works organizations to competitive tender.

Tenders for maintenance . . .

Companies interested in providing traditional maintenance services
such as refuse collection were invited to tender a bid, and the company
offering the lowest price was awarded the contract.

The results were spectacular. Services were often provided at a
higher quality and lower cost by private sector contractors. There were
also a number of dramatic failures.

Nevertheless, improving services by introducing an element of
competition fitted the philosophy of the Conservative government of
the time.

The government was particularly concerned by the inefficient way,
in their perception, in which local authorities were delivering public
services. As early as 1980, an Act of Parliament compelled local
authorities to seek value for money. This was in fairly traditional
maintenance areas of local authority works, such as highways and
housing.

. . .and leisure centres too

At the same time, without any government pressure, a small number
of public authority leisure centres were handed over to the private
sector to be managed and maintained. A few companies started
specializing in this area of work. Again, the results were generally
impressive.

By the middle of the decade, the government was considering a
major extension to the 1980 Act. They were determined that local
authorities should provide services at the least possible cost. In view
of the relative success of a small number of leisure contracts, it was
reasoned that perhaps leisure management could be treated in the
same way as the local authority maintenance services.

THE LOCAL GOVERNMENT ACT 1988

One of the major thrusts of this Act was to introduce competitive
tendering into the provision of many more local government services.
These included vehicle maintenance, grounds maintenance, refuse
collection, street cleansing and building cleaning. Catering was also
added.

The late inclusion of leisure management in the parliamentary Bill
met with a hostile response from local authorities. More surprisingly,

the proposal to require local authorities to seek tenders in leisure management received a lukewarm reaction from the private sector. One major national leisure operator stated publicly that they would not be tendering for local authority services.

As the parliamentary timetable could not be delayed, the Act went ahead without specific reference to leisure management. Further consultations were undertaken. However, the Act was an enabling Act. The Secretary of State for the environment could add more defined services, at any time, with the approval of parliament.

Statutory instruments

Following further consultations, leisure management was formally incorporated into the provisions of the 1988 Act. The statutory instrument (reproduced as an addendum to this chapter) announced the formal ending of some years of hesitation.

However, leisure management was entirely different from the other services which had been subjected to compulsory competitive tendering. All the earlier services related to maintenance. Management is something quite different to maintenance. Nevertheless, local authorities were required to submit their leisure management and catering functions to tender during 1992. To many local authorities, the issues relating to the tender and tendering of leisure management contracts appeared daunting.

This was surprising. Many local authorities had already operated some form of tender in leisure outlets, especially catering. It was perhaps the scale that now gave cause for concern. Also, some local authorities with affectionate regard for their leisure facilities, feared that these facilities were to be taken away from them. They confused compulsory competitive tendering with privatization.

Competitive tendering

Privatization means that a business and all its premises and assets are sold to a private bidder or bidders. This is not the case with a competitive tender. Ownership is unchanged.

The principal change with a competitive tender is that the operation of the service is undertaken by the person who wins the tender by offering the lowest bid. The next chapter examines tendering in more detail.

SUMMARY

The provision of public facilities began with the Victorians and, as with so much of the Victorian era, leisure management styles lasted far beyond their day. Dogmatic management had a life all of its own. Some innovation did occur however, in the most odd places.

Fig. 1.3 The rendition of The Messiah in the swimming pool hall had to be heard to be believed.

The 1960s and 1970s saw both private and public sectors change radically into dynamic and responsive industries. The leisure era had arrived. A game of leapfrog seemed to develop between the two sectors. The 1960s belonged to the private sector and the individual. The 1970s was the turn for local councils who vied with each other to provide better leisure opportunities for their residents.

The early 1980s was a time of general economic restraint. Nevertheless, the decade was notable for the introduction of water-based leisure facilities and theme parks. There were of course many other developments but the changes mentioned in this chapter highlight the principal developments which affected management styles.

The 1990s provides a coming together of the approach to leisure provision by the two sectors. The Local Government Act 1988 as amended, will ensure a much more commercial attitude to leisure management in the public sector. To survive, the public sector will adopt the philosophy of the private sector and seek to maximize income wherever possible. Contract failures will be something new, and difficult to handle initially.

For the private sector, it will be a radical change even to consider submitting tenders for leisure management ventures. Apart from catering, leisure contract management has not been commonplace. However, everyone within leisure will slowly come to adopt similar attitudes and management methods.

Addendum: The 1988 Act. Amended

This addendum provides the principal aspects of the Statutory Instrument (1989: No.2488), by which by which the government added sports and leisure management to the Act. It is reproduced with the permission of the Controller of Her Majesty's Stationery Office.

1. The order extends the activities which must be put out to tender by local authorities under the Local Government Act 1988. The activities include managing facilities for sports and leisure but do not include educational facilities or facilities such as village halls or community centres not used predominantly for sports. The Order adds a new defined activity of 'managing sports and leisure facilities' to section 2(2) (ee) of the Local Government Act 1988. It also adds a new paragraph 8 to Schedule 1 of the Act setting out a definition of the activity. It brings the requirements of sections 4 and 5 of the 1988 Act into effect in respect of the works contracts for managing sports and leisure facilities.

2. Managing any of the following facilities now falls within the Local Government Act 1988:
    (a) swimming pools, skating rinks, gymnasia;
    (b) tennis courts, squash courts, badminton courts, pitches for team games, athletics grounds;
    (c) tracks and centres for bicycles (whether motorized or not), golf courses, putting greens, bowling greens, bowling centres, bowling alleys;
    (d) riding centres, courses for horse racing, artificial ski slopes, centres for flying, ballooning or parachuting, and centres for boating or water sports on inland or coastal waters.

3. Managing any of the facilities described above shall not fall within the Act if the facilities are provided:

(a) on premises not predominantly used for sport or physical recreation

(b) on premises occupied by educational institutions

4. Managing any of the facilities described above shall not fall within the Act
   (a)　if that facility is provided
   　(i) in England or Wales under Section 53 of the Education Act 1944(a) (whether or not also provided under section 41 of that Act) and whether or not also provided under section 19 of the Local Government (Miscellaneous Provisions) Act 1976(b); or
   　(ii) in Scotland under section 6 or 17 of the Education (Scotland) Act 1980(c), whether or not also provided under section 15(2) of the Local Government and Planning (Scotland) Act 1982(d); and
   (b)　(i) where the facility is on premises on which no other facility described in sub-paragraph (1) is provided, if educational institutions have used it exclusively in the immediately preceding financial year for more than 600 hours; or
   　(ii) where the facility is on the premises on which two or more of the facilities described in sub-paragraph (1) are provided, if educational institutions have used exclusively in the immediately preceding financial year facilities of at least half of the descriptions provided (whether concurrently or at different times) and the aggregate periods of their exclusive use in that year of the facilities so described exceeds 600 hours.

5. The term 'managing' includes arranging
   (a) for instruction in the sport or other physical recreational activity provided;
   (b) for supervision of the sport or activity;
   (c) catering;
   (d) the hiring out of equipment for use at the facility;
   (e) the marketing and promotion of the facility;
   (f) the taking of bookings;
   (g) the collection of, and accounting for, fees and charges;
   (h) the physical security of the premises;
   (i) the cleaning and proper maintenance of the facility other than the external parts of buildings;
   and also includes assuming responsibility for heating, lighting and other service charges in relation to the facility.

6. Educational institutions:
   (a) in England and Wales, means schools which are county or
       voluntary schools, or special schools, maintained by the local
       authority; and institutions for the provision of higher or further
       education, or both, which are either maintained by the local
       education authority or are substantially dependent for their
       maintenance on assistance from the local education authority;
       and
   (b) in Scotland, means public schools, or special schools, under
       the management of the local education authority and any other
       institutions provided and maintained by the education auth-
       ority for the provision of further education; and
   (c) in England, Wales and Scotland, for the purposes of
       sub-paragraph (2)(b) only, includes nursery schools.

These details were supplemented by Statutory Instrument 1990: No.
1564, which provides for phasing of the work to be submitted to
tender (in tranches of 35% and 30%).

Chapter Two

Client contract preparations

The only guaranteed way of ensuring that services are provided at least cost is by means of a competitive tender.

This method will not necessarily achieve the best value, or even the most competent service. It may, or it may not. But it will certainly achieve the least cost.

In a theoretical free market, the prices of goods and services are established in the marketplace between a willing seller and a willing buyer. This method has worked well in all civilizations since the days of the Greek Empire. However, such methods are hardly suited to our current state of technological advance. Open competitive tenders provide the nearest alternative.

In fact, seeking competitive tenders is the principal method used by many organizations for the cost effective provision of goods and services.

In the 1990s, public sector leisure management services are being subject to compulsory competitive tender for the first time (as outlined in the addendum to Chapter One). The tenders may be for a total service (for example a swimming pool or a leisure centre); or for a part service (for example, catering within a leisure centre may be a separate tender).

COMPULSORY COMPETITIVE TENDERING

Local authorities are required by law to advertize for, and seek, competent persons interested in tendering for their leisure management operations.

At the time the advertisement appears, copies of the specifications stating how the leisure facilities are to be managed will be freely available to be read in the authority offices or for purchase.

The method

The tendering process can be seen simply in the following steps:

1. The local authority advertizes its intention to let a leisure management contract and invites interested persons to contact its offices.
2. The local authority assesses the relative abilities of those applying.
3. A shortlist of competent contractors is compiled.
4. Those on the shortlist are then invited to tender: in other words, they are invited to offer (or tender) their bid for managing the facility.
5. On receipt of the returned tenders, the local authority will determine the best bid, and award the contract.

The contract documents and specifications prepared by the authority form the basis of everything to do with the tendering procedure and the subsequent contract.

Key terms

Before looking further at tenders and contracts, it is worth listing a few of the more common terms used;

- **contract documentation**
  This is the package of documents supplied by the authority which details all the leisure management requirements of the authority, and how the management and maintenance operations will be carried out and controlled.
- **the tenderer**
  This is the person (or company) who completes the tender and returns it to the authority (for example, a catering contractor).
- **the tender**
  The actual bid made by the tenderer, in accordance with the contract documentation and the tendering instructions.
- **the contractor**
  The tenderer who submits the winning tender bid and is awarded the contract (and thus becomes the contractor).
- **the client**
  The local authority (and its officers) who award and run the contract.

In the next part of the chapter, the basis of the contract is analysed. A brief outline of all the component parts of a contract are provided in Appendix A, at the back of the book.

THE CONTRACT DOCUMENTATION

The contract documentation comprises much more than just the specifications. The specifications will set out what is to be done, but they are quite useless without legal enforcement and all the other integrated aspects of the contract.

A contractor needs to see all the contract documents to be able adequately to price a tender bid. Therefore the client provides all the documents detailed in Appendix A at the time of the tender. At the time of the tender bid, they can be referred to as the draft contract documents. They become the contract documents when both parties sign the legal agreement binding themselves to the contract.

The tendering instructions

These are the simplest part of the document. They simply state how, when and where the tender is to be submitted. The usual method is to submit the completed tender to the authority in a plain sealed envelope by a stated date and time (often noon).

All tenders should be submitted early; even one minute is too late. Late tenders will be declared null and void. It is essential that all tenders are opened at the same time and that the value of all tenders is declared.

The conditions of contract

This section is much more substantial (and can be overwhelming). These conditions need very careful reading, for the winning contractor will be bound by them for the duration of the contract. They set out in quasi-legal form the conditions which will be used to control the contract and will be referred to if there should be a dispute.

At the early stage of expressing an interest in a contract, there is no need to seek legal advice, provided that the conditions are understandable. However, expert legal advice is essential when the time arrives to submit a tender. It is then always advisable for a solicitor with relevant previous experience to be involved.

It is also important to establish legal charges at the outset. The principal advice is to be economical with the (expensive) time of legal and other professionals. This is equally valid for the public sector contractor seeking to submit a bid and for the private contractor. The familiar adage 'check cost before commitment' is an excellent rule.

The conditions of contract are the terms by which the local authority will enforce the contract. Local authorities need to give themselves adequate powers of control over such things as:

- insurance and indemnity
- an adequate financial bond from a third party to safeguard the performance of the contract
- default and penalty procedures
- termination clauses
- provision for annual inflation increases
- and a host of other matters

From the contractor's point of view, these conditions will influence working methods and costings, so it is vitally important to assess the extent of their impact. Anyone submitting a bid needs to ensure that they will be able to comply with all the conditions. The winning contractor will be bound by them.

The specifications

The next section of the contract document will most likely be the specifications. Quite simply, these will specify how the facilities will be operated. Here will be itemized all the familiar leisure management operations to be carried out. The specification will also establish the principcal features of a particular leisure management package. These will include:

- the fees and charges approved by the client for entry to and use of the facilities
- social prices to be charged (for example concessionary fees for the unemployed)
- general policies to be achieved (for example 60 per cent casual use, 40 per cent club use)
- hours of opening

The specifications are invariably the largest section of the contract documents.

Preparing the contract documentation and specifications means a huge amount of work for the client. Successful contracts depend on all relevant details which will affect a contractor's bid being fully stated by the client.

Details in the specifications will include, for example, plans of the leisure centre or swimming pool, the floor area of each room, the cleaning schedules required, the catering requirements and a mass of other information.

The client will also usually provide an indication of the demographic nature of the locality, and catchment area. Also of critical importance to any tenderer is an indication of the recent annual income and usage, from say the last three years.

Client control. . .

However, the extent to which specifications actually provide masses of detail vary greatly. Some specifications run to thousands of pages, others a few hundred only.

The amount of detail is a positive reflection of the degree of control sought by the client. There is a long history to contract management in many other disciplines. Here the importance of detailing every single item within the contract has been learnt the hard way, by something going wrong.

Other tenders are much more modest in the information which they supply. This may merely indicate that the client authority has been left with insufficient time to prepare an adequate specification.

. . . or contractor latitude

Alternatively, a brief specification can be a clear indication by an authority that it wishes to allow the successful contractor the maximum degree of latitude to increase use and income. Such authorities believe that tenders are best when the amount of detail is limited to that essential information which is necessary to provide a fair basis for a contractor to cost.

Other authorities take the view that the leisure facilities have been provided by the local community and that continued close control is essential. Specifications from these authorities are detailed.

This fundamental difference in attitude was recognised by the Institute of Leisure and Amenity Management (ILAM) and the Institute of Baths and Recreation Management (IBRM). They jointly produced a guideline document, *Management of Sports and Leisure Facilities*, published by Longman. The document provides alternative clauses for many situations.

It is possible for a client to select from this document a tight specification with maximum control, or a more basic specification allowing greater freedom to the contractor. The addendum to this chapter provides an extract from the publication which has been so instrumental in setting the industry standards for contract management.

Fig. 2.1 Size of documents = degree of control.

Performance

Leisure management specifications will be a combination of performance based specifications and method based specifications.

The client authority wishing to retain maximum control of its own facilities will often provide exact details of the methods to be used in operating the contract. Such details will include the type and timing of the cleaning to be undertaken in each and every room and corridor and even a painting and refurbishment schedule. This is often called a 'method based' type of contract. In theory, all the necessary methods are stated for adequate service delivery.

A contract in which methods of management and maintenance are not detailed may be a 'performance based' contract. In these contracts, the client requires certain performance targets to be achieved. For example, a throughput of 100 000 juniors at a neighbourhood swimming pool during any one year may be required. The performance target provides both the basis of the contract and the method for its evaluation.

Another example may help explain the difference. If a contract required a room to be heated to a specific temperature, then this is a performance based specification. Providing exact details of how a boiler should be operated to achieve that temperature is clearly a method based specification.

LEGAL FORMALITIES

There are a number of formal legal requirements before a leisure management contract can be operated. In addition to the contract between the client authority and the contractor, the contractor will need, for example, a variety of licences.

Licences

Where alcohol is to be served, the necessary Justices Licence for the sale of alcohol will have to be transferred from the current licensee.

Gaming and amusement machine licences and permits may also be necessary. Control is strict and detailed though actual arrangements for licensing vary from area to area, and also between facilities. For example, where a facility does not serve alcohol, then the permit for gaming and amusement machines is issued by the local licensing authority. In most counties, the local licensing authority is the county or district council. It is also the local licensing authority which will consider applications for a Public Entertainment Licence.

Apart from the licences and the client's conditions, there are other essential rules and regulations which demand total compliance. Examples include the Fire Certificate and food hygiene legislation. Leisure management is always a complex affair.

Use of the premises

Very clear responsibilities will be laid down in relation to the basis of the tenure. Very few contracts will allow the contractor to lease the premises; there are just too many legal difficulties involved in regaining possession. Furthermore, virtually no contract will allow the successful contractor to 'sell on' or assign the contract (in whole or part) to another contractor.

As well as all the standard clauses to be expected in a complex tender document, there will be many clauses which appear odd to a contractor entering leisure management from the private sector.

Full and free use of a leisure centre may be required for the annual Mayor-making ceremony, or for election results. These may puzzle a private sector contractor initially. However, such events are as important to a public sector organization as profit is to the private sector. An annual civic ball will, most likely, be held in a leisure centre, and various specialist annual events will be pre-programmed for the swimming pool.

These will not adversely affect the profitable operation of the centre by the contractor. Provided that the requirements of the client have been stated in the contract documentation at the time of the tender, then the contractor will know that income cannot be expected from the badminton courts while the civic ball is taking place. In the tender bid, therefore, the contractor will allow for the free use required and increase the bid by the amount of lost income expected.

Fig. 2.2 Civic occasions need accommodating.

If, however, the client has not stated in the contract documents the number of hours of free use needed, then the contractor is not required to provide free use. The client will have to pay extra, by means of a variation order (that is, a variation of the original contract).

CUSTOMER CARE FORMALITIES

Going out to tender for leisure management is a new experience for local authorities. The client will therefore take as his starting point the need to reach, at the least, current standards of management and maintenance.

All the client's energies will be directed to ensuring that the customer sees as little difference as possible, and that the same standards of customer care are maintained. Although any improvements will be welcomed, they can be considered later.

It is obviously going to be very different and difficult for the client to work through a contractor, compared with the previous arrangement of managing facilities by directly employed staff. Formality is inevitably increased in a contract situation.

The effects of poor performance and poor customer care are also increased in a contract situation. If one employee is guilty of poor performance or a poor attitude towards customers, then that employee can be disciplined or even dismissed. The effect of one individual has only a small effect on the total management of a facility. Dismiss a contractor and the effect on the management of a facility is total. Everything ceases. The client therefore needs to establish with some certainty that a contractor, if chosen, will be able to perform.

Once all the details necessary for a full contract document (Appendix A) have been established the client is then ready to seek suitable tenderers.

INVITING TENDERERS

Before expressing an interest in a particular tender, a tenderer obviously needs to know the type and nature of the contract to be let. At the time of tendering, the contractor will therefore make a detailed assessment of the nature of the contract, by examining the specifications and the other information supplied by the client. As a copy of the specification is freely available to be read at the client's offices during the period the client is seeking tenderers, no cost will be incurred at this stage.

Most clients also provide a full copy of the draft contract documentation, to allow the prospective tenderers to acquire a full appreciation of the type of contract to be let. This assists both the client and the contractor.

Advertizing

The law requires the client to advertize not only in local newspapers, but also in national specialist publications such as the weekly local government and municipal journals or other weekly and monthly leisure publications. Most tenders will also have to be advertized in Europe, because all large tenders, in any European Community country, have to be advertized throughout the Community. From 1992, the 'common market' aspect of the community takes on increased significance.

The advertisement will invite persons interested in tendering to submit details of themselves. Those expressing an interest will then be the subject of considerable scrutiny by the client.

Clients invariably seek to reduce the number of contractors applying to a competent few. This is not a backdoor method of reducing competition. At least three private sector contractors are required by law to be included in a select list (given, of course, that at least three apply).

The client's foremost task is to select contractors who could adequately perform the contract if it were awarded to them. The client will pay particular regard to the financial stability of the prospective contractor. His technical ability will also be scrutinized together with the company's track record in the management of similar facilities.

Assessing tenderers

The client's assessment of prospective tenderers will be rigorous and searching. The costs of getting it wrong are too great to be countenanced. The addendum to this chapter gives an example of the appraisal form which provides a basis for evaluation of the contractors applying to be considered for an invitation to tender. Site visits by client officers are often made to facilities currently operated by those invited.

The appraisal will be even more thorough in leisure management than for the other disciplines subjected to tender. This is simply because this type of management contract has not traditionally been the subject of tendering. Furthermore, there are relatively few competent contractors about. Added to this background is the fact that the leisure industry in the private sector has a somewhat manic depressive reputation – soaring high one year, down on the rocks the next. Clients will be wary.

Although preparing a tender document is a daunting undertaking for a client, costing and submitting a tender is a formidable experience for a prospective contractor. This aspect of tendering is the subject of the next chapter.

SUMMARY

To help us summarize this chapter, a number of key points need to be emphasized:

- Seeking tenders from specialist contractors is the best method for ensuring lowest cost.
- The Local Government Act 1988 requires that a variety of public services be subject to tender.
- Leisure management was added in 1989, to take effect from 1992.
- Contract documents are big; and are easier to understand when taken section by section:
  - tender conditions relate to the submission of the tenders (e.g. return all tenders by 12 noon on a given date);
  - contract conditions relate to the control and conduct of the contract (e.g. provide adequate insurance);
  - specifications detail the actual requirements, (e.g. open for use at 7.00am);
  - performance based specifications state measurements which the contractor has to achieve (e.g. the temperature of the pool water);
  - method based specifications detail the method to be used (e.g. the temperature at which the boiler shall be operated);
  - the Form of Tender page is left blank for the bid to be inserted by the tenderer;
  - there will be other sections which the authority considers necessary;
  - an outline of a tender is given in Appendix A.
- The amount of detail within the draft contract will reflect the level of control desired by the client authority.
- All systems and procedures will be written down and formalized.
- Contractors invited to tender will be thoroughly scrutinized as to their competence.
- Technical and financial references are especially important.
- Evidence is usually required to show that the contractor has a proven track record in the management of similar facilities.
- Only competent and able contractors will be asked to tender (unless there are less than three private sector contractors, in which case, by law, all will be invited to tender).
- For the successful tenderer, the contract documents supplied at the time of tendering will form the basis of a binding legal agreement lasting up to six years.

Preparing the contract documentation and tender is a major undertaking for any client. The ease of the subsequent contract administration will be largely geared by the detail within the tender documents. For the contractor, the hard work lies in completing and submitting the tender.

The contractor has to assess accurately the value of the leisure business offered in the tender. Expenditure has to be costed, and income assessed. The contractor who wins the contract then has to ensure subsequently that he can achieve his financial forecast. The contractor's view of a tender is given in the next chapter.

ADDENDUM: CONTRACTOR APPRAISALS

The addendum to this chapter provides the basis for the preliminary appraisal of a contractor by the client. A contractor will complete this document as part of his application to be considered as a competent contractor.

The addendum is reproduced from *Management of Sports and Leisure Facilities*, published by Longman. Thanks and acknowledgements are due to the Institute of Leisure and Amenity Management and the Institute of Baths and Recreation Management, who produced these guidelines, and to Longman for permission to reproduce. The guidelines provide an industry standard draft contract document in immense detail.

Specimen questionnaire for evaluation of prospective tenderers

CONFIDENTIAL

PLEASE ANSWER ALL THE QUESTIONS IN THIS QUESTIONNAIRE, FAILURE TO DO SO WILL INVALIDATE CONSIDERATION AS A TENDERER

1   BASIC INFORMATION ABOUT YOUR FIRM

Name of Firm: _____

Address: _____

_____

Person Applying on
Behalf of the Firm: _____

Position in Firm: _____

Telephone Number: _____

WHEN YOU HAVE COMPLETED THE QUESTIONNAIRE, PLEASE READ AND SIGN THE SECTION BELOW

I/We certify that the information supplied is accurate to the best of my/our knowledge and that I/we accept the conditions and undertakings requested in the questionnaire. I/we understand that false information could result in my/our exclusion from the tendering process.

I/we also understand that it is a criminal offence, punishable by imprisonment, to give or offer any gift or consideration whatsoever as an inducement or reward to any servant of a public body and that any such action will empower the Council to cancel any contract currently in force and will result in my/our exclusion from the tendering process.

Signed: _____

For and on Behalf of: _____

Date: _____

PLEASE NOTE the term 'firm' refers to: sole proprietor, partnership incorporated company, co-operative as appropriate. The undertaking should be signed by the applicant, a partner or authorised representative in her/his own name and on behalf of the firm.

A   MAIN CONTRACTORS

GENERAL AND TECHNICAL DETAILS

2   What size of contract are you interested in? Please delete accordingly.

(a)   Contracts up to £25,000
(b)   Contract values £25,000 – £100,000
(c)   Contract values £100,000 – £250,000
(d)   Contract values £250,000 – £595,000
(e)   Contracts over £595,000 – state amount.

3   Please state below the full names of any technical associations or guarantee schemes of which your firm is a member. Where appropriate, please indicate the maximum value of any one contract covered by the guarantee scheme.

Steps to Tendering and Selection of Tenderers

Full Name of Organisation	Registration No. (If Any)	Value of Work Guaranteed

4   Do you undertake any other form of business activity besides managing sports and leisure facilities? If so, please give details.

_____

_____

_____

_____

5   Please list below the addresses of any offices or premises/depots. (Attach a separate sheet if necessary marked A5.)

_____

_____

_____

_____

B   FINANCIAL INFORMATION

WHERE A SOLE TRADER OR PARTNERSHIP

6   Please state full name(s) of proprietor and every partner.

_____

_____

_____

7   Please state date of formation. _____

WHERE A LIMITED COMPANY

8   Please state whether the company is public or private.

_____

9 Please state full names of every director or partner, manager or secretary.

_____

_____

_____

_____

10 Please state date of registration and the registration number under the Companies Act 1946–1981.

_____

OR
11 Please state date of registration and the registration number under the Industrial and Provident Societies Act 1965–1968.

_____

12 If a limited company, please state nominal and paid up capital.

_____

13 Please confirm that the objects of the company as set out in the Memorandum of Association, cover purposes for which this tender is being submitted.

_____

_____

14 Please list wholly owned subsidiary companies (attach separate sheet if necessary marked B14).

_____

_____

_____

_____

15 If the company is a member of a group of companies, give the names and addresses of the ultimate holding company and any other subsidiaries involved in services associated with those offered by you to the Council.

_____

_____

_____

16 Would the group or the ultimate holding company be prepared to guarantee your contract performance as its subsidiary?

Please delete as appropriate: YES/NO

Steps to Tendering and Selection of Tenderers

17   Please give details of any outstanding claims or litigation against your firm or parent company and/or your ultimate holding company. (Attach a separate sheet if necessary marked B17.)

_____

_____

_____

_____

18   Please state names and addresses of bankers (for reference).

_____

_____

_____

_____

19   Please state bank account number.   _____

20   RESERVED.

21   Please state annual turnover for the last five years.

Amount	From	To

22   Please state name and address of insurance brokers

_____

_____

   (a)   Employers Liability Insurance: £
            Insurer:
            Policy No:
            Expiry Date:

   (b)   Public Liability Insurance: £
            Insurer:
            Policy No:
            Expiry Date:

23   Please state your V.A.T. Registration Number: _____

24 Have any of your directors/partners/proprietors ever been directly employed by this Authority?

Please delete as appropriate. YES/NO

25 If the answer to the above is in the affirmative, in what capacity were they employed?

_____

_____

DOCUMENTS TO BE ENCLOSED WITH TENDER

26 Please enclose a copy of the latest published balance sheet and profit and loss account.

Enclosed: YES/NO

27 Please enclose a copy of the Certificate of Incorporation of your firm under Section 13 of the Companies Act 1948 (if applicable).

Enclosed: YES/NO

28 If your firm holds a Tax Exemption Certificate under the Construction Industry Tax Deduction Scheme, please enclose a copy.

Enclosed: YES/NO

29 Does your firm hold a certifying document in line with the provisions of the Finance (No 2) Act 1975, stating:

— the type of certificate held (C, P and I)
— the certificate number
— the name in which the certificate was issued
— address of the issuing office of HM Inspector of Taxes
— expiry date of the certificate

Please delete as appropriate: YES/NO

30 If your answer to the previous question is in the affirmative, please enclose a copy of the certifying document.

Enclosed: YES/NO

C HEALTH AND SAFETY AT WORK

31 Who is the Director, Secretary, Manager or Senior Executive responsible for ensuring that the company policy is carried out in practice?

Name: _____

Position: _____

32 Do you ensure that adequate and suitable facilities for welfare at work are provided?

Please delete as appropriate. YES/NO

33 (a) Are you prepared to make your previous safety performance record, including type of work undertaken and accident record available for examination?

Please delete as appropriate. YES/NO

Steps to Tendering and Selection of Tenderers

    (b)   Has your company or its directors been convicted of an offence in respect of the Health and Safety at Work Act?

        Please delete as appropriate: YES/NO

34 Does your firm agree to be bound in its contracts with the Council to any relevant Health and Safety rules, procedures or codes of practice for the time being in force?

     Please delete as appropriate: YES/NO

     Copies of the current Health and Safety rules should be enclosed.

35 Please enclose a copy of your firm's Health and Safty Policy Statement, as required by Section 2(3) of the Health and Safety at Work Act 1974.

D TRAINING

     Is your firm within the scope of any Training Board, please state:

36 Name(s) of the Training Board(s):

_____

_____

_____

37 List the names of your employees who are registered and trained in accordance with the requirements of the Control of Pesticides Act. (For contracts involving maintenance of outside areas.)

_____

_____

_____

38 RESERVED.

E DETAILS OF WORKFORCE

39 Please state the total number of personnel regularly and permanently employed:

		Full-time	Part-time
(a)	Staff	_____	_____
(b)	Tradesmen	_____	_____
(c)	Trainees/Apprentices	_____	_____
(d)	Registered Disabled	_____	_____
(e)	MSC and YTS Placements	_____	_____

40 Does your company undertake to comply with all current employment legislation including:

	Yes	No
— Race Relations Act	_____	_____
— Equal Opportunities	_____	_____
— Sexual Discrimination Act	_____	_____
— Disabled Persons Employment Act	_____	_____

Steps to Tendering and Selection of Tenderers

(a)   Has your company or its directors been
      convicted of an offence in relation to any of
      the above?
      (Please give details on a separate sheet
      marked 40(a).)   _____   _____

(b)   Do you undertake to provide information and
      access to such documents as the Council may
      require to enable it to satisfy itself that the
      firm complies and will continue to comply with
      the above-mentioned Acts?   _____   _____

41   Please state the names of Employers'/Trade Associations of which your firm is a member.
     Where appropriate, please also state your membership number and the date that your
     membership expires.

     _____

     _____

     _____

     _____

42   What qualifications and experience do you normally seek from the staff described in
     Schedule A? (Please complete and return Schedule A.)

43   RESERVED.

44   RESERVED.

45   Trade/Type   Proportion
                                                          of Work   Sub Let
     Please state the trades your firm would normally let _____   _____
     to sub-contractors on a labour, plant and materials   _____   _____
     basis. Please indicate the proportion of these trades _____   _____
     normally sub-let.

46   Trade/Type   Proportion
                                                          of Work   Sub Let
     Please state the trades for which your firm would   _____   _____
     normally use labour-only sub-contractors (including   _____   _____
     holder of 7141 tax exemption certificates and other   _____   _____
     self-employed persons). Please indicate the   _____   _____
     proportion of these trades normally sub-let.

47   RESERVED.

48   RESERVED.

49   Do you undertake that when engaging, training, promoting or discharging employees,
     your firm will ensure that no discrimination takes place in respect of colour, race, ethnic
     or national origins, religion or sex.

     Please delete as appropriate: YES/NO

50   Is it your policy as an employer to comply with your statutory obligations under the
     Race Relations Act 1976 and, accordingly, your practice not to treat one group of people
     less favourably than others because of their colour, race, nationality or ethnic origin
     in relation to decisions to recruit, train or promote employees?

Steps to Tendering and Selection of Tenderers

51   In the last three years, has any finding of unlawful racial discrimination been made against your organisation or any court or industrial tribunal?

52   In the last three years, has your organisation been the subject of formal investigation by the Commission for Racial Equality on grounds of alleged unlawful discrimination?

53   If the answer to question 51 is in the affirmative or, in relation to question 52, the Commission made a finding adverse to your organisation:

What steps did you take in consequence of that finding?

54   Is your policy on race relations set out:

(a)   in instructions to those concerned with recruitment, training and promotion;

(b)   in documents available to employees, recognised trade unions or other representative groups of employees;

(c)   in recruitment advertisements or other literature?

55   Do you observe as far as possible the Commission for Racial Equality's Code of Practice for Employment as approved by Parliament in 1983, which gives practical guidance to employers and others on the elimination of racial discrimination and the promotion of equality of opportunity in employment, including the steps that can be taken to encourage members of the ethnic minorities to apply for jobs or take up training opportunities?

56   RESERVED.

57   RESERVED.

58   RESERVED.

F   COMPLIANCE WITH THE COUNCIL'S STANDING ORDERS

The Council's Standing Order X.Y. reads as follows:

X.Y.   There shall be inserted in every contract in writing a clause empowering the Council to cancel a contract and recover from the contractor the amount of any loss resulting from such cancellation of the contractor shall have offered or given or agreed to give to any person any gift or consideration of any kind as an inducement or reward for doing or forebearing to do or for have done or foreborne to do any action in relation to the obtaining or execution of the contract or any other contract with the Council or for showing or forebearing to show any favour or disfavour to any person in relation to the contract or any other contract with the Council or, if the like acts shall have been done by any person employed by him or acting on his behalf (whether with or without the knowledge of the contractor) or if in relation to any contract with the Council the contractor or any person employed by him or acting on his behalf shall have committed an offence under the Prevention of Corruption Acts, 1889–1916 or shall have given any fee or reward, the receipt of which is an offence under sections 117(2) and 117(3) of the Local Government Act, 1972.

59   Please indicate that you understand the implications of this Standing Order and will comply with it.

Please delete as appropriate: YES/NO

You will be required to comply with the Standing Orders of the Council, a copy of which can be seen at the main administrative centre.

G DETAILS OF WORKLOAD

60 Approximate annual value of work completed by the firm in respect of managing sports and leisure facilities.

1984–85   £_____

1985–86   £_____

1986–87   £_____

1987–88   £_____

61 Largest contract entered into during the last three years.

Name: _____

Value: £_____

62 Please state on Schedule B, not less than three projects similar in size and character, in relation to each work category for which application is made, carried out in the last three years, together with full names and addresses of the person, firm or council to whom reference can be made.

ALL QUESTIONS MUST BE ANSWERED.

Steps to Tendering and Selection of Tenderers

SCHEDULE A

STAFF QUALIFICATIONS

The tenderer to specify the type of qualification and experience to be provided for the duration of the contract. These details will be an important feature of evaluating the successful tender.

Position	Number	Qualifications	Experience
Facility Manager			
Deputies			
Technical Staff			
— plant			
— engineering			
— buildings			
Technicians			
Nursery Nurses			
Sports Staff			
— general education			
— coaching			
(State all sports)			
Lifeguards			
All Pool Staff			
Groundsmen			
Catering Staff			

Steps to Tendering and Selection of Tenderers

Arts Staff
_____

(Specify position)
_____

Cashiers/Receptionists
_____

Cleaners
_____

SCHEDULE B

Work Category		Project Details			Employer	Supervising Officer/Person to whom reference can be made			
No.	Title	Name	Value £000's	Comp. Date		Name	Address	Tel No.	

Steps to Tendering and Selection of Tenderers

Specimen questionnaire for taking up references from prospective tenderers.

CONFIDENTIAL

REQUEST FOR REFERENCE

Name of referee:

Reference for: (Name of company)

In the work categories of: Managing Sports and Leisure Facilities

Specific projects given as undertaken for referee:

_____

_____

Please answer the questions listed below and return as soon as possible. All information entered below will be treated in strict confidence.

1 Please confirm particulars of the above specified projects and give details of any other works carried out by this company for yourselves, stating when, where and for what value.

2 Please state if these were carried out by the firm as a direct contract or as a sub-contract and give details.

3 Please state the approximate period during which contracts were executed.

4 (a) Was their standard of service:

Please tick the appropriate box:

   (a) More than satisfactory
   (b) Satisfactory
   (c) Less than satisfactory
   (d) Not satisfactory

   (b) If not, why?

5 (a) Was their on-site organisation:

Please tick the appropriate box:

   (a) More than satisfactory
   (b) Satisfactory
   (c) Less than satisfactory
   (d) Not satisfactory

   (b) If not, why?

6 (a) Were the communications between yourselves, the manager on site and the contractors office:

Please tick the appropriate box:

   (a) More than satisfactory
   (b) Satisfactory
   (c) Less than satisfactory
   (d) Not satisfactory

(b)   If not, why?

7 (a)   Was the type of labour employed:

Please tick the appropriate box.

(a)   More than satisfactory
(b)   Satisfactory
(c)   Less than satisfactory
(d)   Not satisfactory

(b)   If not, why?

8 (a)   Were the arrangements for the safety of the public met?

Please tick the appropriate box.

(a)   More than satisfactory
(b)   Satisfactory
(c)   Less than satisfactory
(d)   Not satisfactor

(b)   If not, why?

9 (a)   Have the contracts generally been completed in accordance with the contract period?

Please delete as appropriate: YES/NO

(b)   If not, what were the reasons?

(c)   Would you class these as acceptable circumstances?

Please delete as appropriate: YES/NO

(d)   Did you have cause to complain about delayed, slow or inadequate work in any one part of the contract?

Please delete as appropriate: YES/NO

(e)   If yes, what and in which part?

(f)   Were their reasons for this acceptance to you?

Please delete as appropriate: YES/NO

10 (a)   Were the specifications issued for the contract fully adhered to?

Please delete as appropriate: YES/NO

(b)   If not, why?

(c)   Were their reasons for this acceptable to you?

Please delete as appropriate: YES/NO

(d)   Were there any items of the specification with which the contractor had difficulty in complying?

Please delete as appropriate: YES/NO

Steps to Tendering and Selection of Tenderers

(e)   If yes, what were these and was a compromise reached?

11   (a)   Did you find that your supervision of the contractor was:

     Please tick as appropriate:

(a) Excessive	
(b) High	
(c) Moderate	
(d) Low	

  (b)   If excessive, in what part and why?

12   (a)   Did you experience any difficulty in the agreement of charges for variation orders?

     Please tick as appropriate.

(a) Frequently	
(b) Occasionally	
(c) Never	

  (b)   Have any undue claims been submitted?

     Please delete as appropriate: YES/NO

  (c)   If yes, did you experience difficulty in their settlement?

     Please delete as appropriate: YES/NO

13   (a)   Was a dilapidation schedule included?

     Please delete as appropriate: YES/NO

  (b)   If yes, did the contractor fulfil obligations under the clause and was the attitude to remedy defects satisfactory?

14   (a)   Did you think that the tender price submitted by this contractor was realistic?

     Please delete as appropriate: YES/NO

  (b)   Was their price *much* lower than the other prices received?

     Please delete as appropriate: YES/NO

  (c)   Do you think that they submitted such a low price to ensure they got the job?

     Please delete as appropriate: YES/NO

15   (a)   Would you consider inviting this contractor to tender for works again?

     Please delete as appropriate: YES/NO

  (b)   If yes, specify the types you would be most happy with them doing.

16   Any other general comments you may with to offer regarding this contractor.

Signed: _____   Date: _____

On Behalf Of: _____

Steps to Tendering and Selection of Tenderers

Specimen timetable for sport and leisure compulsory competitive tendering

1 January 1992	Contracts start.
1 October 1991	Successful contractor notified.
1 September 1991	Evaluate lowest tenderer.
1 August 1991	All bids to be submitted.
1 June 1991*	Invite bids having provided details of costs to be taken into account at tender evaluation stage.
1 May 1991	Contractors to formally register interest. Preliminary enquiries and interviews with contractors.
March 1991	Site visits by prospective tenderers. Tenderers' queries to be dealt with.
1 February 1991	Statutory advertisement. All documentation available for inspection (or purchase) by contractors.

(*This date may be up to two months later for small contracts.)

Note:

—   Dates are the latest advisable and for a minimum of 35%.

—   Example incorporates advice available up to and including draft circular on guidance issued for consultation on 9 April 1990.

—   Where large multi-site contracts are due to start on 1 January, then it may be helpful to phase the start dates on different sites. In such cases the whole timetable should be moved forward and all sites started by 1 January.

Chapter Three

The financial basis

In most contract industries, tenders are submitted on the basis of a fixed price. In other words, the contractor offers to undertake services or provide goods for a fixed sum. Examples include the many maintenance contracts within the public sector (grounds maintenance, street cleansing, and so on). The contractor will bid a fixed sum for which he will carry out the contract in the first year. The annual inflation allowance, or variation orders, will be the only reason to increase or alter the originally agreed fixed sum.

Thus the cost to the client will remain the same, more or less, each year. Furthermore, the value of the contract to the contractor will remain the same. This allows for confidence and easy forward planning for both the client and the contractor. A fixed price contract is simple to manage.

Leisure management is different. Unlike most other tenders, the successful contractor will have the opportunity to increase income quite dramatically by successful management methods. Thus, if the successful contractor manages to increase usage of a facility by, say, 20 per cent then a further 20 per cent income would accrue. This could result in a major variation to the bids submitted for leisure management contracts. It could also lead to real difficulty for the client in assessing tenders.

The whole basis of all tendering relies on a like for like comparison of tender prices.

With different tenderers taking a different view of the income earning potential of a facility, the client has a slim chance of making an accurate, like for like comparison. Furthermore, depending on the size of the contract, substantial sums could be at stake.

INCOME

The traditional, service provision, policy of local authorities will be immediately overlaid by the contractor's income maximizing policy. Indeed a contractor with an eye to income could radically change the whole ethos of public sector provision.

The Local Government Act 1988, as amended, allows the local authority to set fees and charges. However, there remains a whole world of other income generating activities a contractor can pursue.

Most clients ponder very carefully on the exact wording of the clauses which are to be inserted into their tenders. There are two extremes, and an infinite number of options in between. Quite clearly, one extreme is for the client to retain all income. The contractor then simply manages the facility and hands the income over to the authority. The other extreme is, of course, for the contractor to retain all income; – which might be thought tantamount to giving an open cheque.

Income sharing

It is doubtful whether the best leisure management operations can be achieved by the client or the contractor retaining all income. The best option is a middle course of action.

The Audit Commission favour the approach in which the maximum possible cost to the authority is set out in the tender bid. They particularly recommend the 'income sharing / deficit guarantee' approach. With this method, the contractor shares income with the client, and at the same time the contractor guarantees the maximum deficit which the client will have to meet.

In the example given in Table 3.1, the tenderer estimates that it will cost £330 000 to operate and manage the swimming pool at Little London. However, this is a gross cost. The tenderer also estimates that there is likely to be an annual income of £180 000. Thus the net cost is £150 000. This is the sum which the local authority will need to agree to pay the tenderer, for the tenderer to agree to operate the swimming pool.

Having agreed to pay the tenderer £150 000 per year, the local authority's financial uncertainties are over. They know that the maximum cost they have to face each year is £150 000. Thus, in this example, the £150 000 can be referred to as;

- the total tender bid
- the operational deficit
- the total subsidy required from the local authority to operate the facility

Table 3.1 An example of a tender offer

	Annual expenditure (£)	Annual income (£)
Little London swimming pool	330 000	180 000
Total tender bid		150 000

In a contract situation, the contractor takes all the risk. If the operational deficit is greater than £150 000, then that is a loss to the contractor. The local authority have a deficit guarantee: the cost (or deficit) to the authority will be no more than £150 000.

However, the contractor may make substantially more income than anticipated. This is where a contract with an income sharing clause benefits the local authority.

LEISURE GAIN?

Many tenders will not allow the tenderers to submit supplementary additions to the bid, because this destroys the like for like comparison so essential to successful tendering.

An example might be when a tenderer offered a higher price in the tender on the understanding that a new health and fitness suite would be provided by the tenderer. The additional income would allow this tenderer to submit a higher priced bid.

Could 'leisure gain' become the feature of the 1990s, that planning gain was in the 1980s?

On a day by day basis, all authorities will wish to know whether increased income received by a contractor is due to achieving a worthy social objective, or is entirely due to the profit maximizing policy of the contractor.

It has been clearly shown that usage and income can be increased substantially by very ordinary methods. In, say, a swimming pool, this has been possible by introducing separate sessions for women and ethnic groups, children's fun sessions and lane-swimming for serious swimmers. Increased income generated in this way is obviously of benefit to everyone.

Who profits?

However, income generation by Sunday markets is quite another thing.

Many leisure centres are well placed to provide a most suitable location for Sunday carpet sales, antique sales, sports equipment sales and the rest. If a contractor has built such use into the tender price, any authority accepting the tender without enquiring into the sources of income could quickly find themselves in an embarrassing situation. Local traders and church representatives will be quick to point out the consequences.

The end results of an open ended, income generating contract will be of intense interest to both the contractor and the client. Both will give the closest scrutiny possible to income generation potential. Both would use binoculars, if that would help, but surprisingly they would find that they were using the same pair of binoculars from different ends.

The key question to be addressed in tender documents must be: who profits by increased income and usage?

- the local community?
- the contractor?
- the client?

Fig. 3.1 Client and contractor see income differently.

And, moreover, if increased usage leads to increased wear and tear, who pays the increased maintenance costs?

Worse, if increased wear and tear leads to plant failures, will the contractor be able to claim loss of income from the client? This is yet another source of income that a skilled contractor will be quick to exploit, unless it is adequately covered in the contract.

BUILDING MAINTENANCE

Critical attention needs to be given to responsibilities in relation to the building structure. For example, either the client or the contractor may be made responsible for the boilers, the ventilation, air-handling plant and other durable items within a facility.

These are very difficult issues to be addressed within a contract. Get it wrong, and it will be the source of unending conflict between the contractor and the client.

Division of reponsibilities

If the client does not make a clear and logical division between the key elements within a leisure facility, then there will always be underlying tension between the contractor and the client.

Tension will especially occur where the contractor believes that inadequate maintenance is adversely affecting customers, and thus reducing income. On the other hand, if the contractor is allowed to maintain fixed plant, there is a danger that maintenance will be neglected towards the end of the contract period. Also some public authorities have a central services department maintaining all fixed plant and equipment. Many authorities have central energy management policies and arrangements.

Contract responsibilities

The central focal point of the contract is the leisure facility which has to be managed. It is the building and other facilities and their management and maintenance which are at the core of the contract. No sensible local authority would let a contract for management without giving due thought to the implications of this contract on the building.

Equally, no sensible leisure management contractor would take on a contract without giving due thought to the buildings and the implications of the contract.

Expert advice

Both contractor and client are well advised to seek the views of a professional building surveyor. All too often this does not happen. The views of Clive Sayer, a professional building surveyor with Alex Sayer Project Services, are given here, to underline this all important, but often neglected, aspect of the contract:

> It seems crazy to us that many management contracts seem to be let with insufficient thought being given to the building. It is essential when the management contracts are let that clear direction is given at the time of tendering as to 'who' should pay for 'what' in the maintenance field.
>
> What exactly is maintenance should be clearly defined in the contract, as should the length of the contract. If it is a short term contract, no sensible contractor is going to wish to take it on a full repairing basis. Equally, no sensible building owner would let a contract with the management contractor not being responsible for any repairs or maintenance as this is likely to encourage wholesale carelessness.

Long term management contracts are normally let on a full repairing basis in the same way that commercial property leases are frequently let on a full repairing and insuring basis (FRI). In this manner the maintenance obligations are placed upon the tenant (in this case the management contractor) so that in theory the building owner receives back, at the end of the term, a building in similar condition to that in which it was let.

If, for any reason, the condition has been allowed to deteriorate below that in which it was let then damage could be payable by the tenant (contractor) to the building owner. In the case of leases, these are normally called dilapidations.

Basic principles

In order to avoid arguments as to who should pay for what, Clive Sayer advises several sensible and prudent steps.

1. Clear definition in the management contract of exactly who pays for what, what is deemed to be maintenance, repairs etc.
2. A thorough survey carried out by a properly qualified and suitably experienced building surveyor at the beginning of the management agreement to determine the exact condition of the building. This survey should be carried out by an impartial surveyor and agreed by both sides of the contract or by a surveyor on each side.
3. The contract should provide for a similar survey to be carried out at the end of the term so that any deterioration can be clearly established and the amount of the damages payable can then be readily agreed. A procedure should be allowed for in the management agreement for agreement to these damages – similar to the dilapidations procedure normally undertaken with commercial property leases.

The key issue to remember is that while effective and intelligent management can make the difference between a successful and an unsuccessful leisure centre or swimming pool, without the buildings and associated facilities there is nothing there to manage.

The buildings are major capital assets. It ill behoves a local authority to let them out on contract without proper thought as to the protection of the asset value. It is also extremely unwise for management contractors to take on a centre not knowing what the potential liabilities for the maintenance and repair of these assets could be.

THE BID

As with all other aspects of the tender, the client will determine the manner in which the tender offer will be submitted. Again, there is a wide difference between authorities.

For the successful contractor, however, there is just one way. Success can be achieved only by accurate assessment of all costs and all income sources.

The contractor therefore needs to predict accurately the net costs of operating the facility specified in the tender document. This can be achieved only by listing all cost centres and all profit centres. Detailed breakdown of income and expenditure allow the contractor to make an accurate assessment of the value of the business.

An example is given in Table 3.2 and Table 3.3; and summarized in Table 3.4.

Table 3.2 Estimated annual expenditure for Little London swimming pool

EXPENDITURE ITEMS	£
Manpower	
Management and office staff	60 000
Operational staff	150 000
Supplies and services	
Utilities: heat, water, and power	30 000
Specialist services	9 000
Supplies, materials and chemicals	12 000
Other costs	
Central establishment charges (head office)	12 000
Business rates, insurances	24 000
Leasing and debt charges	3 000
Expenditure total	£300 000

Table 3.3 Estimated annual income from Little London swimming pool

INCOME ITEMS	£
Entrance fees	
Adult	48 000
Youth	48 000
Unwaged	6 000
Special sessions	
Women	12 000
Ethnic	12 000
Fun sessions	18 000
Learn to swim	15 000
Club	3 000
Vending (net)	
Food	6 000
Drink	3 000
Sales	
Swimwear	6 000
Booklets	3 000
Income total	£180 000

For the contractor, the actual preparation of the bid will be much more detailed. Each item will be subdivided into various cost and profit centres.

Table 3.4 The tenderer's bid for Little London swimming pool, summarized

Totals	£
Expenditure	300 000
Income	180 000
Net cost	120 000
*Add profit/contingencies @ 10 per cent	30 000
Therefore TENDER BID	£150 000

*The profit/contingency element may or may not be detailed on the tender bid submitted to the client. However, it is of fundamental importance to the tenderer/contractor that an adequate element is included for profit or possible loss.

Client requirements

Some clients will require a much more detailed breakdown as well. This will allow a more accurate comparison of different contractors' bids, and facilitate more accurate monitoring once the contract is operational.

A more detailed breakdown will enable the client to make an accurate assessment of the capabilities of the contractor in presenting a bid. It will also allow the client to assess the commercial acumen of the contractor and enable fair comparisons between bids. Furthermore, and more importantly, the client will be able to compare against known costs and income achieved from the same facilities in previous years. This will provide an essential yardstick by which to assess the realistic basis of differing bids.

Detailed analysis of the bid may reveal that a contractor is anticipating increased income by methods which the client would not allow. An example would be cigarette advertising and sales, where the client authority has a strict policy not to encourage such sales where children are present.

The basic requirement for all successful tender exercises for the client is to ensure an exact comparison between a number of contractors bidding for identical workloads. Comparisons are assisted by detailed specifications, and a clear indication of each contractor's estimated costs and income.

After this stage, the client's interest in detailed accounting will wane.

PROFIT OR LOSS

The element of profit or loss cannot be stressed too highly. Quite obviously, if a profit is not made, then the contractor will incur a loss and will be forced out of business. This is equally true whether the contractor is in the private sector or the public sector.

In the private sector, a profit is essential to pay an adequate dividend to the shareholders who have invested their savings in the business. Having shown their confidence in investing in the company, the shareholders will expect a greater return on their capital than if they had invested their savings in a building society.

In the public sector, a profit as such is not required. It may be necessary to achieve a 5 per cent return on the capital employed (e.g. the capital cost of equipment), but as the contractor will have to provide so little capital, this duty should not prove too onerous. However, a loss cannot be allowed. Therefore, the public sector contractor will need at least to break even on the tendered price. In practice a small profit will be essential.

Subsidy payments

The operational loss anticipated by the contractor (£150 000 in Table 3.4) will be paid by the client. Most publicly provided leisure facilities will not be able to operate without client subsidy.

If the competitive tender process has worked effectively, this subsidy will often be less than the costs borne by the client when the facility was managed directly. But although there has been a reduction in cost, the service levels will still be maintained as the contractor will be required to operate the facility according to the specification.

Income sharing

In contracts where income sharing is a feature, the income sharing will usually only start after the estimated annual income has first been achieved. In Tables 3.2, 3.3 and 3.4, this would be any income greater than £180 000; as this level of income is at least needed to break even on the tender.

Beyond the £180 000, it can be argued that the contractor is reaping the just reward for all the effort put in. The question is: should all the extra income accrue to the contractor? The contractor is only able to achieve the income in the first place because of the existence of the leisure facility. A fair share should also accrue to the client who provided the facility in the first place and who has the long-term expense of the upkeep.

A 50 per cent share of additional income is perhaps an equitable arrangement to both parties.

Variable income share

Income share may be varied to favour one of the parties to the contract for a number of reasons. An example would be where the contractor has recently refurbished the facility. The increases in income might be largely due to the improvements. A greater proportion of the additional income should then perhaps go to the contractor: say, 20 per cent to the client, 80 per cent to the contractor.

Special attention needs to be given to catering and other activities where the cost of inputs (food, drink, etc) is a large proportion of the total income. Even a 5 per cent share to the client may be too much. If that occurs, the contractor makes a loss and experiences a very positive deterrent, which leads to a curtailment in the activity. Another example would be a sports course, where a large element of the total income is paid back to the instructors as wages.

As with so much of management, there is no one right answer. Each individual situation has to be judged on its merits and specific arrangements made.

INSURANCE

As part of the contract, the contractor will be required to provide adequate insurance to cover any eventuality. The client authority will demand an indemnity, so that claims cannot be referred to the authority. Again, it is a contractor risk. All contractors will ensure adequate protection from a reputable insurance company.

It is also often advisable for a contractor to be protected by consequential loss insurance. Then, if income is reduced in any area, due to a mishap, the contractor will be financially protected. There are numerous situations where a contractor could face a substantial loss of income due to plant failure or accidental damage.

Some contracts state that the client will not be held responsible for any loss of income howsoever caused. Therefore, if the client is at fault because the roof is leaking, then the contractor needs to ensure that the income generating potential of the facility is not impaired to the extent that it would result in a loss.

Consequential loss insurance has much to offer, and not just peace of mind.

Having settled the financial basis of the contract, it is now time to turn to the planning undertaken by the contactor in preparing to submit a bid. This is covered in the next chapter. First, however, let us summarize this chapter.

SUMMARY

Some of the key elements in this chapter include;

- Most leisure management contracts will not be based on a 'fixed sum' tender bid.
- Many tenders provide an incentive for the contractor to increase income.
- Increased income beyond that estimated in the tender will invariably be shared with the client authority.
- However, the client will not wish to share the contractor's commercial risk.
- The Audit Commission favour a 'deficit guarantee' for client authorities.
- There is no one correct answer. As with so much in management, the best arrangements are those suited to the particular circumstances.
- Any percentage income share will need to vary, to allow for activities where the vast majority of the income only just covers the costs incurred (e.g. catering and sports courses).
- An annual inflation rise will be allowed.
- With a management contract, there will be clear demarcation lines (e.g. who repairs the boiler).
- Particular attention is needed to the appropriate division of responsibilities for building maintenance.
- Professional surveys should be undertaken at the start and at the finish of the contract.
- A tenderer's bid needs to take account of all the details and restrictions stated in the specification.
- The client will need to know the exact detail on which the bid is based.
- No income item will be allowed where this contradicts authority policy.
- The best contracts will increase use for the benefit of customers, client and contractor, which will help them in future tenders.

The leisure industry is volatile at all times. Speculative bidding will do no-one any favours, least of all a loss-making contractor. Successful tendering for both client and contractor has therefore to be based on a firm and fair financial format. Both parties rely on that financial basis to a considerable extent. No matter how detailed or limited, the financial basis of the contract will need to withstand intense client scrutiny and more importantly will need to be deliverable, once the contract is operating.

ADDENDUM: INCOME OPTIONS

The addendum to this chapter reproduces the summary advice given by the Audit Commission in relation to tendering. It is reproduced with the permission of the Controller of Her Majesty's Stationery Office. The Audit Commission have a specific duty to advise local authorities on economy and efficiency measures. Furthermore, the Commission is able to exert pressure on local authorities via their external auditor.

A·U·D·I·T
COMMISSION
REVIEW

The Audit Commission
for Local Authorities
in England and Wales

January 1990

LOCAL AUTHORITY SUPPORT FOR SPORT –
A MANAGEMENT HANDBOOK

The compulsory competitive tendering (CCT) provisions of the Local Government Act 1988 are being extended to the management of sports and leisure facilities; in future local authority employees will be able to manage many facilities only when they have won the work in open competition. But CCT is not privatisation; authorities will still be able to control the way in which facilities are used – opening hours, programme of activities and the prices users are charged. Meeting the competitive tendering requirements will require effort and the time available is not great. The experience of the relatively few authorities which have voluntarily gone to contract shows that there are a number of pitfalls to be avoided. However, the evidence suggests that competition, properly managed, can help local authorities provide more efficient services, better tailored to local needs.

Local authorities in England and Wales have traditionally been major providers and operators of sports facilities largely for social reasons. They now manage over 1700 indoor centres, largely built in the last 20 years, as well as many outdoor pitches and golf courses. They currently spend about £400 million net a year on revenue support for public sport, predominantly in subsidising these facilities. This is separate from expenditure under local education authority duties and powers, which is not covered in this Review. In addition, expenditure charged to parks and open spaces often includes expenditure on sports pitches, which has been estimated as a further £150 million net a year. Local authorities have nearly always employed their own staff to manage the facilities they provide. The extension of CCT to the management of sports facilities will thus create major changes in how sports services are managed.

There is no statutory duty to support sport. In many cases local authorities choose to be involved for social reasons. In other cases provision may be linked to economic development and tourism. Whatever the objectives, they have to be pursued within financial constraints. One of the major challenges facing authorities is to ensure that the balance between social and financial objectives is maintained under CCT.

Exhibit 1
NET REVENUE EXPENDITURE ON SPORT
Expenditure has risen in the 1980s

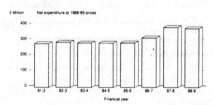

Exhibit 2
BALANCING SOCIAL AND FINANCIAL OBJECTIVES
Each authority will have its own view of where the balance should lie

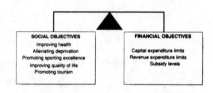

The Order extending CCT to management of sports and leisure facilities was voted through both Houses of Parliament shortly before the end of 1989.

The Government has announced that authorities in England will have to place the management of 35% of facilities in competition by January 1st 1992, 70% by August 1st 1992 and 100% by January 1st 1993. Implementation in Wales will be phased in from January 1992.

WHAT NEEDS TO BE DONE

1. SETTING THE FRAMEWORK

Before putting work out to tender, authorities need to decide their attitude to their Direct Services Organisation (DSO) and to any management buy out proposal, to make a clear client – contractor split, if a DSO bid is to be made, and to undertake a thorough review of their strategy towards sport.

THE FUTURE OF THE DSO

The Commission regards the existence of efficient DSOs as a beneficial influence on the competitiveness of the market. However, if an authority does not intend to allow a bid by a DSO it is not obliged to follow the full rigour of the Local Government Act 1988. Management buy-outs are a possible approach but must be carefully handled (see box).

THE CLIENT – CONTRACTOR SPLIT

Many councils will wish their DSO to bid for work. If they intend to have a DSO they need to distinguish between the authority's client and contractor roles. The Commission favours making the distinction at both officer and member level; member separation at committee or board level is recommended.

THE STRATEGY REVIEW

Councils need to reappraise their involvement with sport in preparation for CCT. Such a reappraisal should be formalised in a strategy review and repeated at least every five years. The exercise is intended to provide a framework for the authority's complete involvement with sport and should therefore cover matters such as sports outreach and development and the management and role of dual use facilities, which are mostly exempt from CCT, as well as new provision issues; it should not

Exhibit 3
OPTIONS FOR THE CLIENT – CONTRACTOR SPLIT
Some arrangements are not acceptable

	UNACCEPT-ABLE	UNDESIR-ABLE	POSSIBLE	IDEAL
MEMBERS	Same committee	Same committee	Same committee but with separate client and DSO sub-committees	Client committee DSO board
OFFICERS	Same officers	Different officers in same department	Client department Stand alone or umbrella DSO	Client department Stand alone or umbrella DSO

concentrate solely on facilities affected by CCT. Client side staffing – numbers, skills required, training needed and organisation – and budget should be covered in the review.

MANAGEMENT BUY OUTS

Management buy-outs may appeal to many authorities. But there are potential conflicts of interest within an authority as a buy out is negotiated. Unless carefully handled, an MBO might bring substantial financial rewards to the managers involved at the public's expense.

Ways of guarding against such problems are discussed in the Commission's recent Management Paper No 6, '*Management buy-outs: public interest or private gain?*' HMSO, January 1990, price £3.50.

Exhibit 4
THE STRATEGY REVIEW
The strategy review involves the following

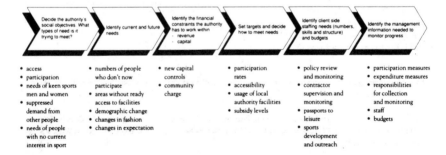

Decide the authority's social objectives. What types of need is it trying to meet?	Identify current and future needs	Identify the financial constraints the authority has to work within - revenue - capital	Set targets and decide how to meet needs	Identify client side staffing needs (numbers, skills and structure) and budgets	Identify the management information needed to monitor progress
• access • participation • needs of keen sports men and women • suppressed demand from other people • needs of people with no current interest in sport	• numbers of people who don't now participate • areas without ready access to facilities • demographic change • changes in fashion • changes in expectation	• new capital controls • community charge	• participation rates • accessibility • usage of local authority facilities • subsidy levels	• policy review and monitoring • contractor supervision and monitoring • passports to leisure • sports development and outreach	• participation measures • expenditure measures • responsibilities for collection and monitoring • staff • budgets

2. THE COMPETITIVE TENDERING PROCESS

Once the client and DSO roles have been separated and policy objectives set, the prime task is deciding how to achieve those objectives – the contract strategy to follow, the specification to use, how to handle shortlisting and tender evaluation, how to supervise and manage contracts and how to monitor performance.

Many authorities will already have tackled similar issues when letting contracts for other services covered by CCT. And the Audit Commission has discussed them in its Occasional Paper No 7, *'Preparing for Compulsory Competition'* (HMSO, January 1989, price £5.50).

Some problems will, however, be unique to sports management contracts – how to control the programme of activities and the prices users are charged, how to continue to subsidise facilities which are being managed under contract and some aspects of tender evaluation.

PROGRAMMING AND PRICING

Under CCT, contracts will run for four to six years. No detailed programme and set of prices drawn up in advance is likely to be valid at the end of the contract. Since increased use is likely to promote social objectives, detailed client control of programming might be counter-productive by preventing a rapid response to changing user needs. Approaches which give contractors some programming discretion, within the client's policy guidelines, will often be best.

Authorities do not currently possess the power to devolve pricing decisions to contractors. They need nevertheless to ensure that their control of pricing does not hinder contractors' ability to respond to changing public needs.

FINANCIAL ARRANGEMENTS

Under CCT the client will deal directly with some costs such as debt charges and external building maintenance while the contractor will meet others. Six main approaches are used in existing, voluntary contracts to provide the contractor with income to help meet costs and generate a profit.

Authorities should not normally use contracts under which the council bears the losses if the contractor's performance is poorer than expected. The Commission thus favours approaches in which the maximum possible cost to the authority is set out in the contract, such as the income sharing 'deficit guarantee' approach.

TENDER EVALUATION

Tender evaluation poses some interesting issues. Under many contracts, tenderers' prices will be based not simply on an estimate of operating cost but also on an estimate of the income the tenderers expect to generate from users and thus on the

Exhibit 5
FINANCIAL OPTIONS
There is a range of options

OPTION	CLIENT	CONTRACTOR
Franchise	Meets debt charges and external maintenance of buildings.	Meets other costs. Retains income from users. Pays a fee to the client.
Deficit guarantee	Meets debt charges and the external maintenance of buildings. Pays fee to the contractor.	Meets other costs. Retains income from users and uses this and the fee to meet costs and provide profit.
Profit sharing deficit guarantee	Meets debt charges and external maintenance of buildings. Pays fee to the contractor.	Meets other costs. Retains income from users and uses this and the fee to meet costs and provide profit. Pays a proportion of any profit to the client.
Income sharing deficit guarantee	Meets debt charges and external maintenance of buildings. Pays fee to the contractor.	Meets other costs. Retains income from users and uses this and the fee to meet costs and provide profit. Pays a proportion of income to the client irrespective of whether or not the operation is profitable.
Risk sharing	Meets debt charges and external maintenance of buildings. Meets a proportion of any operating loss.	Meets other costs. Retains income from users. Shares any profit with the client.
Open book management fee	Meets debt charges and external maintenance of buildings. Meets contractor's costs. Pays contractor a fee.	Passes all income to the client.

tenderers' predictions of the number of users they expect to attract to a facility. An over-optimistic assessment may mean that an operator will not receive the income needed to cover costs and may fail or withdraw part of the way during contract life.

Exhibit 6
INCOME SHARING 'DEFICIT GUARANTEE' CONTRACTS
The contractor uses the 'deficit guarantee' and income from users to meet expenses and provide profits. A share of income is returned to the authority

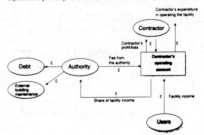

3. PREPARING THE DSO FOR COMPETITION

Competition alone may not be enough to ensure that authorities receive keen bids from tenderers. Evidence from other Commission studies suggests that authorities tend to receive better prices, irrespective of who wins, when efficient DSOs bid against private contractors; but many recreation DSOs need to improve their performance if they are to compete realistically against the private sector.

COST CONTROL

Pay and conditions of service should reflect the local labour market. Other costs also need to be controlled. DSO managers require delegated authority; standing orders and financial regulations may need to be altered. Information systems should be tailored to DSOs' needs.

MARKETING

DSOs' bids for contracts will be based not only on estimated running costs, but often also on predictions of the income the DSO expects facilities to generate. Marketing is central to success. Though it is improving, weaknesses are still common. Marketing is more than advertising; it is the whole process of deciding what service to provide, whom to provide it for, what prices to charge, how to persuade people to use services and how to monitor success. Promotion is a part of marketing, persuading people to use services; and advertising is one, but only one, way of promoting use.

Each recreation DSO should therefore have someone designated as marketing manager and should have a marketing plan which is regularly reviewed and updated. DSOs also need to pay particular attention to customer care – only a few hundred people may provide the bulk of the use of a sports facility and a single person who stops using a facility may represent a loss of income from over 100 user visits a year.

THE NEXT STEPS

The Commission's auditors will be conducting value for money reviews of local authorities' support for sport, and of their preparations for CCT, during 1990.

DUAL USE

Many dual use facilities are likely to be exempted from CCT. Authorities which do not wish to place management of such facilities to competition will need to check whether the exemption applies, for example by examining the powers used in their provision and the number of hours of educational use.

A clear understanding of managerial responsibilities will also be needed following recent education legislation. Care is required to ensure that schools are not forced to subsidise public use from their share of the education budget and that they are not overcompensated for the existence of dual use facilities. The actual costs of public and educational use may need to be identified more accurately than at present.

Even when management is not put to competition, managers of dual use centres should be given subsidy targets and the delegated authority to manage facilities, and meet those targets, within the policy guidelines set by a clearly identified client.

IF YOU WANT TO KNOW MORE

The Audit Commission's findings and recommendations are contained in its recent report *'Local authority support for sport – a management handbook'*. Complimentary copies of this report have been sent to each local authority. Further copies can be obtained from HMSO, price £8.50.

The *'Management Handbook'* is a companion to a shorter report, *'Sport for whom? – clarifying the local authority role in sport and recreation'* which was published in August 1989. That report was aimed primarily at those with responsibilities for strategic issues; the *'Management Handbook'* is aimed primarily at those responsible for preparing an authority for the extension of CCT to sports management. It is recommended that *'Sport for whom?'* is read before reading the *'Management handbook'*.

Exhibit 7
THE MARKETING PLAN
To develop a marketing plan DSOs need to follow this procedure

Chapter Four

Business planning and tendering

Business planning is, surprisingly, not an exact science. No two academics can even agree on the same definition. This perhaps explains the great variety of approaches to business. Business planning for leisure therefore needs to take account of the specific requirements of the industry.

Leisure is much more variable than many industries, although this is not necessarily so true when considering leisure management contracts. In leisure management, the basic business is already provided for the contractor. This is not only the existing leisure facility, but also the contract documents and the business environment. These aspects are outlined and analysed in this chapter.

INCOME PROJECTIONS

A leisure management contract will normally be up to six years' duration. Thus, at the time of tender, the tenderer needs to consider all the likely major changes which may occur during that period. This is extremely difficult. During any five year period, there are a multitude of leisure fashions and crazes which come and go. Leisure is nothing if not dynamic.

It would clearly be financial suicide to base income levels for the next five years merely on the income received in the last five years. There could be a downward trend in some key activities.

Equally, a tender bid will be less than successful if account is not taken of those sports and activities which are enjoying increased popularity. For example, in the early 1990s a leisure operator could plan with some certainty for increasing income from ten pin bowling and health and fitness suites. It was a far different story, however, for squash and skateboarding.

What are important to a tenderer are the likely trends and patterns of use.

FORWARD PLANNING

Although usage patterns vary enormously, it is essential to make a reasoned assessment of likely usage and income patterns for the length of the contract.

For sound financial reasons nearly all businesses annually review their future plans and try to anticipate possible major changes. Many businesses plan both one year ahead and five to six years ahead.

Some of the questions which need to be taken into account when looking forward over the next five to six years include:

- May there be a possible change in government?
- Or a possible change in government policy?
- Will the national economic climate alter?
- Will there be economic growth, stagnation or decline?
- Is leisure spending likely to increase?
- Is leisure spending likely to increase within the facilities being managed?
- Is the political colour of the client authority likely to change?
- If it did, could the contract change, adversely?
- Is the political composition of the authority marginal?
- Could the policies of the client change over the period of the contract?
- Could increased social provision be at least offset by increased profitable activities?

The element of risk in any business venture is reduced when accurate assessments can be made of these matters. But accuracy in these issues for small companies is extremely difficult.

However, any business is greatly strengthened by at least trying to predict some of the major trends which will affect trading over the period of the contract. For small businesses, far too often this analysis is not even attempted.

COMPANY REVIEW

A fair assessment by the contractor of his own strengths and weaknesses is also essential. There is no point in analysing the client authority if the same rigorous analysis is missed for the contractor. SWOT analysis is often used in these circumstances. SWOT stands for:

- strengths
- weaknesses
- opportunities
- threats

All businesses have their own peculiar blend of strengths and weaknesses. For example, one leisure contractor may be strong on sports, but weak on catering: no point, then, in bidding for a contract with a large banqueting and wedding trade.

Opportunities come in all shapes and sizes, and are limited only by the rational judgement of the business manager.

One opportunity could be, say, the prospect of considerably increasing catering income by the introduction of a wide range of high qualtiy functions. An opportunity for perhaps another bidder could be the prospect of gaining additional contracts with the same client or in the same vicinity.

Threats emanate from the marketplace. One threat could be a possible change in client policy; another, the competitor down the road. A wide variety of leisure providers compete for local residents'

Fig. 4.1 Leisure trends are volatile and exciting.

disposable income. It may be more exciting for a family to go the new ice centre, than return to the old swimming pool.

The biggest threat is undoubtedly a radical shift in leisure spending patterns, away from the attractions specifically provided in the leisure centre being managed.

Leisure is a volatile industry. Today's boom is tomorrow's gong.

Having assessed the marketplace, a prospective contractor is ready to prepare the financial bid. The success, or otherwise, of the ensuing five to six years will rest on that bid.

PREPARING THE BID

Preparing the financial bid is the most exacting task required of the contractor.

In the draft contract documents, the client will have set the financial format and thus the parameters of the contract, as explained in the previous chapter.

For the contractor, pricing the tender starts with the business planning principles already explained. The contractor will need to be able to fully appreciate the environment surrounding the contract.

The client committees of local authorities differ.For example, one local authority may willingly seek bids and thus welcome the attention of contractors. Another may be submitting the leisure facilities to tender only because they are compelled to by law. A world of difference lies between the two.

Fair competition?

Some private sector contractors believe that some authorities are providing a soft option for their in-house teams. If this is so, the Act allows any unfair decision or uncompetitive practice to be challenged via the Secretary of State. An aggrieved party would be well advised to take that route. But an in-house contractor would be foolish indeed to rely on perceived protection. Competition just does not allow for favouritism.

Competitive tendering has rules and regulations in the same way as most sports. All sports managers will quickly understand the boundaries of the pitch, and the rules of the game in tendering. Also, as with most games, the rules are open for all to see. The referee may sit in Whitehall, but he has yellow and red cards to use if necessary. Sections 13 and 14 of the Act provide for that (brief details of the legislation are contained in Appendix C).

So, given the rules of the game and the nature of open competition, all contractors need to analyse the situation carefully and submit their best bid.

Getting started

Having assessed the environment, completed a SWOT analysis, and looked to the future, the contractor is then ready to itemize all aspects of income and expenditure in great detail. To be successful in leisure management, a contractor will need to undertake painstaking and detailed analysis of each and every operation.

Many contractors start by estimating their heating and lighting cost; this is a large fixed annual overhead. It also lends itself to relatively easy analysis. Once the quantity of water in the swimming pool is known, or the cubic footage of the sports hall, then it is a fairly simple arithmetical exercise to calculate the cost of heating to reach the required temperature.

Client information

The client may or may not provide key background information, such as the heating and lighting costs over the last three years. But in any case such information needs to be treated with care. It is surprising how inaccurate information can be, even when the client is trying to help to provide an adequate base for tenders to be made. A case study in the next chapter illustrates the point.

An experienced contractor will always consider and compare the information supplied using his own judgement, based on past experience.

STAFF COSTS

The other major fixed cost is that of salaries and wages. This is not as straightforward as the heating and lighting calculation. Indeed there are an infinite number of variables. Detailed planning is essential for a successful and workable contract.

First a detailed assessment of the staff required to run the operation will be needed. With the right incentives in place, this may be fewer than in a pre-contract situation. Although a number of key specialists will be required, any contractor will seek the greatest flexibility between all staff.

Rate of pay

It is, of course, essential to choose the right payrate for the locality. If that equation is wrong, then either no-one will work for the contractor because the wages are too low or, if they are too high everyone will want to work at the leisure centre but any chance of profit will be in jeopardy.

The leisure facility staff at any leisure centre, are a prime asset. It is essential for success to ensure that the fundamental equation of payrates and staff numbers are correct at the planning stage. Subsequently annual inflation in wages will need to be allowed for, to retain staff.

Income to offset an annual inflation award will be derived from the annual increase in fees and charges as allowed in the contract, and also the increased client payments. Any promise to staff regarding annual pay awards can be no higher.

It is also essential that the contractor apportions all overhead costs onto the basic wage rate. The actual pay to the employee is much less than the cost to the employer.

The contractor will therefore build up a composite wage rate. Some of the key elements in the wage rate will include:

- The wage paid to the member of staff.
- Costs directly attributable to employees, such as National Insurance, sick and holiday pay.
- Office and payroll administration.

In this manner the contractor can ensure that all costs incurred in operating the contract have been included in the tender bid.

COMPILING THE BID

Finally, the contractor has to collate all the costs into a total expenditure estimate. This will allow for sufficient heating and lighting, advertizing and promotions and most importantly adequate staff to run all the facilities.

The contractor can then confidently state the total cost of managing the facility.

The details necessary to satisfy the contractor that all items have been taken into account will be more numerous than the summary shown in Table 3.2.

Having calculated expenditure, the contractor will turn to the more interesting side of the equation: income.

DETERMINING INCOME

Income is a variable. The principal battle for competitiveness in leisure management will be waged on the income front. A successful contractor will increase income and usage.

Fees and charges

To maintain social balance, many clients will specify certain target groups whom they want to attract into the facility. Examples might include ethnic minority groups, women and solo parents. Some clients will require free use by some of these groups.

Other contracts will allow fees and charges to be levied against all users, whether or not from a special interest group. The contractor then has an immediate incentive for increasing usage. This will be the most beneficial relationship between a client and contractor.

Improved income to the contractor also means improved usage for the client and thus more activity taking place by local residents. This will, no doubt, meet many authorities' objective of increasing leisure and recreation opportunities for all groups.

Increased usage

The contractor will be constrained as to the prices which can be charged by the specification. Fees and charges will be set by the local authority in the contract documentation. Increasing usage will therefore be an aspect which the contractor should consider in detail when preparing the tender bid. Furthermore, once operational, the contractor will be keen to do everything possible to increase usage and thus income. Advertizing and promotions will, no doubt, be boosted.

Particularly in leisure management, there are many more subtle ways to increase usage.

If not already available, most leisure centres will soon be provided with a crèche or a poolside playpen. This allows the parents of young children the freedom to enjoy a swim. There is a multitude of other restrictions preventing people taking part in activities, which any self respecting leisure manager will wish to address. Some of these include:

- price
- opening times
- fear of the unknown
- lack of sporting ability
- embarrassment
- lack of knowledge

Where possible, the contractor will seek to reduce these impediments. Lessons for special groups can be arranged. Newcomers can perhaps be attracted by the provision of free lunchtime swimming sessions. A client will rarely object to reduced fees being charged. If new users can be introduced to an activity this way, a proportion will undoubtedly return.

Fig. 4.2 Increased income and use please both client and contractor.

Splash sessions in the swimming pool attract children. This is a chance to encourage parents and relations to join in activities or to inform them of other events which may interest them at some other time.

Realistic estimates

The contractor should not allow unbridled optimism at the prospect of increasing income. Overenthusiasm at the tender stage is the first step to bankruptcy. A realistic assessment of income is very important. It should be based on the type of usage allowed and the contractors' perception of the potential to increase and improve usage.

Leisure facilities operated by contractors who have previously been within local government have often shown dramatic increases in usage. Even after paying 50 per cent of the surplus income back to the client, a contractor can still make a worthwhile profit on an existing operation.

CLIENT PERMISSIONS

All this is totally complementary to the client's objective of increasing usage, especially among target groups. Both client and contractor benefit by a marketing approach. However, an estimate of increased income can never be based on an assumption that the client will allow a variation in the contract.

Frustration occurs where there is insufficient detail within the specification as to the type and nature of use which the client will allow.

Clarification from the client would be sought. The client will usually receive many enquiries from prospective contractors during the course of the tendering period. In answering the query, the client will inform all other tenderers, thus keeping the like for like basis of the tender intact.

Dialogue and . . . . .

In contract management, there has to be meaningful dialogue at all times between contractor and client. This will allow change to take place within the duration of the contract to take account of a new leisure pursuit, or changes requested by customers and users. A contractor cannot rely on client acceptance.

. . . . . change

However, it will often make sense for the client and the contractor to change and amend the programme of use of a leisure facility. Increased use makes good sense to almost everyone. It increases income to the contractor and to the client as well, if the contract is income sharing. This in turn might allow a slight reduction in the local community charge. Moreover, the increase in participation must be of real benefit to those participating.

There is one very real danger.

Programme changes will undoubtedly be resisted by those who have grown used to a set programme over the years. They will not see the benefits. If this involves clubs, they will bring pressure to bear. Hopes of change can be easily dashed.

The point to be appreciated in relation to tender bidding is that no bid should ever be built on assumption. That is an easy way to financial loss.

TENDER SUBMISSION

Once the tenderer has been invited to bid, has analysed the situation thoroughly (by reference to the tender documents, the likely economic climate and a SWOT analysis), all that remains is to complete the expenditure and income tables and submit the tender on time. The competition then enters its final and most gruelling stage.

Post tender negotiations

Many tenderers are surprised to find that there is no immediate announcement of the outright tender winner. The various bids may need clarification by the client, or error correction or even negotiation to achieve a better offer for the client.

The tenderer/contractor needs to be absolutely sure of the income and expenditure basis of the tender before entering negotiations. The tenderer needs to know where to concede amendments, and where any change to the tender bid would lead to impossible financial risks. If, for example, the client suggests deleting a particular activity from the contract, the tenderer must know immediately if that activity is a high income earner and whether the loss of it from the operation is likely to jeopardize the tender bid submitted.

A contractor at this stage cannot help looking over his shoulder at his competitors. Invariably the current in-house contractor will have been invited to bid. However, by law, at least three other contractors have to be invited to tender (provided of course, that at least three contractors are forthcoming). The award of the contract will then almost certainly go to the most favourable financial bid, after negotiations if necessary.

Winners and losers

For any tender, there are more losers than winners. In many, there will be three losers for every winner. Thus three contractors will have spent time and money submitting a bid to no avail. That will hurt.

If they believe that unfair practices have been used in awarding the contract, they should appeal to the Secretary of State for the Environment.

Fairness to all

The rules governing acceptance of tenders are quite clear. Furthermore, all contractors submitting a bid should be informed of the value of the winning bid. In this way the competition is seen to be fair and open. More importantly, the range of tender values will be known. Tenderers will know how near, or how far away, their own bid was from the successful bidder. This key information can be used profitably for the next tender submission.

In certain limited circumstances, the contract may be awarded to the in-house bid, even where it does not make the best offer. An example would be where the costs of redundancy outweighed the financial benefits of the lower tender offer. However, this is a card which can be played only once, and all local authority leisure management contracts will be renewed before six years.

Once a tender has been let, all the leisure management contractor has to do is to achieve the budget plan of income and expenditure submitted with the tender. Simple – in theory. But in practice, all too many deflections and variations can and do occur to alter the original planning. This is a subject of another chapter, but in the meantime let us summarize this chapter, before looking at some actual tender case studies in the next.

SUMMARY

- To minimize commercial risk, the contractor needs to assess the future accurately.
- Key assessments are needed in relation to:
    - possible policy changes during the life of the contract
    - the contractor's own strengths and weaknesses
    - opportunities and threats
- An accurate assessment of the business environment as it could affect the contractor for the following four to six years is essential.
- This would include:
    - any likely change to council policy
    - any likely change to leisure trends
    - the trends in the national economy
- Very detailed costings are needed in relation to all expenditure items.
- Wage and salary levels should be locally comparable, perhaps with a profit share link.
- Realistic estimates of income are imperative.
- It is easy, and fatal, to be overconfident at the tender submission stage.
- There will be many ways to increase use and income, within the terms of the contract.
- There will be even more methods to increase income, given approval.
- All contracts rely on mutual goodwill once operational.
- The ability to change to meet new circumstances is important for everyone.
- The alternative is disillusioned contractors and customers and a fossilized leisure facility.
- Invariably the lowest tender bid will win.
- Clear rules and regulations govern the analysis of all bids, including in-house bids.
- When the value of all bids are known, tenderers will be informed of the value of other bids, which will help them in future tenders.

A successful tender bid by a contractor is based on a solid commercial judgement of the tender documents, the prevailing economic climate, the likelihood of change from the client and, perhaps most importantly, the contractor's own strengths and weaknesses.

ADDENDUM: MANAGEMENT DATA

The details supplied in this addendum give an example of some of the commercial data necessary for the successful ongoing operation of a leisure management business. The information has been supplied by Quota Computer Associates Ltd, office computer systems consultants, of Shrivenham, Wiltshire who have produced a range of leisure centre management applications.

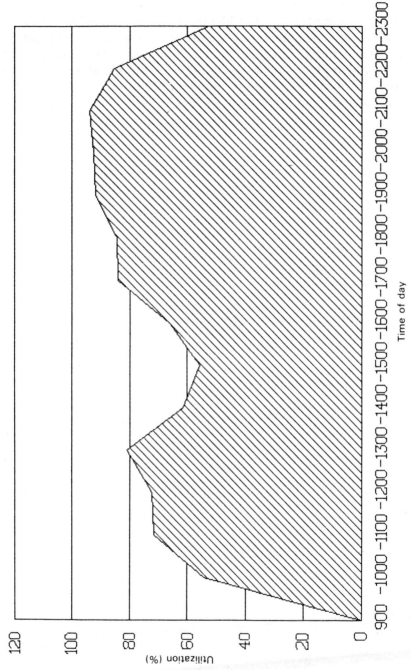

Squash court utilization.

Utilization (per cent) of squash courts, January

Period	SUN 1	MON 2	TUE 3	WED 4	THU 5	FRI 6	SAT 7	SUN 8	MON 9	TUE 10	WED 11	THU 12	FRI 13
Pre 0900	0	0	0	0	0	0	0	0	0	0	0	0	0
0900–1000	100	100	0	8.3	0	100	58.3	8.3	100	16.7	0	0	0
1000–1100	100	100	50	33.3	0	100	58.3	8.3	50	83.3	66.7	0	100
1100–1200	100	100	25	50	50	100	66.7	16.7	8.3	50	100	33.3	100
1200–1300	100	100	91.7	16.7	100	100	66.7	0	75	66.7	100	50	100
1300–1400	100	100	33.3	0	100	100	16.7	0	100	16.7	0	50	100
1400–1500	100	100	50	16.7	100	100	0	0	100	50	0	50	100
1500–1600	100	100	0	12.5	100	100	58.3	0	50	33	50	50	100
1600–1700	100	100	16.7	12.5	100	100	75	33.3	100	100	33.3	50	100
1700–1800	100	100	33.3	16.7	91.7	100	83.3	8.3	66.7	91.7	100	50	100
1800–1900	100	100	83.3	50	91.7	100	100	25	100	91.7	100	41.7	100
1900–2000	100	100	100	45.8	100	100	83.3	16.7	100	100	100	50	100
2000–2100	100	100	100	45.8	100	100	83.3	16.7	100	100	100	50	100
2100–2200	100	100	91.7	50	100	100	58.3	0	100	100	100	50	100
2200–2300	100	100	41.7	16.7	83.3	33.3	25	0	33.3	50	100	50	50
2300–2400	0	0	0	0	0	0	0	0	0	0	0	0	0

Utilization (per cent) of squash courts, January (contd)

Period	SAT 14	SUN 15	MON 16	TUE 17	WED 18	THU 19	FRI 20	SAT 21	SUN 22	MON 23	TUE 24	WED 25	THU 26	FRI 27
Pre 0900	0	0	0	0	0	0	0	0	0	0	0	0	0	0
0900–1000	25	66.7	33.3	25	8.3	100	100	33.3	33.3	33.3	33.3	0	100	100
1000–1100	91.7	100	16.7	91.7	75	100	100	66.7	83.3	83.3	100	66.7	100	100
1100–1200	58.3	100	66.7	50	100	100	100	58.3	91.7	0	66.7	100	100	100
1200–1300	91.7	100	66.7	66.7	50	100	100	91.7	75	66.7	83.3	50	100	100
1300–1400	0	100	0	66.7	8.3	100	100	16.7	66.7	83.3	50	8.3	100	100
1400–1500	16.7	83.3	66.7	50	8.3	100	75	16.7	83.3	33.3	50	41.7	100	91.7
1500–1600	100	100	83.3	100	8.3	100	75	66.7	100	100	100	33.3	100	58.3

Period	SAT 28	SUN 29	MON 30	TUE 31	AVERAGE
Pre 0900	0	0	0	0	0
0900–1000	83.3	33.3	100	50	54.3
1000–1100	66.7	83.3	33.3	100	71.8
1100–1200	66.7	100	66.7	91.7	72.6
1200–1300	100	100	66.7	91.7	81.2
1300–1400	75	75	66.7	83.3	61.8
1400–1500	75	41.7	0	50	55.9
1500–1600	100	100	50	66.7	66.5

CANCELLED BOOKINGS – December

This report shows details from the list of cancellations held on file. No default is created and no details are written to WP files by printing this report.

VENUE:- Carn Brea LC

BOOKING DATE	BOOKING REF	VEN	LOC	TIME	ACTIVITY	TO PAY	CUST NO	CUSTOMER NAME/ ADDRESS	TEL	CANC. CODE	RE-USED	BOOKING CANCELLED BY	AT
8/12	A501864	001	01	1730	SOCCER 5	.00	000000	WESTLAND S	67541	A	?	1/12	JOHN 11:59
9/12	A501818	001	02	1500	SNOOKER	.00	000000	WESTLAND S	67541	J	?	1/11	JOHN 12:02
11/12	A501342	001	01	0900	MAINTENANCE	.00	999999	MANAGEMENT ADMIN		G	?	6/12	JOHN 14:46
16/12	A501818	001	02	1500	SNOOKER	.00	000000	WESTLAND S		J	?	1/11	JOHN 12:02
18/12	A501342	001	01	0900	MAINTENANCE	.00	999999	MANAGEMENT ADMIN		G	?	6/12	JOHN 14:46
18/12	A501883	001	01	1530	BADMINTON	.00	1000001	Scarth Quarry Walk Littlehampton	TEL HOME	A	?	13/12	JOHN 11:02

CANCELLATION CODES:

A = Cancelled at customer request, no penalty.
B = Cancelled at customer request, within penalty period, default possible.
C = Customer NO SHOW with money outstanding DEFAULT set ON.
D = Booking cancelled – unpaid by due date – NO DEFAULT and NO penalty. (See overnight report for these details)
E = Customer no show but paid – NO DEFAULT and NO penalty. (See overnight report for these details)
F = Cancelled by management – facilities unfit.
G = Cancelled by management – referee/umpire declared facilities unfit.
H = Customer NO SHOW after booking HELD. DEFAULT set ON if customer details are on file.
I = Cancelled by management – facilities unfit. (Like type F but for repeated bookings.)
J = Cancelled by management – booking incorrectly made or needed changing.

Periodic CASH ANALYSIS PART 2 – DESCRIPTIVE ANALYSIS FOR PERIOD October 1.

DESCRIPTION	ANALYSIS	UNITS	+	VALUE
No description		3	+	.70
ICE HOCKEY TICKET SALES	A80730S	707	–	1805.00
ICE HOCKEY PROGRAMME SALES	A80731S	156	–	215.46
RINK SKATE – ADULT PEAK	A80904S	204	–	436.50
RINK SKATE – CONC PEAK	A80906S	461	–	772.05
RINK – GUARDIANS	A80915S	25	–	12.50
RINK – SKATE HIRE	A80916S	78	–	35.10
RINK SKATE – COACH PARTIES	A80917S	12	+	.00
RINK – COURSES	A80920S	100	–	152.45
RINK – PATCHES	A80921S	5	–	7.50
RINK – LOCKER HIRE	A80928S	4	–	.80
HELMET LOCKER TOKENS	A80929S	0	–	.40
SNOOKER	A80934S	85	–	55.00
SQUASH	A80935S	42	–	36.30
SWIMMING – ADULT	A80936S	67	–	60.30
SWIMMING – CONCESSION	A80937S	134	–	51.20
BADMINTON	A80942S	75	–	60.65
HALL HIRE	A80943S	6	–	2.95
TABLE TENNIS	A80944S	15	–	3.85
CLIMBING WALLS	A80946S	8	–	9.20
HEALTH SUITE	A80950S	36	–	94.20
EQUIPMENT HIRE	A80955S	0	–	2.85
COURSES	A80962S	5	–	9.80
BIRTHDAY PARTIES	A80963S	27	–	26.00
RECREATION SESSIONS	A80964S	30	–	22.50
LINK ARTS TICKET SALES	V23019S	4	–	10.00
BOOKING CARDS	Y16573Y	0	–	15.00
SUBTOTAL				3896.86
CASHIERS UNDER/OVERS	AB0500Y		+	1.60
TOTAL INCOME	Y01302Y		+	3895.26

Chapter Five

Recreation contractors – tender experiences

A picture is worth a thousand words, so it is said. Similarly, real life case studies provide a clear insight into the operation and practice of tendering. However, case studies are but snapshots of the experiences of one company at a particular moment in time.

In any tendering situation there are certain features which are peculiar to that situation. It is therefore dangerous to generalize from the experience of one contractor. Taken together, however, the experiences of a number of contractors do tend to underline common features. That is the purpose of this chapter.

Pathbreakers

The companies who have agreed to be case studies have all been leaders in the new world of leisure management by competitive tender. They have all been party to starting a new industry and setting procedures and guidelines for others to follow.

In some industries where contract management has been a feature for decades, the methods employed for tendering and contract management have become standardized across the industry. An example is housing maintenance where national detailed specifications are available for a multitude of tasks from replacing tap washers to repairing roofs.

As leisure is a relative newcomer to contract management, tender documentation has not yet had time to become standardized.

The amount of written detail available within all contract industries tends to reflect the number of years in which contract management has been a feature. In the leisure industry, contract management documents will be somewhat less variable and perhaps more detailed by the end of the 1990s than they were at the start of the decade.

Initially tender documentation varied greatly in size. Some contained only a few hundred pages, others a few thousand. All tried faithfully to reflect the desires and aspirations of the client authority.

Once draft contract and tender documents are prepared, the client will advertize for the intention to let a contract. All contractors regularly check the press for details of contracts being advertised, and then express their interest.

Management without restrictions

Services directly provided by local authorities tend to have inbuilt restrictions. These include inflexible pay arrangements and a lack of capital resources to exploit a new leisure fashion. The leisure contractors in these studies were not bound by such restrictions. Their sole objective is to maximize use of the leisure facility for everyone's benefit. This they have done with great success.

CROSSLAND LEISURE

Crossland Leisure (Holdings) Ltd. was pehaps the first company to be formed with the intention of operating leisure centres by contract.

It was formed in 1983 by David Cross and John Staniland. Their stated objective was to manage leisure centres free of the constraints normally imposed by local authority operation, and thus provide a better service for the customers and the local authority.

Deficit guarantee

The company offered local authorities the opportunity of having leisure facilities managed for them on a deficit guarantee basis. In other words, the company guaranteed the maximum deficit which the local authority would have to meet.

This was a radical departure from the practice up to then. Before this offer was available, local authorities had to accept the deficit, whatever its size, on their leisure facilities, as they were directly managed. There was no intermediary third party who acted as a buffer.

Furthermore, the company was perhaps the first to offer a profit share to the local authority. Any income received in excess of the amount estimated in the original contract was shared equally between the local authority and the contractor.

On this basis, Crossland developed a number of partnership business ventures up and down the country. It became known as an 'income sharing/deficit guarantee' contract.

Basis for the contracts

Most contracts were for a five- to ten-year term. The exact length of the contract often depended on whether capital improvements were involved to the buildings, for example a new reception area. If capital improvements involved extra initial expense by Crossland, a longer contract term was then essential to allow the company to recover the outlay made.

At the outset of each contract, agreement was reached with the local authority as to the recreation programme to be provided at the leisure facility, and the type of operation which the client wished to see was in place. An example for a sports hall would be 20 hours of badminton, five hours of indoor cricket and so forth.

A price was then submitted on this basis. This invariably allowed the local authority to set the fees to be charged to customers. Once the contract had been let, changes were allowed by discussion and agreement.

Employment policies

Beginning to operate a contract, at a stated price, is only the start of any business. Thereafter success in a leisure facility depends heavily on the motivation of the staff. A strong feature of the company therefore relates to staff policies. Crossland Leisure go to great lengths to ensure that the right staff are employed. Monthly appraisal of all staff is undertaken to assess and re-assess their success in any particular post.

'We have always believed that staff are our greatest asset,' John Standiland explains. 'It is essential for the company's long-term viability to have a team of committed, well trained and enthusiastic staff keen to provide the highest possible standards of service.'

Financial control

The company undertakes a thorough monthly examination of accounts for all centres, and for all activities. These monthly accounts allow an accurate assessment of each business.

Any change in trend is thus quickly pinpointed. If, for example, an income lower than forecast is received, then immediate analysis can be undertaken, the difficulty diagnosed and corrective action taken. This is sound business practice. Furthermore, all income and expenditure figures are made available to the local authority.

Elements for success

Crossland Leisure have secured an excellent reputation for managing leisure facilities. Their success is based on the application of fundamental business principles. These principles emphasize first, the importance of the agreed contract between client and contractor and, second, the importance of the staff employed.

AN ANALYSIS OF DOCUMENTS

Before looking at other companies, it is valuable to reassess the fundamental importance of the draft contract supplied at the time of tender.

The size and nature of the documents supplied at the time of tendering give the tenderer an early indication of the type and nature of an authority. A clear understanding of the nature of the client authority is essential for a tenderer to be successful. All contracts are, in the end, based on confidence and trust. Building this confidence and trust begins with draft contract documents and the tenderers' appraisal of them.

Having decided to tender for a specific contract, the hard work then begins for the tenderer. Evaluation of the worth of the business is the most essential aspect for the tenderer. There is a multitude of other factors to be analysed, assessed, valued and put in place before completing the tender.

CITY CENTRE LEISURE

One of the first local authorities to offer all the leisure facilities in their borough to tender was the City of Westminster. Here the council decided, as a political decision, to put the leisure facilities in the borough out to tender, ahead of any legislation.

The officers employed within the leisure department re-evaluated their careers in a very different light. Challenged by the new arrangements, they formed their own company.

City Centre Leisure Ltd was the name chosen for the new company, composed of the local government officers employed by the City of Westminster. They were thrust from their protected environment into the intense pressure of not only submitting a tender bid, but also forming a new company. Their biggest advantage was knowing the client authority intimately and having a fair assessment of the business value of the five leisure centres within the borough.

Income projections

Their principal disadvantage was their lack of experience of the business world. They rectified this by seeking the advice of a specialist who could provide the necessary guidance. Phil Reid, the operations director, explains:

> We particularly analysed the income growth likely for the five years of the contract period. We then gave more detailed attention to income and expenditure during the first 18 months. This highlighted the likely peaks and troughs of our business.

Fig. 5.1 A sympathetic city financier.

December and January were easily identified as the months with the lowest turnover. This was essential information to determine the projected cash flow of the business, allowing attention to be given to the financial balances needed to sustain the business. A business plan was prepared. This business plan, prepared in conjunction with their financial adviser, had to be sufficient to achieve credibility with the bank. This aspect of the company is the subject of a case study in Chapter 10.

With the basis of a company formed, and the business plan established, the team had the confidence to set about submitting a tender.

Staff terms

Before the tender submission, it was necessary to agree terms and conditions for the members of staff, and thus enable the calculation of the staff budget.

Critical attention was also given to the number of staff to be employed. Staff numbers were then compared with the projected attendance and income figures. The number of staff employed was reduced by six by streamlining the engineering section and a further slight reduction of two was made possible when coin-operated lockers were introduced.

Arrangements for payroll management were made with the bank. For a payment of slightly over £1 000, a desk top computer and telephone modem were purchased, providing direct access to the bank. Arrangements were made for some aspects of the payroll to be undertaken by the bank for the company, although a significant input of time by City Centre Leisure staff was still needed.

The newly formed company decided to maintain similar rates of pay to those already in place. Unlike many similar leisure operations, this included shift pay and other enhancements to the basic wage. This was a bold decision. However, the company was one of the leaders in taking on existing staff in existing leisure facilities. The maintenance of pay levels was seen to be an important stabilizing factor in entering this new contract situtation.

Sick leave

Nevertheless, arrangements for periods of illness were totally changed. This is an area of staff control often inadequately addressed in many industries. Without clear guidelines, resources can be wasted, and in a contract where every pound counts, such waste can quickly lead to financial loss. A firm and fair policy in relation to sick leave was considered essential.

No pay was to be provided for the first three days of absence. Subsequently, full payment was agreed for the following 14 days, with a further 14 days on half pay. The management board would consider more favourable arrangements according to individual circumstances, and at their discretion.

Incentives

The company also believed in incentives. This extended to extra annual leave of up to one week to award a good attendance record. Other incentives included the provision of a monthly cash bonus scheme, awarded to the employee of the month. Although total staff numbers were reduced, there was a huge improvement in staff morale and customer awareness. The success of the business, and the obvious customer satisfaction expressed at the centres, is a clear indication that the original planning was well thought out.

A tender is submitted. . . .

With their business plan in place, and employment practices agreed, the company was able to finalize its tender submission. There was a last minute nightmare obtaining a performance bond (very difficult for a company with no track record). Nevertheless, the tender was submitted on time.

Once a tender had been submitted, most tenderers can settle down for the nervous wait until the winner is announced.

. . . . and a winner announced

However, in reality, what followed was possibly an even more difficult period.

City Centre Leisure and the City of Westminster entered into post tender negotiation. There were a number of meetings at which the City of Westminster made demanding new requirements. Phil Reid recalls:

Eventually, by negotiation, these requirements were met. Both parties can be said to have taken some credit from this negotiation process: the City of Westminster for achieving a far better contract, and CCL for being able to respond positively and to withstand the pressure of the continued negotiating procedures.

By all accounts it was a very difficult and traumatic time.

In the end, the negotiations resulted in the five centres within Westminster being divided between two companies. City Centre Leisure Ltd was awarded the contract for the prestigious Queen Mother Sports Centre, located half way between Victoria main line station and Vauxhall Bridge on the Thames and opened in 1981 by the Queen Mother.

The second centre awarded to the company was the Seymour Leisure Centre, built in the 1930s, with a very traditional programme of activities.

Although disappointed by the change in financial circumstances, and having been awarded only two of the five centres, the company set about putting their new practices and ideas to the test. Their subsequent success is clear evidence of the firm foundation provided by the business plan, and the on-going management expertise within the company.

Further down the River Thames, a similar political picture was unfolding in the small Essex District Council of Rochford.

CIRCA LEISURE plc

Circa Leisure, based in Essex, had a unique experience with their tender for the Rochford District Council leisure facilities, which comprised three sports centres and three public halls.

Circa Leisure was formed in 1988 from, and by, the employees of the leisure department of Rochford District Council. Their buyout experiences are detailed in Chapter 10. They had to tender, along with four other companies, only a few months after the trauma of the company's birth.

The new company had, however, put those early months to valuable use. The employees invested heavily in the company, and rigorous marketing research analysis paid dividends by increasing use and income. The company believed that, armed with the information it had, it could beat off any challengers.

It did so. However, it was successful by only the tightest of margins. The five tenderers all gave very competitive bids to the council.

Personal commitment

Peter Johnson, chairman of Circa Leisure remembers:

> It was not an easy time. Everyone in the company had invested
> their own personal savings. This cash had been used up front,
> in improving our marketing position. Although this was vital to
> long term success, it was not without real personal risk. For
> example, whilst completing the tender, I was well aware that
> failure would financially ruin me and my wife and family.
> I cannot emphasize too strongly to anyone taking a tendering
> route where their own finances are involved, that there are very
> real risks. At Circa, for all of us, the fear of risk was balanced
> by the total sense of commitment by everyone. Also we had the
> benefit of sound financial advice from one of the largest com-
> panies of accountants in the country.

Tendering strategy

Circa Leisure quickly expanded from their base at Rochford. The next
step was to secure additional local contracts. They now operate a leisure
pool and sports centre for Maldon District Council on a 10-year contract,
and a bars contract for the adjacent local authority of Castle Point. In
this way the new company established a strong home base in Essex.

Circa feels that contracts, if they are to be successful, need to be
based around an effective partnership with local authorities. The
company seeks to obtain tenders with those authorities who can see
the real benefits that the private management of their leisure facilities
can bring. Consequently, the company has a positive development
strategy which takes it all round the country and into many tendering
situations. Their early success is a clear indication of their future
potential. Peter Johnson comments:

> We place tender bids where we believe a viable operation is
> possible. It is particularly important to us to be able to secure
> good quality senior staff locally. Also, we look at each tender
> and each operation from a marketing point of view. Our market
> research at Rochford forced us to rethink our perceptions of what
> the community wanted and proved to be well worth the £80 000
> that we invested.

In their experience of tendering, they have found that tender
documents vary enormously. Some require detailed statements

Fig. 5.2   Tenders vary in the detail required.

of income and expenditure for up to five years ahead. Others are more modest in their requirements.

Two senior members of the company are allocated to tendering. The philosophy is simple. If the company does not allocate resources to tendering, its long-term future is much less secure. Company policy is the long-term expansion of the company, at a gradual rate.

The main lesson then, from the Circa experience, is perhaps the very positive assessment of all expenditure and income heads prior to tender, and an ongoing marketing approach once the contract is awarded.

SUMMARY

Leisure management by contract is a new industry. The experiences of tendering are therefore more varied than would be the case in an established contracting industry. For example, some draft contracts are barely a few hundred pages in length, others run to a thousand or more.

The more important points illustrated in this chapter include:

- Most tender situations start with the client's advertisement in the local paper and specialist national press.
- Sharing of surplus income is often a feature; (surplus income means income additional to that expected when the tender was submitted).
- For the first time, local authority clients now have the financial security of knowing the maximum deficit which will occur on their facilities.
- The contractor absorbs any losses.
- Contracts are generally for four to six years, although some of the earlier contracts were up to ten years.
- Programming and pricing are stated by the client.
- The size of the tender documents give an early indication of the level of control to be exercised by the client.
- The client controls everything in a tender situation.
- Tenderers often feel used by the client, especially when the client introduces late changes.
- Critical attention needs to be given to all items of expenditure and income, as part of the tender submission.
- A top quality financial adviser is almost essential in a competitive situation.
- A marketing approach is also invaluable.
- Staff are a major cost in any tender submission, and thus need to be very carefully considered.
- Terms and conditions for contractor staff are usually very different from traditional local government terms and conditions.
- The numbers of staff to be employed, and the provision of attractive terms and conditions (linked to performance), is a key feature.
- Tight income and expenditure monitoring is built into the subsequent contract operation.
- Leisure managers are, by their very nature, innovative. Their dynamic energy should be harnessed.

Total personal commitment to winning the tender, and subsequently delivering the service, is an essential ingredient for all successful tenders. This attitude needs to be in place with all the staff, and not just the management team at the top.

ADDENDUM: CLIENT CONTROL

A wide variety of client control documents will be used in many leisure management contracts. The documents in this addendum provide three examples where critical client control is seen to be essential.

The documents are from *Management of Sports and Leisure Facilities*, jointly produced by the Institute of Leisure and Amenity Management and the Institute of Baths and Recreation Management, published by Longman and reproduced with their permission.

Monitoring, supervising and controlling the contract

USER COMPLAINT RECORD

```
┌─────────────────────────────────────────────────────────────┐
│ NORTHDEN DISTRICT COUNCIL                                     │
│ DEPARTMENT OF AMENITIES AND RECREATION                        │
├─────────────────────────────────────────────────────────────┤
│ USER COMPLAINT  RECORD                                        │
├──────────────────────────────────────┬──────────────────────┤
│ CONTRACT:............................ │ Date:                │
│ Contractor:..........................                        │
│ Address:............................. │ Time:                │
│          ............................ ├──────────────────────┤
│          ............................ │ Project No.          │
│          ............................ ├──────────────────────┤
│          ............................ │ File Ref.            │
├──────────────────────────────────────┴──────────────────────┤
│ LOCATION [AREA/SITE/ESTABLISHMENT]:                          │
│ ............................................................ │
│ ............................................................ │
├──────────────────────────────────────────────────────────────┤
│ Complaint received by:.................. Acknowledged: Y/N   │
├──────────────────────────────────────────────────────────────┤
│ NAME OF COMPLAINANT:........................................ │
│ ADDRESS:.................................................... │
│         .................................................... │
│         .................................................... │
│         .................................................... │
│ TELEPHONE NO............................                     │
├──────────────────────────────────────────────────────────────┤
│ Complaint submitted: BY LETTER/BY TELEPHONE/IN PERSON        │
├──────────────────────────────────────────────────────────────┤
│ NATURE OF COMPLAINT:                                         │
│ ............................................................ │
│ ............................................................ │
│ ............................................................ │
│ ............................................................ │
│ ............................................................ │
│ ............................................................ │
├──────────────────────────────────────────────────────────────┤
│ CLIENT'S COMMENT/ACTION PROPOSED:                            │
│ ............................................................ │
│ ............................................................ │
│ ............................................................ │
│ ............................................................ │
│ ............................................................ │
├──────────────────────────────────────────────────────────────┤
│ INCORPORATE ON DEFECTIVE WORK NOTICE/VARIATION ORDER NO..... │
├──────────────────────────────────────────────────────────────┤
│                                                              │
│ Signed......................................for Contractor   │
│                                                              │
│ Signed...................................Authorised Officer  │
│ [Copy to : Client Officer/Contractor/Contract File]          │
└──────────────────────────────────────────────────────────────┘
```

DEFECTIVE WORK NOTICE

NORTHDEN DISTRICT COUNCIL DEPARTMENT OF AMENITIES AND RECREATION	
DEFECTIVE WORK NOTICE	Notice No.
CONTRACT:............................. Contractor:..........................	Date:
Address:.............................	Project No.
....	File Ref.
....	
LOCATION:	
SCHEDULE REFERENCE NO.:	
CLIENT'S INSTRUCTIONS : Signed on behalf of Contractor.............................	
ACTION TAKEN : 	

Date Work Completed		Time	
Date Work Inspected		Time	
Work carried out	SATISFACTORILY	UNSATISFACTORILY	
Date Work Re-inspected		Time	
Work carried out	SATISFACTORILY	UNSATISFACTORILY	
Date Work Re-inspected		Time	

WORK COMPLETED TO SATISFACTION OF AUTHORISED OFFICER

Signed.................................Authorised Officer
[Copy to : Client Officer/Contractor/Contract File]

Monitoring, supervising and controlling the contract

AGENDA FOR PROGRESS MEETING

NORTHDEN DISTRICT COUNCIL DEPARTMENT OF AMENITIES AND RECREATION	
AGENDA FOR PROGRESS MEETING	Meeting No.
CONTRACT:............................ Contractor:..........................	Weekly/Monthly
Address:............................	Date:
....	Project Ref.
....	File Ref.

AGENDA

     1.   Attendance

     2.   Apologies for Absence

     3.   Action on Minutes of last meeting

     4.   Work carried out to date/Work Programme

     5.   Orders/Instructions outstanding

     6.   Review of performance

     7.   Response times in rectifying defects

     8.   Correspondence/complaints/compliments

     9.   Financial Report/Performance Indicators/Usage

    10.   Additional work requirements

    11.   Any other urgent business

    12.   Date of next progress meeting

Signed.................................Authorised Officer

[Copy to : Client Officers/Contractor's Reps/Contract File]

Chapter Six

Delegation and contract management

Strong financial forward planning forms the solid foundation for all successful business. This has been highlighted in the earlier chapters. Positive delegation comes next. There are two areas for delegation:

- technical and recreational
- financial

TECHNICAL AND RECREATIONAL DELEGATION

A manager's first priority is to ensure absolute confidence in the provision of all the technical and recreational input necessary for operating a leisure facility.

These range between the technical competence essential to operate a facility like a swimming pool with chlorination, water treatment and water safety requirements to the specialist knowledge needed for, say, offering weight training opportunities.

Each area has its own, specific requirements. The simplest mistake can have the most traumatic consequences.

Great emphasis has always been placed on technical training over the years. Once a person is trained and qualified, delegation easily follows. This, unfortunately, often leads to rigid working practices. Perhaps for too long, technical and recreational ability has been assumed to be of overriding importance. In a commercial business environment that is no longer true. There is more to management than technical competence.

We live in a technically competent society. Management demands, and expects, constant and unswerving skill and technical ability to be infinitely available. This is not to belittle technical and recreational ability, but rather to enshrine it. Without it nothing works. Every business manager will be at pains to ensure its continued consistency.

Right first time, every time

The business manager therefore needs to ensure that a range of competent specialists are available in all aspects of operation. A wide variety of specialist staff will be employed. These will include receptionists, lifeguards, plant mechanics and engineers, swimming instructors, catering managers, sports coaches and a host of other specialists. All will have one thing in common: each will be qualified and experienced in his or her own particular field, and take pride in an individual area of delegated responsibility.

However, for business success, there will need to be totally flexible working between virtually all staff. There can be no arbitary demarcation lines. All staff will need to be interchangeable.

Those staff who undertake tasks which require a specialist technical or recreational qualification are still fully competent to undertake a wide variety of other tasks. Furthermore, they are in an excellent position to train new staff. That way, many staff become competent to carry out a wide variety of work. This not only helps in the management of the centre or the facility, it also leads directly to increased job satisfaction for everybody.

Flexibility

For example, there is no inherent reason why a lifeguard cannot also clean the changing rooms. Indeed this is recommended working practice as it provides necessary variety for the employee, so that peak concentration can be maintained when on lifeguard duty.

Furthermore, many progressive pool managements have taught their lifeguards the skills associated with backwashing, and other technical operations. This is good personnel management; again, it increases job interest and satisfaction. It also makes obvious economic sense. There is no point in employing a specialist plant attendant who cannot be used on other duties.

Business management demands a total, abstract, and objective view over everything, with each specialism and each technical skill fitting correctly into the corporate jigsaw. The business manager cannot allow attention to be diverted from the management of the business, by a continual succession of day to day problems of a technical or customer care nature. These should be undertaken by competent subordinates. Delegation and motivation go together.

Fig. 6.1 Flexible staff learn backwashing.

DELEGATION AND MOTIVATION

Much has been written about motivation and delegation. Some of the key elements include:

- shared values
- appropriate experience
- appropriate training
- clear definition of responsibilities
- achievable goals

Leisure has always been able to offer real satisfaction to those seeking a career, whether in a technical specialism, sports, arts, recreation, catering or one of many other areas. Long may it continue. In this manner everyone gains – the career motivated specialist, the customers and users, and the business.

Motivation is enhanced by the right working environment. Key environmental features include:

- pay and conditions
- provision of suitable staff clothing
- good rest and recreation facilities on site
- for some posts, hours to suit home commitments.

More than anything, a person at work needs to understand how worthwhile their contribution is to the organization as a whole.

And there is one factor which ensures continuing motivation. That is a sense of winning.

Everyone needs to feel that they are winning – at something. It is a fundamental human need (once all the basic necessitites of life are provided). Winning, however, comes in many guises.

Winning with a difference

In any game, there are, in fact, often two games being played. One is the formal game, with goals and points to be won, which all can see. The other is the game within the mind of each individual player. It may be as simple as a weekend football player showing off to his girlfriend on the touchline. It can manifest itself as a personal vendetta against another player, to be settled when most players are looking the other way.

At work the interior game can show itself in being the best dressed person in the centre, or in some other personally esoteric way. Another player is the persistent petty pilferer. Both, believe that they are winning – but winning according to their own rules.

Managers need to be acutely aware of all the games people get up to. Many of life's games can bring real improved quality without cost. Some games however, are merely corrosive. The players in these games have to be removed from the scene immediately.

Setting the goals

Once aware of life's games, and how to tackle them, the manager can then concentrate on setting management oriented goals. Management goals have a very simple and easily understood common denominator: cash.

The tender bid will have been compiled from all the many elements of income and expenditure within the centre. That exercise will have set the ultimate goal which has to be achieved (i.e. the bottom line, tendered cash total). Failure here cannot be countenanced.

Having achieved technical and recreational delegation, and flexible working, the business manager can now turn to the financial dimensions of the business.

OPERATING TO A BUDGET

The ability to predict future income levels and, more importantly, to be able to deliver the income, is the hallmark of the competent leisure management contractor. Regular income and expenditure monitoring is essential for delivering a contract service to a given price. This is true for all sources of income (sports, recreation, health and fitness, catering, machines and so on) and all sources of expenditure.

The secure foundations of the business must be built on the bedrock of technical and recreational competence. Once that is provided for, financial responsibility and delegation should follow on.

FINANCIAL DELEGATION

In a contract situation, delegation in financial terms is (in theory) very simple. The bottom line tendered figure has to be achieved. The manager of a unit or facility is the person who is held entirely responsible for achieving that goal.

Although no football manager scores any goals directly, the players know that scoring goals depends in turn on strategy, good tactics and teamplay. In management too simple tactical targets of income and expenditure have to be set for individual activities; and then activity managers appointed.

Activity managers

For those in the public sector, financial delegation will be a fundamental and essential change. It is one of the single biggest changes which is directly attributable to the competitive environment.

If an activity manager is to be responsible for part of a budget, then that manager should have been largely responsible for preparing it, at the tender stage. If that has not been possible, then the activity manager must be allowed an opportunity to state the target income which is achievable. Having agreed target figures (of income and expenditure), then the activity manager has to deliver.

For this to be possible, an all encompassing itemized statement of income and expenditure for each and every cost centre and profit centre is essential. Nothing less will achieve effective financial delegation.

Profiled budgets

It is easy to prepare a budget of income and expenditure from the tendered bid. This then needs to be profiled for each expenditure and income item. This profiled budget becomes the principal management tool for monitoring. An example of a monthly profiled budget is given in Table 6.1.

Table 6.1 A profile of monthly expenditure

| | Month 1 | | Month 2 | |
	Estimate £	Actual £	Estimate £	Actual £
Manpower				
Management	5 000.00		5 000.00	
Staff	12 500.00		12 500.00	
Supplies				
Utilities (heat, water etc.)	2 500.00		2 500.00	
Specialists	750.00		750.00	
Materials	1 000.00		1 000.00	
Other costs				
Central costs (head office)	1 000.00		1 000.00	
Rates, insurances	2 000.00		2 000.00	
Leasing etc	250.00		250.00	
Totals	25 000.00		25 000.00	

ORGANIZATION AND STRUCTURE

For a small facility, there will be only one manager. For example, a small swimming pool with ancilliary rooms will be directly managed by one person. This manager will be wholly responsible for all aspects of plant, equipment, expenditure on heating, lighting and expenditure on wages.

Nevertheless, proper delegation of a wide range of duties to receptionists, lifeguards and other staff is essential for the manager to succeed. In this example, the activity managers will be one of the receptionists, one of the lifeguards and so on. Rostering, programme control, training schedules can all be delegated; even financial control.

Division of responsibilities

A receptionist is just as able to account for the weekly income as to tally the day's takings. A fulltime lifeguard is easily able to keep track of all the duty rosters. The staff nearest to the source of delegated activity (weekly takings, duty rosters), are the staff with the greatest interest. The office staff may well process all payments, but genuine interest lies nearer to the source of the income and expenditure.

Job enrichment is not just for the textbooks.

More importantly, the facility manager is then freed to give sufficient attention to total income and expenditure control, and to the key areas of customer care, facility management, and promotions to increase use. No longer should the manager be locked away in the office looking after the paperwork. For the first time in many cases, the manager will manage and, furthermore, be seen to manage.

Specialist managers

A large, complex, leisure centre will need, and be able to afford, a business manager in overall control, and specialist managers in addition. Again, it should be emphasized that these specialist managers must be competent in income and expenditure forecasting, as well as qualified and experienced in their own specialism.

A busy leisure centre may have the following managers:

- Sports manager
- Catering manager
- Front of house and administration manager
- Plant and equipment manager

It is interesting to note that many small private businesses have a more managerial division of responsibilities for their senior management team than that encountered in most leisure centres.

A typical business management team, would often be limited to:

- Managing director
- Finance director

- Marketing and sales director
- Technical or production manager

The difference in approach is worth analysing. There is strength in both.

FINANCIAL RESPONSIBILITY

Whatever the title of the manager, the financial task is at least known once the tender value is set. The operation of the leisure management contract needs only to achieve the planned budget each year. Regrettably, in business, all too often inadequate attention is given to accurate financial monitoring.

Each manager needs to produce a budget for income and expenditure for his or her area of responsibility. Specific attention is necessary

Table 6.2 A profile of monthly income at Little London Swimming Pool

INCOME ITEMS	Month 1		Month 2	
	Estimate £	Actual £	Estimate £	Actual £
Admissions				
Adult	4 000.00		4 000.00	
Youth	4 000.00		4 000.00	
Unwaged	500.00		500.00	
Special sessions				
– women	1 000.00		1 000.00	
– ethnic	1 000.00		1 000.00	
– fun sessions	1 500.00		1 500.00	
– lessons	1 250.00		1 250.00	
– club	250.00		250.00	
Vending (net)				
Food	500.00		500.00	
Drink	250.00		250.00	
Sales (net)				
Swimwear	500.00		500.00	
Booklets	250.00		250.00	
Client				
Subsidy payment	12 500.00		12 500.00	
Income total	27 500.00		27 500.00	

during the first year of operation. Many businesses fail in their first year. Often this is entirely due to lack of attention to income and expenditure control on a regular basis.

To succeed, each manager has to achieve the targets preset by the tender submission.

Local authority management

These principles of management are equally valid for local authority contractors, as the competitive environment becomes more pervasive throughout the 1990s.

Formal authority will still rest with a committee or board. However, reference to committees to set the budget will be a thing of the past. Once the tender bid has been made, each facility manager will be held accountable for meeting business targets.

Due to its very variable nature, constant income monitoring is most important. Again, working from the tendered submission, constant comparisons need to be made between estimated income and that income which is actually achieved. This should be prepared as shown in Table 6.2.

INCENTIVES

The extent of delegation will in turn bring about further change. Some form of incentive payment for managers and key staff is unavoidable if long-term success is to be achieved.

This can be as simple as a twice yearly profit share. Alternatively, a more complex system can give more substantial financial incentives to key staff. Such staff would undoubtedly include the manager, and those staff who have the direct ability to increase income, for example instructors, and the marketing specialist.

YEAR ON YEAR COMPARISONS

Expenditure and income must be compared and contrasted with the original budget as tendered, and also the income and expenditure of previous years. Every corner shopkeeper knows whether trade is up or down compared with the same period last year. Nothing less, surely, can be allowed for the much larger business of the local leisure centre.

The real benefit in comparing income year on year is to detect early any changes in trends. This is invaluable marketplace information. If income is reducing, perhaps special promotions are necessary; or alternative attractions and activities may need to be considered. But without that basic information in the first place, no trend will even be detected.

A simple method of financial comparison can be easily formed by amending Table 6.2 to show the income from last year. This form of profiling will be more keenly attuned to actual variations; there may, for example, be an offpeak associated with the summer.

Profit and loss

Particular attention will be given by the board of directors, or council committee members to the annual profit and loss account. Again, the manager does not need to wait for an accountant to announce the annual result. The true business manager will keep an ongoing check. Table 6.3 provides a simple monthly analysis.

Table 6.3 A simple profiled monthly profit or loss account for Little London Swimming Pool

TOTALS	Month 1		Month 2	
	Estimate	*Actual*	*Estimate*	*Actual*
	£	£	£	£
Expenditure	25 000.00		25 000.00	
Income	27 500.00		27 500.00	
Surplus/profit	2 500.00		2 500.00	

BUSINESS STRATEGY

A leisure management contract will be different from all other local authority contracts. Success will depend not only on the tender price submitted but also on achieving, day by day, the income targets. It is therefore necessary to prepare a business structure which will successfully deliver this income. There is no simpler method of assessing the effectiveness for the contractor than by meeting financial and usage targets. This is of direct benefit to the contractor and client alike, and most of all to the customers who use the facility.

To achieve profitable success, key elements of a business approach need to be implemented. Some of the key essentials to a commercial and competitive approach can be summarized as:

- A clear family tree showing responsibilities;
- Clear areas of performance delegation;
- Financial accountability for each and every cost centre, and income activity;
- Staff training for all personnel;
- Keeping a motivated environment for all staff;
- The employment of outside specialists to provide services where it would be too expensive to employ someone fulltime;
- A monthly review of each business unit;
- A monthly review of changes and opportunities for income expansion;
- An annual review of the financial success of the facility;
- An annual review of possible refurbishments which will benefit both the client and the contractor and, most importantly, the customer;
- An annual review of major recreational changes and possible new income generating activities;
- An annual review of all staff and their targets.

Directional management

Most important of all, it is essential to ensure that everyone employed within a facility knows the direction in which the organization is heading.

People who win races know where the finishing line is and have devised a clear plan to ensure that they reach the line before their competitors. Competitive tendering and competitive management are just the same. Targets will have been clearly identified in the tender submission. What is then required is a plan of action to ensure that the targets are hit.

There is no way other than monitoring expenditure and income. Expenditure needs to be checked against target at least monthly. Income, however, demands daily assessment. The slim profit margin on most leisure management contracts will not allow for any appreciable variation.

If income does take a sudden downturn, special events (with client agreement), or specific promotions, may be necessary to boost income levels. The client will usually agree to new events, provided that they stay within the authority's policies.

Contractor clout

The client has a vested interest in keeping a good contractor in business.

If a client is faced with the alternatives of allowing a changed recreation programme for a centre or the likely prospect of the contractor terminating the contract or going bankrupt, then the client will sensibly agree to a reasonable programme variation.

No client will lightly consider the expense and uncertainty of seeking an alternative contractor due to a bankruptcy which could have been avoided. It takes time and money to readvertize, to say nothing about the upheaval to customers, the loss of income for weeks, and the likelihood of appointing an even less satisfactory contractor.

Methods of measuring performance are studied in more detail in Chapter 9. Now a summary is given of some of the key elements within this chapter.

SUMMARY

Some of the critical elements for success in contract business management include delegation and firm financial control. The key essentials to success here are:

- Once committed to a tendered bid, the successful contractor has then to deliver the service within this price.
- This commitment will last the full length of the contract – usually between four and six years.
- Income and expenditure need to be kept within the tendered values.
- Higher than anticipated expenditure or lower than forecast income means bankruptcy sooner or later, even for a public sector contractor.
- Regular income and expenditure analysis is essential.
- First, however, attention needs to be given to establishing clear and responsible lines of management delegation
- Technical management and plant maintenance cannot just be assumed.
- Staff must be competent.
- Technical competence needs to be linked to flexible working between all staff.

- Also technical competence must be matched to financial responsibility.
- Delegation is required to keep staff motivated.
- Delegation is simply defined as setting agreed and achievable goals for all staff.
- Everyone then can win. . .
- . .or almost everyone. Constant guard is needed to spot the petty pilferer or other disruptive staff members.
- After that, it is a question of providing the incentive for staff to achieve their own goals.
- The prime motivator, with the right staff, is a delegated budget, and financial incentives.
- This will be a big change for those in the public sector.
- Success here can only be monitored by producing a profiled budget.
- This gives a crystal clear indiction of the expected income and expenditure.
- Each activity manager with a delegated budget then has an accurate measurement of success.
- Furthermore, each manager is then in charge of his or her own destiny.
- A large leisure complex may have a number of specialist managers.
- Smaller facilities will have only one manager covering all functions.
- The key features of successful management are the same for both, and are summarized as;
  - financial control
  - marketing
  - technical competence
  - staff motivation
  with all aspects linked to profiled budgets.
- With a tendered contract, the income and expenditure to be achieved is set at the start.
- Profiling is then easy.
- Achieving targets requires constant attention to meeting customers' needs.
- Market research and targetted marketing may well be useful tools.
- As both client and contractor can benefit from good market research, both will benefit from sharing the costs incurred.
- Success then lies in competent and motivated staff, and constant monitoring.

Success does not end with winning the tender. In fact the hard work then starts.

Winning the ensuing contract means constant attention to income and expenditure control. This is only possible with a well motivated and disciplined group of employees. They need to feel that they are contributing to the overall success of the business venture.

Attention to results compared with estimates is an essential ingredient to that business success. The same applies to those who are employed in the enterprise. They also need to know when they are winning.

ADDENDUM: DEFAULTS, PENALTIES AND CONTROL

This addendum, and indeed the whole book, seeks to provide an indication of current good practice as an operational guide to leisure management. It does not attempt to give any legal advice on procedures or interpret any aspect of the law.

Anyone involved in a default claim should study the specific contract documents carefully and then seek the advice and assistance of a solicitor or legal expert, experienced in contract law. All default situations relate to specific instances and specific contracts.

The purpose of this addendum is to give a practical guide to controlling contracts; and summarize some of the principal systems of default correction in common use.

THE BASIS OF CONTROL

Any contract needs a system of control. An example of contract control familiar to many managers is that relating to contracts of employment.

A disciplinary procedure is required by law in respect of all contracts of employment. This procedure has to be followed before an employee can be fairly dismissed. Disciplinary procedures provide a fair and impartial form of employee control (the impartiality is provided by the independent industrial tribunal, if and when a dismissal leads to an appeal).

The disciplinary procedure for most companies normally applies where the performance or conduct of an employee is inadequate for the work being undertaken. The disciplinary procedure, therefore, provides the formal method for drawing inadequacies to an employee's attention, stating what improvements are necessary, and applying some sanction.

Many disciplinary procedures have the following steps.

1. Oral warning.
2. First written warning.
3. Second written warning.
4. Final warning.
5. Termination of contract of employment.

On each occasion the aspect of inadequate performance or misconduct is investigated, the employee's attention drawn to the inadequacies, and a clear statement made as to the performance or conduct required in future.

Beyond the first step, all discussions are held within the context of a formal meeting.

Broadly similar arrangements apply to written contracts with contractors. There are a number of different methods of contract control but all have the same ultimate intention: to eradicate poor performance or inadequate conduct and ensure that performance is as required in the contract documentation. Failure will result ultimately in termination of the contract, and could lead to independent arbitration or to a court of law; both are able to provide that all-essential impartiality.

DEFAULTS

For any control action to be contemplated by the client, some default must have occurred. In other words, the contractor will have failed to meet the specification or the terms of the contract in some way.

All contracts work on the basis of confidence. It is therefore important to deal with all defaults in a fair and reasonable manner. Usually a discussion between the client and contractor, confirmed in writing, will be sufficient to rectify the situation and ensure that a repetition does not occur.

Having said that, if a default has occurred, then clearly the contractor should not, and cannot, be paid for work which is unsatisfactory, nor work which has not been undertaken.

Some examples of defaults include:

- Water in the pool not at the stated temperature;
- Air temperature in a room less than specified;
- Late opening of facilities.

Client control can be exercised in a number of ways. An example at the end of this addendum is a method which can be used to cover some aspects of contract performance at a swimming pool.

FORMAL ACTION

The method of formal control will be stated in the conditions of contract (a brief example is given in Appendix A.5). Only this agreed form of control, which is specific to a particular contract, can be used within that contract.

There are a number of different forms of formal contract control.

Penalty points

Some contracts rely on the imposition of penalty points on the contractor by the client. This is an area of some difficulty at law, as it is relatively untested. However, it is a system in wide use.

The penalty point system, does meet the necessary criterion for indicating to a contractor that defaults have occurred. The difficulty lies in placing a financial value on the default. In law, a financial penalty is not normally allowed where it is not related to a loss incurred. Also, in many leisure management contracts, the contractor will receive the income direct from the customers. Therefore the contractor does not rely solely on the client for payments, unlike all maintenance or construction contracts.

However, for the purposes of this addendum it is important to note that a specific number of points will be allocated for different defaults. More points will be imposed for defaults which are of greater importance, and fewer for matters of less importance. It is also important to note that a penalty points system cannot be used arbitrarily to 'fine' a contractor.

The principal purpose of the penalty points system is to give a positive, and quantified, indication of the degree of default incurred.

Warnings

Some clients rely on warnings. The client indicates the default, and deducts payment where this is justified in exact financial terms.

More importantly with this system is the grading of the warnings. This may be very similar to an employee disciplinary system of control. Examples in a contract situation could include;

- gross default
- default

Of fundamental importance is that the action taken by the client invariably relates to the use of another contractor for part (or all) of the service, where the original contractor has defaulted. The costs of the new contractor are payable by the original contractor. This is a most effective form of control.

Non performance

Most contracts will provide for termination of the contract where there is a default against any of the conditions of the contract or any of the specifications.

CONTRACT TERMINATION

Eventually, if defaults continue and a contractor is not able to perform within the terms of the contract, then the contract will be terminated. This always means failure for both parties.

Termination really is an action of the last resort. It means considerable difficulties for both the client and the contractor.

The contractor will be placed in substantial financial and contractual difficulty. The client's problems will relate to the need to seek another contractor. By law, the client will not be able to carry out the work using directly employed staff. Before the Act became effective, there were situations where local authorities took control of leisure facilities when the facility otherwise would have closed; examples can be found as far apart as Chelmsford, Aberdeen and Croydon.

Both parties will be well advised to ensure that the contract does work to the benefit of everyone, rather than attempt to be punitive or seek termination of the contract. Even so, contract terminations have occurred and always will.

SUMMARY

It is important to stress that specific control measures will be defined in each specific contract. These measures, and these alone, can be used within that contract. Contract law itself is an immense subject in its own right. In leisure management it is essential to be firm and fair, not punitive, and to seek the advice of an experienced legal expert at all times. It is far better then to ensure that adequate contract control is maintained at all times. This will involve both the client and the contractor. The daily control form illustrated on the following pages provides an indication of a method for monitoring which will benefit both the client and the contractor.

For the contractor, it allows regular checks to be undertaken by a range of staff to ensure standards are maintained. The client can use the form for the same purpose, while on the lookout for any default. It is thus most important that the contractor uses the forms regularly to reduce any possible incidence of defaults or penalties being imposed.

LITTLE LONDON SWIMMING POOL

CONTRACT PERFORMANCE CHECKS

Date _____   Time _____

Completed _____   Position_____
by: _____   _____

Pool Hall
Activity (eg casual, club): _____

Number of bathers in pool (approximately): _____

Number of lifeguards on duty on the poolside: _____

Lifeguards

Name	*Qualifications and date*	*On poolside duties since:*

Water   Time of last test _____
Temperature _____   pH _____   TDS_____
Chlorine; total _____free_____ combined _____

Staff on duty (state all)

Name	Position Duty officer	Activities this shift

Emergency Equipment
Resuscitation Equipment (eg. checked? spare oxygen?)

_____

Fire extinguishers (eg. last checked?)

_____

Ambience
Staff Clothing (all in agreed clothing?)

_____

Cleanliness (litter? clean surfaces? clean windows?)

_____
_____

Lockers

_____

Vending Machines

_____

Air temperatures

_____

Defaults
Specific reference to any defaults ie. any aspect of the service which does not conform to the specifications.

Default	Specification	Major/Minor	Action

General comments

_____
_____
_____
_____

Signed _____   Signed _____

Date _____

Chapter Seven

Hotels: the leisure experience

For many people hotels offer the ultimate leisure experience. They are associated with holidays in attractive surroundings, good food and a high standard of service.

For the many tourists going abroad, good hotels offer exactly this kind of experience.

Back at home in Britain, the quality is the same but our use is different. There has been a massive change within the last few decades away from the family holiday in a hotel. Hotel business in the UK now relies heavily on bed and breakfast, the business traveller and the conference trade, not to mention our insatiable appetite to eat out more frequently.

A ROLE MODEL

Hotels stay in business by ensuring continued customer satisfaction. Competition ensures that anyone who is dissatisfied can readily find alternative accommodation. Each hotel has therefore to balance customer care with sound business practice to achieve a profitable operation.

Hotels provide an excellent example of leisure management at its best; not perfect, but good and reliable and to a consistent quality.

Just as leisure facilities vary greatly in their range and size, so do hotels. Hotels range from small, individually operated establishments through to massive national (and a few international) chain groups. Local authority leisure facilities vary from small, relatively independent units (such as a neighbourhood swimming pool), through to comprehensive leisure complexes offering a great range of activities and leisure opportunities.

In business terms, the similarities are clearly evident. The principles of management are the same. With a small independent hotel, the total management is within the capability of one person; whereas with a larger facility, the manager is invariably reporting to a board.

Fig. 7.1 Hotels are associated with the best in leisure management.

Standards

The question is are the standards of customer care and service in local council leisure facilities comparable with those of the hotels in their locality? If not, why not?

There are a number of good reasons why the comparison is unfair: higher income groups use the hotels; management style is dissimilar; an entirely different experience is being sought by the hotel guest . . . , the list is endless.

However, this should not deflect from the similarities, and the methods which hotels use to achieve their end result are very relevant.

Most particularly, this shows itself in an intense pride, reflected by all members of staff in the hotel. If the same ethos can be developed in leisure centres and swimming pools as exists in hotels, improved services and standards will result.

It is worthwhile, therefore, to examine some examples of hotel management practice. The starting point in this chapter, which is easily confirmed by brief consideration, is that there are many common elements between hotel management and leisure management. Some examples include reception services, administration and bookings catering, and the general basic management tools of delegation and performance monitoring.

LOCAL AUTHORITY HOTELS

Some local authorities already own and operate their own hotels, either as a social service, or to provide seaside holidays for selected groups. Some are directly managed, others are let out on contract.

One such is the Harperley Hotel, lost in the undulating landscape of County Durham, and owned by Derwentside District Council. The development and management of the Harperley Hotel over the years is a good example of the ups and downs of a local authority in a leisure contract management situation.

The Harperley Hotel is now a first class local leisure facility. This has not always been the case.

The original buildings date back to the 17th century. They were in use for centuries as a granary, and only latterly were they turned to a variety of leisure uses.

Before local government reorganisation in 1974, the local authority set about developing a country park near to the small township of Tantobie. The decision to create a country park reflected the desire of the council to make best use of land holdings in the area, and to provide improved leisure opportunities for local residents while attracting more tourists to the area. Perhaps a little civic pride also played a part in the decision to develop the park. In keeping with the country park movement of the late sixties and early seventies, a neighbouring authority had developed a large country park. Harperley followed.

THE HARPERLEY HOTEL

The council substantially altered and extended the old buildings to provide the hotel, which was seen to be an essential complement to the country park.

The hotel was initially operated directly by the council and proved to be a loss making venture. To rectify this, the Council sought an experienced tenant to run the business, in the belief that it did not have the necessary expertise to operate the hotel directly, but that specialist management was required. Unfortunately, this worked out even less successfully.

The council then sought competent and interested hotel managers by public advertisement. They received a number of enquiries, and as a result a seven-year contract was awarded. The council intended to keep the hotel under close review, and a seven-year term was the maximum that it would consider. This time, success was at last achieved.

The hotel management

The new manager, Mr Morris, had a lot to prove. Long hours and hard work by Mr Morris and his wife began to reap rewards. Between them, they turned a loss-making venture into a thriving and successful business. Not only was this a source of satisfaction to the Morrises, but also, of course, to the council.

Due to their satisfactory performance, the contract was extended in 1990 for a further 25 years. Mr Morris explains his views:

> The key to success lies in satisfying the customers, Dedication and commitment have achieved results. There are only five bedrooms in the hotel, so the income derived from that side of the business is limited. Over the years, therefore, I have improved the restaurant trade in addition to the hotel trade. My business principles have been simple but effective.

Management delegation

Together Mr and Mrs Morris have established clear lines of delegation. He is responsible for all catering; she is responsible for accommodation, accounts and the hotel side of the operation.

A head chef is in charge of the kitchens, and works to precise percentages in relation to food costs, and wages. Thus the resulting sale price has set profit margins. Nothing is left to chance. The costs of food and its preparation are too heavy to allow unnecessary wastage. A head waitress is responsible for the restaurant service to customers.

The head chef and head waitress are entirely responsible for their own rosters and for ensuring they have sufficient staff to fulfil their functions. Local people are employed and a taxi is provided at night to ensure that all staff return home safely and conveniently.

Performance measures

Performance measurement is built into the business.

Independent stocktakers call monthly to carry out a complete stockcheck. In addition to providing an audit of the stock, these independent stocktakers provide a monthly business analysis, broken down between the various sources of income. Furthermore sales are compared and contrasted to the costs of wages and food.

Fig. 7.2 Detailed costings result in profit.

Basic business principles underpin the operation. The personal touch is also vital, says Mr Morris:

> We strive to provide a pleasant atmosphere and excellent service. I do not use a wholesaler to purchase food. I personally select most of the food from local independent suppliers. In this way, I can ensure that I achieve the quality which I demand for meat and vegetables and all other provisions. By these means, I have achieved an excellent local trade in addition to the hotel accommodation.

Indeed, Mr Morris is a success by any performance indicator. He has turned a loss-making business into profitable venture; wedding receptions are booked into the hotel virtually every week; and his own personal attention has won local popularity. Furthermore, the local authority owners have sufficient confidence to extend his lease for a much longer period.

HOTEL MANAGEMENT PRINCIPLES

Before looking at larger hotels, the basic business principles need to be emphasized. The experience at the Harperley Hotel can be easily translated to a small leisure facility. Indeed, the key elements of hotel (or leisure) management are all in place at the Harperley Hotel. These include;

- Delegation;
- Key staff working to performance percentages;
- Each supervisor preparing his or her own staff rosters;
- Personal flair and commitment.

These are all features which can be successfully brought to bear on any leisure management operation.

For the next case study, we travel from the Pennine foothills into the very centre of London. Similar, but slightly different, principles apply here. It is important to note that perhaps the biggest difference relates to the size of the operation, rather than the actual principles of management themselves.

THE GREAT WESTERN HOTEL

The Great Western Royal Hotel is adjacent to, and forms part of, Paddington British Rail Station in the very heart of London. It was built in the days when to travel was an adventure in itself. Designed to the highest standards, and located at the top of the railway system, the hotel provided well for the rich and affluent of the day.

Sold off by British Rail in the 1970s, the hotel nowadays maintains high standards, but for an entirely different clientèle. The hotels 17 function and banqueting rooms give an indication of its size and business orientation. A more common indication of a hotel's size is its number of bedrooms: in the case of the Great Western, this is about 200.

Food and beverages

The food and beverage side of the business caters for a wide variety of cosmopolitan tastes, and an extensive range of meals. Provision is made for the usual dinner, bed and breakfast market. In addition there is a large trade in lunches for conferences and the seminars held in the function rooms. As is to be expected, there is also a variety of food and beverages for travellers. The catering bill is huge.

With the amount of business generated by a hotel of this size, it might be expected that the hotel could easily negotiate competitive prices from its suppliers. However, this is not necessarily their case. Mr Kneer, front of house manager, explains why:

> The hotel is privately owned now and is therefore a single business unit. It is not part of a chain of hotels. Although we make considerable purchases of food and beverages, we can make greater economies by buying through a consortium. We belong to a consortium which specializes in providing for hotels. Their buying power commands a far greater discount than we could ever expect, by tender or any other means.

Consortia

In addition to providing food and beverages to the hotel, the consortium also supplies other hotel requisites such as linen, stationery, soap and many other accoutrements associated with hotels. Most deliveries are made direct from the original supplier to the hotel, to reduce costs to a minimum. There is no wasteful third party involved with storage, transport and paperwork.

The hotel also pays an annual membership fee to a marketing company. This company undertakes market research and a number of other marketing activities necessary to the hotel.

Even the name and location of a hotel of the stature of the Great Western is insufficient by itself to attract enough business. To be successful, the hotel requires constant advertizing and publicity, especially in the international air tour brochures. For example, an all inclusive flight and hotel package rate is offered to overseas customers. This benefits everyone involved, from the customer to the transport carrier.

Delegation and information

For the daily complexity of running a business the size and breadth of this hotel, there has to be absolute confidence in the information systems. Surprisingly perhaps, an integrated computer system is not used. Mr Kneer explains:

> The hotel relies entirely on each unit manager. We have a comprehensive computer system for cash and accounting but not

for, say, the banqueting business. Each unit relies on a paper-work system and the knowledge and expertise of the banqueting manager. A simple checklist system for booking functions would be totally inadequate. Cancellations and alterations to functions can be expected up to within days or even hours of a planned function.

The ability to rebook a function room at short notice, and thus reduce income loss, is as important as ensuring that all the arrangements requested for a function are provided. Intimate knowledge of functions is needed. Often when a booking is made, the unit manager needs to ask searching questions to establish all the essential details. Last minute variations have to be accommodated.

Customer care with a difference

With a large hotel in the centre of London, there are a number of specific requirements associated with certain customers. This goes far beyond coffee at 11am and tea and biscuits at 3pm.

For example, it is not sufficient to know that a television crew is attending a particular function. The hotel needs to know whether a camera is to be set up in a fixed position or to be held on a shoulder. The hotel may also have to insist that a mobile generator be provided by the television company. Otherwise, not only would the television equipment drain the electricity supply to the hotel, it would also blow every fuse.

There are a host of other specialist requirements and needs to be accommodated with each booking.

The paperwork systems are therefore under the control of each unit manager, who is then entirely responsible for ensuring the success of his or her own business area.

Yet again, the basic business principles of leisure management can be seen to be operating here in a large city hotel. Particular impor-tance is placed on delegation and the unit manager. Leisure is nothing, if not person oriented.

SUMMARY

Hotels are often considered to be the ultimate leisure experience. They are associated with high standards and holidays and all that is best about leisuretime activities. The only down side is that they tend to be expensive and therefore not in general use.

A study of hotels provides a fascinating insight into a very different environment from most other leisure facilities. A casual observation or a formal study are both instructive and informative to the dedicated leisure manager. The ability to study a local hotel is an opportunity available to everyone.

The key management principles highlighted in this chapter can be easily summarized.

- People count: whether staff, customers or delegated unit managers.
- Leisure and hotels both operate in the people business.
- People are the biggest asset.
- People also demand high standards; a leisure experience cannot be easily repeated.
- Leisure centres should provide for customers in the same way as local hotels.
- Hotels are easy to study and locally based.
- Personal pride and commitment are essential to successful customer care and business profit.
- Appropriate delegation is elementary.
- A consortium helps to reduce costs, by creating awesome buying power for a number of relatively small units.
- Consortia are as viable in the public sector as the private sector.
- To be cost effective, a consortium should not be involved in the ordering and delivering, just the bulk negotiations.
- Marketing expertise is worth buying in.
- A range of technical competences is needed in hotels, from food and beverages to control of television companies.
- Computers are essential to our complex lives, but they do not solve everything.
- People and manual systems can be more economical with paper, and perhaps more effective in certain circumstances.
- Commercial accountability is helped by a logical division into separate business units within the hotel:
  - Food and beverages
  - Front of house
  - Administration
  - Accommodation
- It is often more economical to use the services of specialist agencies than to employ staff direct.

These principles can and should be applied to the management of all leisure facilities.

A peculiar trait of the stiff upper lip British is that we complain all too infrequently (and, for that matter, are far too slow to praise as well). Someone in this country has to be really pushed to make a complaint.

But people do lodge their concerns. They do it quietly, without telling anyone. They ensure that they do not suffer again by the simple expedient of going elsewhere. The leisure facility operator (in whatever line of business) will then hear the unspoken complaints through the sales figures.

Hotel managers are acutely aware of this simple truism in their day to day dealings with customers. Success for hotels, as well as leisure centres, is summed up in that one simple sentence: 'The key to success lies in satisfying the customers'. Nothing can be allowed to impede that objective.

ADDENDUM: SERVICE STANDARDS IN HOTELS

This addendum provides a brief insight into some specific aspects of hotel management. Control of standards is particularly important. This is provided by a variety of training schedules and by standard control forms.

In a contract situation, the categories good, fair and poor, will often be changed to pass or fail, in relation to the specification.

LONDON HOTEL – CLEANING AND MAINTENANCE SCHEDULES

ROOM	Frequency*	STANDARD

DAY ROOM — Good Fair Poor Action

Floors
- vacuum carpet + edges — D
- damp clean skirting — D
- spot clean — D
- damp mop bare floor — D

Curtains
- track and runners — D
- dry clean — A

Furniture/Fittings
- polish — D
- empty ashtrays, clean — D
- empty bins, clean — D
- vents, clean — D
- lights, clean — M
- mirrors, clean — D
- signs, clean, clear — D
- clean all ledges — D

Check/Report
- cigarette burns — D
- chairs, broken; dirty — D
- doors, squeak; dirty — M
- paintwork, chipped — M
- lights, out — D
- other — D

LIFTS
Vacuum — D
Clean vertical surfaces — D
Clean, check telephone — D
Clean coves — D

TOILETS
Clean
- inside — D
- outside, back — D
- cistern — D
- seat — D

Check/Report/Remedy
- seat, loose; chipped — D
- toilet paper — D

BEDROOMS
Open windows — D

*D, daily; M, monthly; A, annually

LONDON HOTEL – RECEPTIONIST TRAINING

1. The importance of posture, facial expression.
2. The importance of calling people by their name.
3. The importance of listening – giving individual attention.
4. Making the customer feel important – and the importance of doing this with sincerity and conviction.
5. The importance of not arguing – how an argument can be won and a customer lost.
6. The importance of admitting mistakes emphatically and frankly, and rectifying them quickly.
7. The importance of understanding the customer's point of view.
8. The importance of letting a customer 'save his face' when he has made a mistake.
9. The importance of recognizing regular customers.
10. The importance of developing sensitivity to requirements.
11. The importance of dealing with complaints:
    - no room for guest with confirmed reservation;
    - complaint about other departments.
12. The importance of being well informed about arrangements within the hotel, local events etc.

Chapter Eight

Catering and subcontracting

The provision of catering services in leisure centres is often the subject of a franchise or a subcontract because catering is seen as a specialized area of operation.

Subcontracting is a particularly important aspect of leisure management by contract, and needs to be considered carefully. Before looking at the major service of catering, it is worth addressing the whole issue of subcontracting. It has a particular relevance across a range of essential (yet minor) services contained within a larger contract.

SUBCONTRACTING

In any leisure management contract, there will be areas where limited specialist expertise is required, for example the provision of physiotherapy services. Depending on the actual leisure centre, there could be many forms of specialist operation which lend themselves to a subcontract.

The main rationale for using a subcontractor should be when a necessary specialist service does not justify the employment of a full-time or part-time member of the in-house staff.

The arrangements for subcontracts are an essential part of the tender preparation process. The appointment of specialist subcontractors is a useful way of reducing costs and increasing income potential thus improving the overall bid.

ARRANGING SUBCONTRACTS

The client must agree to subcontracting. A clause in a tender is likely to limit subcontracting to those subcontractors specifically named and approved by the client. This provision in the contract allows the client to be satisfied that the contract will be delivered adequately to the required performance by the principal contractor.

With the approval of the client. . . .

The client will not agree to the use of poor subcontractors, and will undertake a thorough appraisal of nominated subcontractors in a way similar to that used for the main contractor.

The other key issue which will concern the client is the extent to which the subcontractor will be used. If the contractor is intending to use the subcontractor for an extensive part of the contract, then the client may as well employ the subcontractor directly and benefit by the lower price offered.

. . . and the contractor

Incorporating a subcontractor into a tender requires forward planning by the tenderer, who must be aware of those areas or services where a subcontractor will be desirable. The tenderer needs an intimate knowledge of the subcontractor to establish sufficient confidence to incorporate the subcontractor into the business. Furthermore, a clear indication of the subcontractor's price will be needed, before preparing and submitting the tender to the client.

All this requires the tenderer to have a full and early knowledge of appropriate subcontractors. The period for tender submission is limited (normally two to three months), which does not allow time for a tenderer to go and find suitable subcontractors and then discuss the tender in detail with them.

Forward planning is the key. Successful tenderers will already know of a number of subcontractors who could be of value to specific contracts. Furthermore, the tenderer needs to have approached the subcontractor in plenty of time to allow the subcontractor to prepare an accurate assessment of expenditure and income. Otherwise both will suffer.

Collusion

It is essential that the client is aware of the subcontract arrangements, even at an early stage. Otherwise a client may be mistaken in thinking that arrangements for a subcontract constitute some form of collusion. Almost all contracts have a clause which prohibits collusion.

Collusion exists where two or more tenderers on a select list fix the tender bid between them. It works only if all the tenderers are party to the deal, and agree between themselves who shall be the winner. This, of course, totally negates the purpose of tendering in the first place and is against the whole intention of the tender. Anyone involved in collusion, in any walk of life, will sooner or later find themselves in court, and paying the appropriate penalty.

Key issues

The purpose of a subcontract is to produce exactly the opposite effect to that achieved by collusion. A successful subcontract will provide specialist services at reduced cost. This will benefit the tenderer in submitting a competitive bid and the client by ensuring the best bid is made. The key to successful subcontracting for any serious tenderer is:

- Seek prior client approval
- Maintain an up to date list of suitable subcontractors.
- Give early warning that a tender is being considered to those subcontractors likely to be used.
- Seek their bids early so that they can be incorporated into the main tender submission

And finally, make sure that the legally binding contract with the subcontractor is in place before commitment to the main tender submission.

Small business opportunities

Submitting a tender for even a moderately sized leisure centre is far too onerous a task for any one person wishing to set up his or her own business. Even for the smallest leisure centres and swimming pools, there is little possibility of one person being able to submit a tender successfully or even satisfy the initial appraisal criteria.

Nevertheless subcontracting does offer an opportunity for a number of small business ventures. Many subcontractors have gone on to become successful in more major contracts.

The key to success for subcontractors is to ensure that all likely tenderers are aware of their availability and interest. A tenderer cannot invite an unknown subcontractor to submit a price.

So although leisure management tenders will naturally favour the already competent contractor, there is room for specialists too. Catering provides one particular opportunity for a subcontractor.

CATERING AS A SUBCONTRACT

Individuals operate catering establishments up and down the country, including public houses, hotels, cafes and snack bars in leisure centres.

Leisure centres perhaps provide the best and the worst examples of subcontract catering. At its best, a catering subcontract is unbeatable. At worst, it can mean soft drinks and prepacked snacks provided in poorly decorated premises tucked away in an unattractive corner of the leisure facility.

Clear failure is evidenced when a sign appears at reception which says: 'If you wish to complain about the catering services, do not bother us – contact . . . . . '. All the management of such a leisure facility should resign forthwith.

The rest of this chapter concentrates on the best practices for catering whether by subcontract or by the main contractor.

Fig. 8.1 Management should resign.

To subcontract or not

Initially, the tenderer must decide whether to seek a subcontractor for a specialist area of work. In contract terms, the only valid reason for doing so is when the work is so specialized, and the area of operation so relatively small a proportion of the overall contract, that it would pay dividends to subcontract.

All too often, a leisure management contractor automatically seeks to franchise out the catering element of the operation. This is a common example of management abdication at its worst.

Successful leisure management depends on the skilful combination of a wide variety of trades and professions. There is no reason why catering should not be one of those specialist professions. Catering will form a significant proportion of many leisure management contracts, and furthermore it is used by most customers. Get the catering wrong, and there is little hope for the main contract in the long term.

All successful business relies on the correct application of methods and procedures. Catering is no different. It is a technically complex service with statutory controls via the food hygiene legislation and regulations which were greatly extended again as recently as 1990.

Success relies on sound management, and adherence to the well tried and tested practices of catering. In this book, it is the management critera which are being examined, many aspects of which are equally applicable to other areas of management.

CATERING MANAGEMENT

Catering management can offer some excellent examples of business management at its best. For success, management controls must ensure a day by day, and week by week, analysis of all income and expenditure. Critical and constant attention to income and expenditure is of paramount importance. It is all too easy to make a loss in catering.

A thorough knowledge of catering management and the ability to deliver a quality, and customer oriented catering service is complementary to the successful provision of a leisure service. These principles of catering management hold good for all leisure management.

As with all businesses, delegation is necessary for success. For delegation to be possible, there must be a clear division of responsibilities.

Catering delegation

Delegation is greatly assisted by dividing the business into separate accounts. The subdivisions need to take account of the actual catering facilities in the leisure centre. Two possible divisions of responsibility could be:

1. café
2. bar
3. vending machines
4. amusement machines

1. food
2. beverages
3. administration
4. customer services

Depending on the size of the leisure facility, these could be treated as separate business accounts and delegated to specific employees to operate. For example one person could be in charge of the cafe (or food), another the bar (or beverages), and a third the machines.

There is no inherent reason why three people could not work on all services, yet have specific responsibility for one. There is much to commend this division of workload within one combined catering unit. Job satisfaction is increased, responsibility is clarified, and lines of accountability improved.

The customer care side is the most often overlooked. Put simply, this all-important side of the service requires a manager to view the service throught the eyes of the customers. It is too easy for managers to think that they know the customers' views because they are serving the customers all day. It is what the customer does not say that is more important. All managers should regularly check their services from the customer's side of the counter.

A simple example will illustrate the point. The volume and type of music being played (or the choice of television channel) is invariably set to the satisfaction of the counter staff. Because of the general noise at the counter, the volume is higher than some categories of customer prefer. Delegation works best when positive steps are made to involve customer desires and choices.

Costings

After delegation, profiled budgets of income and expenditure are the next requirement.

To profile a budget demands prior attention to the major cost and income items within the budget. Examples of profiled budgets have been given in a previous chapter. These can be adapted for the special requirements of catering.

Some of the key variables within a catering business include the following:

- Appropriate numbers of staff, rostered to meet the peaks and lows of demand.
- A pricing policy which is kept under constant review.
- Adherence to basic paperwork procedures like checking delivery notes against deliveries and the subsequent invoices.
- Keeping stock levels to the minimum possible (most stock should be used within one to three weeks), thus not tying up cash unnecessarily.
- Wastage monitoring reports, setting a maximum allowable, for each category.

All these are basic business practices in catering. Some detailed examples of catering methods and procedures are given in the Addendum to this chapter. It is important to note that all the procedures are finely tuned to achieve the best possible customer satisfaction and best income.

Very similar practices are needed in sports management, technical management and all the other skills which make for a successful leisure operation.

TRADING REPORTS

Having prepared and profiled a budget, the next step is to ensure that critical attention is given to constant monitoring of both income and expenditure. Daily, weekly and monthly monitoring is essential.

All tills will be reconciled at the end of each day. Furthermore, by the start of the next day of trading there should be a full analysis of all income. This can then be compared with the same day of last week, last month and last year. Only in this way can a trend be identified early.

A theme which is seen in all the areas of leisure management covered in this book is the need for constant and critical analysis of use and income and expenditure.

It is no use waiting for the annual accounts to expose or confirm a downward trend. By then it is too late. A loss will have been made and the total leisure business may be in jeopardy. Furthermore, it will be a long haul to turn around an unprofitable business.

The monthly accounts are of critical importance. These should include a complete stocktake of all stores, orders, deliveries and sales of the past month. Most caterers use independent stocktakers for this exercise, to ensure absolute impartiality.

Computer aided accounting

Most businesses rely on computers for all accountancy practices. There are a number of specialists in the hotel and catering industry. Some of the best examples of current practice can be found in up to date trade journals and the specialist press.

Of course, computers are excellent at crunching numbers. However, the correct numbers have to be fed into the system in the first place. If this basic and fundamental requirement is fulfilled computers can be an invaluable asset, providing, for example, an indication of the gross profit margin (income less the cost of purchases, often referred to as the cost of sales).

Computers are also excellent at providing graphic displays. A graphic display of the previous month's income and overall trading situation is worth pages and pages of figures.

Fig. 8.2 Graphs are so much easier to understand.

Percentage mark up

The actual percentage return varies on each commodity.

The cost of the ingredients is less than half of the total price paid for prepared food but is matched almost equally by the cost of staff time taken in preparation.

Running a cafe with fresh food can be both popular and profitable. However, it can also be a disastrous loss maker where there is insufficient trade. If staff are underemployed, then obviously there is a larger wage cost to be shared among a lesser number of sales. That is why it is so important to give attention to the actual gross percentage margin of sale.

PROFIT OR LOSS

The profit and loss situation is controlled by regular monitoring. Some of the key issues to be constantly monitored in addition to the trading accounts include the following:

- Portion control on hot food sales.
- The level of wastage, especially of prepared food.
- Pilfering: difficult to identify but essential to control.
- Wasted time on activities which do not directly lead to sales or income
- Control of overheads

The annual accounts will be prepared by a chartered accountant. Professional auditing and accounting are essential at this stage. The resulting annual accounts are relatively simple. However, they give a very clear indication of the profitability of a business. They are not so much of value to the manager, as to the shareholders, board members or councillors as the case may be.

SUMMARY

A grasp of the key business principles involved in catering is not only essential for a successful catering business, but also invaluable to any leisure centre or business manager. The key aspects highlighted are as follows:

- Subcontracting offers real advantages to the contractor and client.
- Minor specialist services can be provided more efficiently, and at less cost, by a subcontractor.

- Prior written client approval will nearly always be required.
- The client will accept only competent subcontractors, for clearly defined activities.
- The contractor should seek subcontractors only for small specialist areas of work, like boiler maintenance for example, to be most effective.
- A contractor needs to know of possible subcontractors, and their prices, before completing the tender submission.
- This requires forward planning and evaluation.
- Subcontractors should always keep possible tenderers informed of their availability.
- Subcontracting offers an excellent method for a person to set up his or her own business.
- Catering is often subcontracted in a leisure facility.
- This is a pity. Although catering is a specialized area, it is no more so than other activities.
- If catering is operated directly by the contractor, a more integrated approach is possible to the management of the facility.
- Catering affects all customers.
- Specialist staff are essential.
- Specific catering management controls are required;
    - trading reports (weekly, monthly, annual)
    - stock control
    - accurate percentage costings
    - matching staff resources to peaks and troughs
    - food hygiene checks
  - constant auditing
- Graphical displays help.
- Successful catering is achieved only after attention to a mass of detail.
- Most importantly, this detail includes rigorous control of inputs, which in turn deliver profits.

Catering is a specialist area of activity in which only qualified staff should be employed. Whether the staff are employed directly is a matter for the contractor to decide. But leisure managers will benefit from the application of the same business principles to all other areas of activity within the same leisure facility.

ADDENDUM: CATERING CONTROLS

The details in this addendum are provided by courtesy of Innsite Hotel

Services Limited. They give working examples of documents necessary to retain exact control.

For non-caterers, attention should be given to similar exact detailing of the business, and the resulting management financial information.

This is a first class example of financial management as applied rigorously to a leisure industry.

BC INNSITE CONSOLIDATED MANAGEMENT REPORT

Period Covered: From 16/09/XX To 30/09/XX Days 15 Date of Report 30/09/XX

Opening Stock	1158.82	Net Revenue	1345.98
Add Receipts	992.68	Add Allowances	40.00
Add Stock Profit	2.00		
	------------	Gross Revenue	1385.98
	2153.50		============
Less Closing Stock	1576.61	Potential Revenue	1343.97
Less Stock Loss			
	------------	Shortage Re Potential	
Consumption	576.89		
		Surplus Re Potential	42.01
Less Cost of Non Rev Outlets	2.20		
Add Miscellaneous Receipts	5.00		% Cost % Gross
Less Miscellaneous Usage	5.55		of Sales Profit
	------------	Net Revenue	42.66 57.34
Cost of Sales	574.14	Gross Revenue	41.42 58.58
	============	Potential Revenue	42.72 57.28

	Op.Stock	Receipts	Issues	Stock P/L	Cl.Stock	Consump
Stores	462.74	992.68	796.39	2.00	661.03	
Adjustments						
BAR	431.70		162.77		434.20	160.27
REST	91.70		48.29		91.70	48.29
KITCHEN			2.20			2.20
FUNCTIONS	172.68		583.13		389.68	366.13
Total Outlets	696.08	0.00	796.39	0.00	915.58	576.89
Total	1158.82	992.68	0.00	2.00	1576.61	576.89

	Net. Rev.	Allowance	Gross Rv	Poten.Rv	Shortage	Surplus
BAR	430.01		430.01	403.01		27.00
REST	193.74	40.00	233.74	193.74		40.00
FUNCTIONS	722.23		722.23	747.23	25.00	
Total	1345.98	40.00	1385.98	1343.97		42.01

BC INNSITE   MANAGEMENT REPORT   RESTAURANT

Period Covered: From 16/09/XX To 30/09/XX Days 15 Date of Report 30/09/XX

	Spirits	Beers	Wines	Others	TOTAL
Net Revenue	126.61	0.00	46.96	20.17	193.74
Add Allowances	20.00	0.00	20.00	0.00	40.00
Gross Revenue	146.61	0.00	66.96	20.17	233.74
Potential Revenue	126.61	0.00	46.96	20.17	193.74
Shortage					
Surplus	20.00		20.00		40.00
Opening Stock	42.50	0.00	34.00	15.20	91.70
Add Issues	24.00	0.00	21.30	2.99	48.29
Less Closing Stock	42.50	0.00	34.25	14.95	91.70
Consumption	24.00	0.00	21.05	3.24	48.29
Add Misc. Receipts					0.00
Less Misc. Usage					0.00
Cost Of Sales	24.00	0.00	21.05	3.24	48.29
%Cost Of Sales (Gross)	16.37		31.44	16.06	20.66
%Cost Of Sales (Net)	18.96		44.83	16.06	
%Cost Of Sales (Pot)	18.96		44.83	16.06	24.93

BC INNSITE   MANAGEMENT REPORT   FUNCTIONS

Period Covered: From 16/09/XX To 30/09/XX Days 15   Date of Report 30/09/XX

	Spirits	Beers	Wines	Others	TOTAL
Net Revenue	90.18	591.05	12.78	28.22	722.23
Add Allowances	0.00	0.00	0.00	0.00	0.00
Gross Revenue	90.18	591.05	12.78	28.22	722.23
Potential Revenue	100.17	606.05	12.78	28.22	747.23
Shortage	9.99	15.00			25.00
Surplus					
Opening Stock	17.00	136.00	13.60	6.08	172.68
Add Issues	26.00	543.50	8.75	4.89	583.13
Less Closing Stock	27.50	342.50	13.70	5.98	389.68
Consumption	15.50	337.00	8.65	4.98	366.13
Add Misc. Receipts					0.00
Less Misc. Usage					0.00
Cost Of Sales	15.50	337.00	8.65	4.98	366.13
%Cost Of Sales (Gross)	17.19	57.02	67.68	17.65	50.69
%Cost Of Sales (Net)	17.19	57.02	67.68	17.65	
%Cost Of Sales (Pot)	15.47	55.61	67.67	17.65	49.00

BC INNSITE   MANAGEMENT REPORT   BAR

Period Covered: From 16/09/XX To 30/09/XX Days 15   Date of Report 30/09/XX

	Spirits	Beers	Wines	Others	TOTAL
Net Revenue	190.18	606.05	12.78	28.22	747.23
Add Allowances	0.00	0.00	0.00	0.00	0.00
Gross Revenue	190.18	606.05	12.78	28.22	747.23
Potential Revenue	155.83	171.27	30.52	45.39	403.01
Shortage	55.65		17.74	17.17	
Surplus		434.78			344.22
Opening Stock	42.50	340.00	34.00	15.20	431.70
Add Issues	27.50	105.00	21.30	8.97	162.77
Less Closing Stock	42.50	342.50	34.25	14.95	434.20
Consumption	27.50	102.50	21.05	9.22	160.27
Add Misc. Receipts					5.00
Less Misc. Usage					5.55
Cost Of Sales	27.50	102.50	21.05	9.22	159.72
%Cost Of Sales (Gross)	27.45	16.91	164.71	32.67	21.37
%Cost Of Sales (Net)	27.45	16.91	164.71	32.67	
%Cost Of Sales (Pot)	17.65	59.85	68.97	20.31	39.63

```
BC INNSITE              SLOW MOVING STOCK REPORT              30/09/XX

    Date of Report 30/09/XX  Date of Last Receipt 30/09/XX  Last Issue 30/09/XX

-----------------------------------------------------------------------------
Stock                    Unit    Min.    No. In   Stock    Last    Last
Code    Stock Name       Type    Stock   Stock    Value   Receipt  Issue
-----------------------------------------------------------------------------
B1   CARLSBERG LAGER     11GL    4.000   6.000    219.00 20/09/87 26/09/87
B2   TETLEY BEST BITTER  9GL     4.000   5.000    160.00 20/09/87 25/99/87
O1   DRY MARTINI         75CL   24.000  12.000     22.68 21/09/87 26/09/87
O2   DRY SHERRY          50CL   24.000  11.000     12.10 21/09/87 26/09/87
S1   SMIRNOFF VODKA      75CL   24.000  25.000     87.50 30/09/87 26/09/87
S2   GORDONS GIN         LTRE   12.000  13.000     65.00 21/09/87 26/09/87
W1   SOAVE               LTRE   12.000  13.000     64.35 21/09/87 26/09/87
W2   CARILLON RED        75CL   24.000  16.000     30.40 21/09/87 26/09/87
                                                 ============
                                         Total    661.03
```

BC INNSITE   STOCK TURNOVER REPORT   30/09/XX

Date of Report 30/09/XX   Period to 30/09/XX

Stock Code	Stock Name	Unit Type	No. In Stock	No. Days For Stock Turnover
B1	CARLSBERG LAGER	11GL	0.600	5
B2	TETLEY BEST BITTER	9GL	0.500	5
01	DRY MARTINI	75CL	1.200	*
02	DRY SHERRY	50CL	1.100	*
S1	SMIRNOFF VODKA	75CL	2.500	*
S2	GORDONS GIN	LTRE	1.300	*
W1	SOAVE	LTRE	1.300	*
W2	CARILLON RED	75CL	1.600	*

Chapter Nine

Performance indicators

Performance indicators are exactly that: indicators of performance. That may seem so simple as to need no explanation. But what does need emphasizing is that they are only indicators.

This simple fact needs stressing because of the surprising and widespread distrust of performance indicators, often due to a misconception or lack of knowledge.

Some managers rely too heavily on them, forgetting that they are indicators only. Other managers do not use them, believing that their use reduces management and performance measurement to a numerical value. Both approaches are wrong.

Key performance indicators provide an objective assessment of the success of a leisure management operation. They are valuable for both client and contractor.

There are many performance indicators. The addendum to this chapter gives quite a variety, and some have been included in other chapters. However, to be of real value, a specific performance indicator is needed for each function within leisure management. The best performance indicators are simple to apply, readily understood, and have often been designed for a particular task.

THE BASIS FOR PERFORMANCE INDICATORS

A good performance indicator gives a measurable indication of performance year by year, month by month or even day by day. They are of particular value to a specific manager and a specific activity. Performance indicators quickly become meaningless when comparisons are made between two different activities.

A great disservice has been perpetrated to performance indicators by attempting to compare like with unlike.

For example, the total expenditure on leisure is often compared between one local authority and another. The inference is that one authority can be shown to be better or worse. Nothing could be further from the truth. All that is shown by a comparison of such figures is that one authority spends more than the other.

GENERAL BUSINESS INDICATORS

The most effective performance indicators are also the simplest. A good example is that used by a small corner shopkeeper. A shopkeeper operates a business not so dissimilar to leisure management. Instead of providing a leisure service to local residents, he sells them food and household products.

The shopkeeper knows exactly how one week's takings compare with those of the same week in the previous year.

Once adjusted for inflation, the shopkeeper knows exactly whether the business is improving or not. Many shopkeepers have never heard of key performance indicators, but the comparison of the same week's taking from one year to the next is exactly that. It is a critical and precise measurement of business success. It relates specifically to that particular business and is obviously an exact comparison with the same period in the previous year. For that particular businessman there can be no better indicator.

Management is at its best when it is simple.

In a multifunctional leisure facility, no one indicator will suffice. Different indicators are appropriate for different activities. Furthermore, the client will be more interested in one set of indicators and the contractor in another set. The client's indicators address how well the residents of the locality are being provided for by the facility and by the contractor. The contractor's indicators concentrate on income maximization. Both are interested in customer satisfaction.

CLIENT INDICATORS

The client's role is to set policies and then ensure their satisfactory delivery. In the case of leisure management this requires that the client monitors and controls the contractor. More particularly, the client needs to ensure that the contractor provides for the residents of the locality as stated and specified in the contract.

All client performance indicators should start and finish with the views of local residents. The management contract can then be regularly varied to accommodate their demands and desires.

There is no other way than to undertake detailed market research. Research within a leisure facility will provide an exact indication of the satisfaction of a range of individuals using the leisure facility. However, this method has distinct limitations. These need to be addressed before beginning a market research survey.

Setting objectives

Market research carried out in a leisure centre or swimming pool will obviously only identify the views of those people already committed to a sport or recreational activity. The views of non-users are equally important.

Market research must therefore be carried out in the general community as well. For example, if a council, for social and community reasons, wishes to encourage increased sport and leisure activity by, say, single parents, then market research is better carried out in shopping areas or health clinics.

Before a council can test whether local facilities are being well used, it needs to have established objectives. Some of the usual range of leisure objectives for a local council would include the following;

- To encourage children to learn to swim.
- To encourage women to swim.
- To help those who are unemployed to keep a sense of value in life.
- To encourage greater participation in physical activity by people over the age of 50.
- To encourage excellence in sport by gifted youngsters.
- To encourage community-wide improvement in health through increased sport and recreation.

Some of the objectives are very specific (for example, encouraging children to swim), while others are more general and social in their application.

Without operational concerns, the client committee of the council will be freed to check on the success of their policies in the community at large. The client side of a council will undertake objective community research on the very issues they seek to address. The full and beneficial impact of tendering in this respect will be gradually realized as the decade unfolds.

Methods

To achieve these policies, the client committee of a council will

Table 9.1 Questions for the leisure strategy review

All authorities should ask themselves these questions

Questions	Considerations
What sports related services do we currently provide? Who does and doesn't use them, and why?	• user surveys • contact with clubs, leagues etc. • surveys among people who don't use the services
Who else is providing services to our community and what are those services?	• provision by adjacent authorities, voluntary and private sectors
What are we trying to achieve and who are we trying to help?	• accessibility orientation (attention concentrates on location of facilities, no price barriers to use by the poor) or • participation orientation (actively seeking to increase participation)
What needs are we trying to meet?	• expressed needs • suppressed demand or • needs as determined by the authority (paternalistic approach)
What constraints are we working under?	• legal (e.g. CCT) • financial (capital, revenue)
How will needs change?	• demography • fashion
What will we do as they change?	• respond to trends or be innovative • support a wide range of activities or concentrate on a selected few (a 'core curriculum')
What should we leave to the private or voluntary sectors?	• activities • facilities
How can we best meet needs?	• what to provide • which activities to support • pricing and subsidy policy • special arrangements for target groups
What resources are required?	• budgets (capital and revenue) • staff (numbers, skills, training needs)
How do we monitor what we are achieving?	• management information needs
What do we need to do to implement our ideas?	• organisational change • assignment of responsibilities

Source: Audit Commission report 'Sport for Whom?'

invariably employ a number of methods to attract participation by the target groups. An example of the methods in use would be the following;

- Junior learn to swim: a programme of courses
- Women swimmers: women-only sessions
- Unemployed participation: reduced fees
- Over-50s: sessions limited to that age group
- Gifted youngsters: schools of excellence
- Community health: interdistrict competitions

In the past, councils have limited themselves to providing the methods by which to achieve their policies. Too often they have stopped short of checking whether the policies have worked.

Concessionary fees were often seen as being sufficient stimulus to increase usage by juniors, the unemployed, senior citizens and those on supplementary benefit. Many councils may not be aware that even their cheaper prices are too expensive for a young person to afford a particular sport or activity.

Furthermore, there are a number of very real fears to be overcome before a person will participate in a new activity.

A survey should therefore be undertaken among non-users as well as users. There can be no other way of assessing how successful a policy has been in achieving its objective. With the increased marketing orientation in local government generally, authorities will no doubt become increasingly concerned to ensure that their leisure policy objectives are actually met.

Community measurements

Many clients see a market approach as being too commercial. Nothing could be further from the truth. The marketplace is of course commercial in concept, but that is as far as the analogy needs to go.

The words 'market research' could be just as easily changed to community research, or community measurement. Different sections of the community have different needs and demands. Just as a market research company will identify a target group of people for a particular product, so community research will establish those sections of the community most in need of a particular activity.

Market, or community research need not be costly. A strong combination occurs where a local council and nearby college combine to undertake research. Such a survey is invaluable for both. The council gains an in-depth insight into local residents' perceptions and views.

Meanwhile college students gain experience in interviewing, statistical analysis and the experience of a live project.

Financial measurements

There are a number of performance indicators specifically provided to monitor the financial effect of the contract on council costs. Some client oriented performance indicators are reproduced in the addendum to this chapter. Some popular client indicators include:

- Subsidy per user;
- Usage figures;
- Expenditure per community charge payer.

These indicators are invaluable for the task required of them. However, they do not address specific target groups. Only by assessing the use made of facilities by specific target groups can a council ascertain whether its policies have been successfully achieved.

Indeed, the principal performance indicator for any council as client needs to start from the council's stated policies. Measurements of use and participation should then be assessed against those objectives.

The average recovery rate (ratio of income to expenditure) varies with type of facility

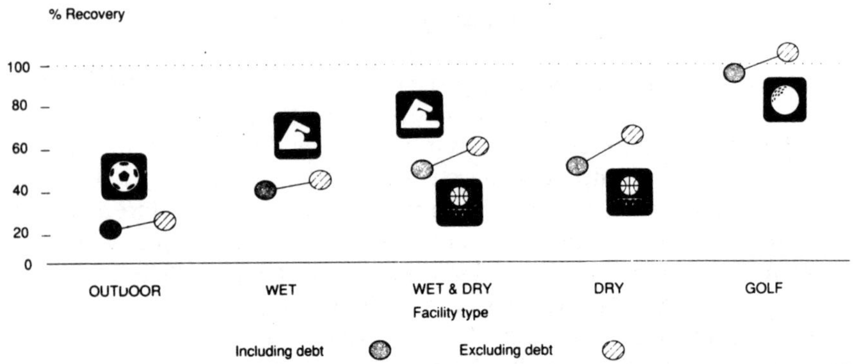

Source: Audit Commission analysis of CIPFA 'Leisure and recreation statistics 1988-89 estimates'. The analysis excludes support for sport charged to urban parks and open spaces

Fig. 9.1 Recovery rates.

Within each authority, the average subsidy for wet and dry users differs

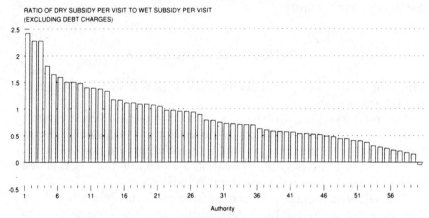

*Source: Audit Commission analysis of CIPFA 'Leisure and recreation statistics 1987-88
estimates'\|and 'Leisure usage statistics 1987-88'*

Fig. 9.2 Subsidies for wet and dry facilities.

CLIENT AND CONTRACTOR MEASUREMENTS

It should never be forgotten that both the client and the contractor
have very similar objectives. These may or may not be formally stated
in the contract documents, but relate to target measures such as:

- Percentage of time allocated to club use;
- Percentage of time allocated to casual use;
- Percentage of time allocated to ethnic users;
- Other percentage allocations;
- Target numbers to be achieved for learn to swim courses;
- Percentage increase in disabled users.

This type of indicator lends itself to easy factual analysis from records
kept at the facility.

But usage figures are not everything. Equally important is the
customers' perception of the facility. Subjective judgements come
into play here, and this issue is more fully covered in Chapter 12.
What is important to note is that much research is of direct benefit
to both contractor and client and thus perhaps should be jointly
funded. Even more important, the information resulting from the
surveys should be jointly assessed. Poor perceptions of a facility

may be due as much to poor client building maintenance, as to poor contractor performance.

CONTRACTOR INDICATORS

The contractor's key performance indicators will stem directly from the business plan.

The business plan will have estimated income from a range of activities in the centre. The key requirement of a successful operator is now to achieve these targets and if possible surpass them. The only effective way to manage this situation is to ensure that each activity manager has individual performance indicators.

This allows a real sense of management responsibility. It also cuts out, at a stroke, hierarchical decision making, the type of decision-making which has characterized local authorities over many years. Traditionally, decisions have not been made at the point of sale or operation, but referred up the management tree to be taken at a higher level. Such systems can be confined to the history books.

Successful leisure management operation requires immediate action. Given a good client specification, there is no reason why immediate decisions cannot be taken.

Delegation not abdication

As discussed earlier, managers and supervisors within a facility need targets. These should be financial targets wherever possible, agreed between management and the individual activity manager or supervisor concerned, and derived directly from the tendered price.

Having set a tender price, accurate monitoring of all the relevant targets must take place. A good facility manager always delegates, then constantly checks. Only a fool abdicates control, and takes no interest in subsequent performance.

Having given responsibility for expenditure and income centres to activity managers or supervisors, simple ratios or indicators then need to be provided to ensure continuing success. An accurate financial indicator is given in Tables 9.1 and 9.2. They pay specific attention to the need for actual income and actual expenditure to be at least equal to that estimated in the tendered bid.

These indicators are a natural follow-on from the budgeted income levels predicted in Chapter 6.

Table 9.2 Profiled estimated daily income form, for Little London swimming pool

INCOME ITEMS	Estimated daily income Week ending							
	Monday £	Tuesday £	Wednesday £	Thursday £	Friday £	Saturday £	Sunday £	Totals £
Tickets								
Adult	120.00	120.00	120.00	150.00	150.00	150.00	180.00	990
Youth	90.00	100.00	100.00	100.00	100.00	200.00	300.00	990
Unwaged	20.00	20.00	20.00	20.00	20.00	10.00	10.00	120
Specials								
– women			120.00	110.00				230
– ethnic		120.00			110.00			230
– fun					250.00			250
– lessons	100.00	100.00	100.00					300
– club	60.00							60
Vending								
Food (net)	15.00	15.00	15.00	15.00	15.00	20.00	20.00	115
Drink (net)	5.00	5.0	5.00	5.00	10.00	15.00	15.00	60
Sales (net)								
Swim wear	10.00	10.00	10.00	10.00	20.00	25.00	30.00	115
Booklets)	10.00	10.00	10.00	10.00	10.00	5.00	5.00	60
Totals								3.520

1. This table reflects the anticipated income in a school term weekday.
2. Income during the school holidays will be separately estimated.
3. Closures of approximately 10 days per year are anticipated.

This is the list of estimated income, derived from the budgeted income contained in the tender bid (Table 6.2). This can be easily and regularly checked against the income actually received.

Table 9.3 Daily actual income summary form for Little London swimming pool

INCOME ITEMS	Actual daily income Week ending							
	Monday £	Tuesday £	Wednesday £	Thursday £	Friday £	Saturday £	Sunday £	Totals
Tickets								
Adult								
Youth								
Unwaged								
Specials								
– women								
– ethnic								
– fun								
– lessons								
– club								
Vending								
Food (net)								
Drink (net)								
Sales (net)								
Swim wear)								
Booklets)								
Totals								

This simple daily total provides a powerful management tool when collated by the senior cashier (or activity manager). The completed table allows accurate analysis of actual income received and can be easily compared with the budgeted estimates (Table 9.1). Furthermore, the information caught in these records gives excellent base data on different patterns of use. This is essential information with which to launch a publicity drive.

Expenditure control

Income is fluid. It varies from day to day; that is why it is so important to keep a constant check.

But with all this emphasis on income, attention should not be lost on the all important task of keeping expenditure within budget.

Unlike income, much expenditure is regular, sizeable and predictable. Bills are generally for monthly and quarterly periods. Provided that proper procedures have been set to control expenditure at the outset, there should be no great surprises suddenly sprung on management by unexpected expenditure.

There is one area of expenditure where weekly assessment is essential – wages. Salaries and wages form the greatest expenditure within most management contracts. It is all too easy for salaries and wages to run ahead of income. There are dozens of genuine reasons in any one week why extra staff, or a little overtime, is needed. If the extra staff result in income received being greater than the expenditure incurred – fine. If not, immediate action is necessary. Only rigorous weekly control will be adequate in this critical area of performance.

Staff incentives

Local authorities have, for many decades, paid incentive bonuses to manual staff and yet not to officer staff. The reason is that work output is relatively easily measured in the manual trades, and can be rewarded accordingly.

However, the intention behind productivity payments is to enhance performance and relate pay to work output. It is the oldest and strongest motivator, once the basic necessities of life are provided.

Leisure centre management will become increasingly linked to performance pay. A number of examples are given in the book where incentive payments are made. All have achieved the desired objective of improving performance.

The best pay schemes incorporate the following principles:

- Incentives are linked to actual increased income.
- Improved incentives are paid as income to the centre increases beyond that originally budgeted.
- Allowance has to be made for any income shared with the client, before paying staff incentives.
- There is no outright entitlement to incentive pay; different employees will earn different rates.

- The incentive payments are linked directly to a rigorous quarterly performance interview and assessment with each individual employee.
- The incentive payments will increase and decrease according to performance and income.
- There is a ceiling to the performance payments (commonly 10 – 20 per cent of basic pay).
- Additional special payments are made for income generating, or cost cutting, initiatives.

All staff, by their attitude and behaviour, affect the profitability of a centre or facility. A few will have significant ability to increase income, or reduce expenditure. Incentive payments need to take this into account, but at the same time must reward those staff who have no direct income increasing or cost cutting abilities. The system has to be fair.

It cannot be over-emphasized that incentive payments should be linked to individual personal quarterly assessment, and the total profitability of the facility.

Monthly analysis

The danger is that a manager can become inured to the meaning of the information before him. The repetitive day by day flow of figures can dull the senses. After a number of years a manager can be completely switched off from the very information which measures the health of the business.

Thus monthly analysis is also imperative. Critical monthly analysis of information has an impact much greater than daily analysis, especially when this information is compared and contrasted with the annual budgeted expenditure and income. If presented graphically, this information cannot fail to highlight trends.

CONTRACT PERFORMANCE

A contract only works between two willing partners. Thus although there will be different key performance indicators between client and contractor, there will also be a lot of common ground. Customer monitoring will produce the most useful data for client and contractor. It will also identify areas for action for both parties.

A simple customer monitoring form is included in Appendix D. This will benefit both parties to the contract. It is not, however, a market research survey; it is purely a simple method of checking customer preferences. Easy to complete, it will provide an objective assessment to the subjective area of perceptions.

The addendum to this chapter includes perhaps the most definitive list of leisure performance indicators available up to 1990, assembled by the Greater London and South East Region of the Sports Council. The secret is to choose one or two simple indicators which suit the particular circumstances of the contract.

As all contracts vary so much, the best performance indicators are those generated by the management and staff of a facility. The indicators provided in the addendum should help.

SUMMARY

The principal message of this chapter is that both client and contractor have some key differences in performance criteria. The client is more interested in social and community benefits; the contractor in usage and income. Both, however, are keenly interested in customer views, and customer perceptions.

The other critical issues identified in the chapter include:

- Performance indicators do have set limits to their value; they are just an indication of performance.
- To be of value, performance indicators must compare like with like.
- The corner shopkeeper has an excellent indicator in the level of sales from one week to the next, and from one year to the next.
- A multifunctional leisure facility will need a greater number of indicators.
- All indicators are extracted from a mass of detail, and highlight trends and attitudes.
- The basic essential before the introduction of indicators is to have quantifiable objectives in place, against which to measure.
- For the contractor, this will be some form of income and expenditure comparison.
- Financial incentives to staff will be a corollary to financial performance measurements.
- For the client, some form of quantified measure of social performance is needed, like the number of primary school children learning to swim.

- Results should be critically examined in a positive manner, not as a means of finding fault with the other party to the contract.

Freed of operational management, council client committees should be able to concentrate (increasingly through the 1990s) on policy issues and their effective implementation. This will be one very positive result of competitive tendering, provided that councils have the necessary will to monitor and check for themselves who benefits from the subsidy payments made. The financial benefits should not continue to accrue to those who can afford to pay more for their leisure.

The biggest disadvantage that could result from competitive tendering is that client committees of local authorities abdicate their responsibilities to the contractor. This can, and to an extent does, happen whether the contract is operated in-house, or by an outside contractor. It is an easy and comfortable relationship; but it will not benefit the wider community.

Sports development programmes operated by most local authorities should ensure that this level of abdication does not occur.

ADDENDUM: PERFORMANCE INDICATORS

The performance measures on this addendum are reproduced with the kind permission of the Sports Council, Greater London and South East Region, who first published them as one of their Occasional Papers in recreation management. A particular debt of gratitude is owed to the authors, Chris Hespe, Alan Sillitoe and John Thorpe.

MANAGEMENT PAPERS
Occasional papers in recreation management

Measuring Performance

INTRODUCTION

Managers of sports and leisure facilities have always measured performance, if only by keeping records of levels of use or of income year by year. Increasingly, the measures of *financial* performance which are commonplace in the commercial sector have come to be applied in the public sector, and with the advent of competitive tendering there will be an increasing need to measure the performance of a facility in a fair and realistic way.

The purpose of this Management Paper is to provide a tool for managers, mainly in the public sector, who wish to apply performance ratios to their facility, either for the use of their own employers or for the specification which will be the basis for a competitive tender. By using ratios in this way they can compare one aspect of performance with another. The paper has been written on the assumption that most public leisure centres have been provided to offer a service to the public rather than primarily to make a profit, and the ratios included do not therefore measure profitability in the commercial sense.

The expression 'ratio' is used fairly generally in this paper to describe a range of measures many of which are expressed as proportions or as percentages, and are not ratios in the strict mathematical sense.

THE STATE OF THE ART

Some ratios which have been used by public leisure providers in the past have included:

► Recovery Rates (Income as a proportion of expenditure)

► Subsidy per attendance

► Average spend per visit

► Staff costs as a proportion of operating expenditure

These measures have been used primarily to compare a facility's performance with other known facilities (for example in a neighbouring borough), or against known standards and targets, or with the previous year's performance.

In 1981 the Greater London and South East Council for Sport and Recreation took the lead in measuring performance by calculating levels of income recovery in the region. Using figures for annual income and expenditure provided by the Chartered Institute of Public Finance and Accountancy, it set targets for both 'recovery rate' and 'subsidy per user'. The report, entitled 'Making Better Use of

ACKNOWLEDGEMENTS

For their comments on a draft of this paper, we would like to express our thanks to

Audit Commission	Steve Studd
Crossland Leisure	Grant Thornton Ltd
Hywel Griffiths	George Torkildsen
Roger Quinton	Bob Kimmis

Resources', recognised that while no two swimming pools or leisure centres are identical there are enough similarities between broad types of facility (eg. post-war 25m pools with learner pool) to justify the setting of targets to encourage managers to raise their sights. The average recovery rates and targets from that report were:

	1981 Averages		
	London	Counties	Region
Pools	27%	46%	30%
'Wet & Dry' Centres	43%	59%	50%
'Dry' Centres	48%	70%	56%

	Targets	
	Outer London & Districts	Inner London
Pools	50%	40%
'Wet & Dry' Centres	65%	55%
'Dry' Centres	75%	65%

For this exercise, central management charges were omitted (because they are calculated in such an uneven and non-comparable way) and loan charges were also excluded.

Subsidy per user was calculated and a number of targets were advocated, ranging from 60p per head subsidy for pool users in Inner London to 20p per head for 'dry' centres in outer London and the counties (1981 prices).

Since this report was published CIPFA have made and published their own calculations of recovery rates, and now include a summary table showing the proportion of gross expenditure met by income from sales, fees and charges.

Using CIPFA figures based upon local authority estimates for 1987-88 the following are the recovery rates for sports centres and swimming pools in Greater London and the South East. Recovery rate is defined by CIPFA as all income divided by all expenditure other than loan charges.

	London Boroughs	*Counties*
Pools	32%	53%
'Wet & Dry' Centres	51%	55%
'Dry' Centres	57%	56%

In 1983, the Audit Inspectorate published its report entitled 'Development and Operation of Leisure Centres.' This study stated that "although there are inherent difficulties and dangers in preparing ratios of performance, we believe that a set of ratios would be useful to both management and those interested in leisure provision". The study proposed a number of ratios, both operational and financial, which are included among those in this paper.

The report did not apply these recommended ratios to facilities and thus arrived at no statistical information which could be of operational use to facility providers and managers.

It is vital that performance monitoring should be seen within the wider context of management practice. The Sports Council, through its 'Recreation Management Award', advocates the process of 'management by objectives' (MBO) in which the establishment of detailed objectives and targets is undertaken for all aspects of the centre's management. This process will then provide the framework within which performance ratios will be used by the manager to evaluate the way in which the centre performs.

CALCULATING THE RATIOS

(a) *Recovery Rate*

Recovery rates are relatively simple to calculate. Gross recovery rates can be expressed as

$$\frac{\text{Income} \times 100}{\text{All Expenditure}}$$

Operational recovery rates consist of

$$\frac{\text{Income} \times 100}{\text{Operational Expenditure}}$$

where operational costs exclude loan charges, central management charges, and rates. Gross recovery rates are sometimes called (eg by CIPFA) 'service recovery rates'. The Audit Inspectorate recommended that bar and catering should be excluded from this calculation.

(b) *Subsidy Rates*

The Gross Subsidy (or 'service' subsidy) is: Total Gross Expenditure, less total income.

This figure can be expressed as an amount per user:

$$\frac{\text{Gross Expenditure, less Income}}{\text{No of Attendances}}$$

Similarly, the Operational Subsidy is:
Total Operational Expenditure, less total income, and:

Operational Subsidy per User can be expressed as

$$\frac{\text{Operational Expenditure, less Income}}{\text{No of Attendances}}$$

(c) *Occupancy Rates*

A broad measure of the level of use of a facility is the occupancy rate, expressed as a percentage:

$$\frac{\text{No of Bookings Made x 100}}{\text{Total No of Space Bookings Available}}$$

This figure can then be calculated as a 'unit' occupancy rate for each distinct element of the building, eg. occupancy rate for squash courts, sports halls, fitness room. Whenever possible it is important to record any 'excess' demand (over 100%) and to log the number of 'turn-aways'. For some parts of the building, weekly throughput is a better indicator than percentage occupancy rates.

(d) *Measuring Income*

As a starting point for measuring income, gross amount spent per user is a widely employed figure. It is then important to be able to analyse income into its component parts, normally expressed as a percentage:

$$\frac{\text{Income from Activities x 100}}{\text{Total Income}}$$

and income from activities could be further divided into courses or casual use.

Major sources of income are important to identify:

$$\frac{\text{Income from all Catering x 100}}{\text{Total Income}}$$

or

$$\frac{\text{Income from Special Events x 100}}{\text{Total Income}}$$

or

$$\frac{\text{Income from Educational Use x 100}}{\text{Total Income}}$$

Within a leisure centre, activity spaces can be singled out and the income from each can be calculated:

    Income per activity area (squash court; badminton court)

or   Income per square metre

or   Income per hour

and income from customers can be calculated as an average spend per head by separating

$$\frac{\text{Income (Excluding bar/catering)}}{\text{No of Admissions}}$$

from $$\frac{\text{Bar/Catering Income}}{\text{No of Admissions}}$$

as used below.

Income from special events, from courses, and from sale or hire of equipment should all be capable of being identified and measured separately.

(e) *Measuring Expenditure*

Expenditure can be analysed in a similar way, for example:

$$\frac{\text{Energy Costs (heat, light, power) x 100}}{\text{Operating Expenditure}}$$

and

$$\frac{\text{Repairs and Maintenance} \times 100}{\text{Operating Expenditure}}$$

as well as

$$\frac{\text{Rates} \times 100}{\text{Operating Expenditure}}$$

and

$$\frac{\text{Allocation of Central Charges} \times 100}{\text{Other Operating Expenditure}}$$

Wherever possible, the expenditure incurred by a centre in staffing and providing each element of the building should be calculated separately, as in the 'cost-centre' approach set out in section (d).

A valuable indicator is 'cost efficiency', which reveals the number of admissions per £1 of operating costs. Cooper and Lybrand Associates define cost efficiency as:

$$\frac{\text{Number of Admissions}}{\text{Operating Costs}}$$

where operating costs mean total costs, less loan charges and central administrative costs.

(f) *Turnover*

For the purposes of competitive tendering the 'target level' set by the Secretary of State may well be expressed as the 'net profit on turnover'. This can be calculated in the following way:

Facility Income:

Income from users	250,000
Income from Rate Fund	250,000 (ie. net deficit)
TOTAL INCOME	500,000 (ie. turnover)

If net profit on turnover were set at 5%, it would equal £25,000. The tender figure would therefore be turnover plus profit, less income from users. = £275,000.

(g) *Staffing Costs*

A major element of expenditure, and one which it is important to monitor, is the cost of providing staff. Total employee costs are the crudest and most obvious measure, and this can be broken down in a more revealing way:

$$\frac{\text{Payroll Cost}}{\text{Revenue generated}}$$

or

$$\frac{\text{Employee Costs} \times 100}{\text{Operating Expenditure}}$$

The staffing element in the hourly cost of running a centre can be calculated, either for the entire centre or for separate elements which might be hired independently, eg. the swimming pool. In addition, it is suggested that managers should be clearly aware of the relationship between plain time and overtime payments, probably on a month by month basis, so that staff numbers and shift patterns can be planned in the most economical way.

It can also be useful to calculate the relationship between total income and the total number of staff employed (income divided by number of staff) to give a rough measure of the 'productivity' of staff.

Within overall staff costs, it is worth analysing the costs of cleaning the building, in order to compare cleaning costs with those of other similar centres:

$$\frac{\text{Square Footage}}{\text{No of Cleaners (full-time equivalents)}}$$

and, where cleaning is contracted out:

$$\frac{\text{Contract Cost of Cleaning}}{\text{Square Footage Cleaned}}$$

(h) *Catering*

Assuming that the profit or loss on the catering can be calculated by management as part of the centre's operation (as opposed to franchising, or catering as part of a remote central catering department), there are a number of useful ratios which can be employed:

$$\frac{\text{Bar/Catering/Vending Gross Profit}}{\text{Bar/Catering/Vending Revenue}}$$

or, more usually, Gross Profit — represented by total income from sales less cost of goods sold.

As a measure of catering spend per head, the following calculation will be of value:

$$\frac{\text{Bar/Catering/Vending Income}}{\text{No of Admissions}}$$

(i) *Marketing*

Marketing is the Achilles heel of public sector management, and is a much wider concept than merely advertising and printing. As a first step it is important to know:

$$\frac{\text{Marketing Expenditure x 100}}{\text{Total Operating Expenditure}}$$

This gross percentage figure can then be refined and augmented by calculating:

$$\frac{\text{Marketing Expenditure}}{\text{Catchment Population}}$$

and

$$\frac{\text{Marketing Expenditure}}{\text{No of Admissions}}$$

(j) *Collecting the Information*

It will only be possible to calculate many of these ratios if a centre is equipped with a modern data collection booking and payments system, which staff are trained to use. More and more leisure centres are being equipped with micro computers, thus allowing managers to use graphic display to highlight trends and also to programme different variables into their calculations.

THE LIMITATIONS

(a) *Variables*

Apart from SASH centres, no two sports centres are identical in terms of design. Ratios comparing one facility with another must be tempered by taking into account variables, some of which can be varied by the local authority or by managers:

► pricing policy

► operating hours

► staffing levels

► agreed levels of subsidy (stemming from social objectives)

and others which lie outside managerial control:

► catchment size

► the design and scale of the centre, and whether 'wet' or 'dry'

► The nature of the catchment area, including age and socio-economic levels

► competition from other facilities

(b) *Objectives*

Most recreation facilities now have a set of written objectives, and the performance of the centre must be judged against these objectives. These may be social as well as financial, and are likely to aim at a varied recreational programme which balances club use with casual use, recreation with 'excellence', and social 'target groups' with the recreationally active and prosperous.

Applying financial ratios on their own will not therefore show whether a facility is well-managed or badly-managed. Monitoring of the first nine SASH sports centres of similar design showed that the 'recovery rate' in 1987 ranged from 33% to 83%, and much of this variation can be explained by the differing objectives set by the managers and local authorities.

As 'Making Better Use of Resources' pointed out, the purpose of public recreation centres is usually to provide a broad-based service to the public, and therefore 100,000 swimmers paying 50p a swim must be a better return to the authority than 50,000 paying £1.

(c) *Standardising the Measures*

There has been little standardisation in the format of ratios. There are good arguments for including or excluding some elements of the cost of running a centre, particularly

▶ loan charges (which may not exist if the centre was financed from capital receipts)

▶ rates (a proportion of which are returned to the authority)

▶ central administrative costs (where there is no marginal cost to the central department)

▶ insurance and licences, ie. other 'non-controllable' costs

but it is very important to state clearly which have been included so as to compare like with like and to identify genuine 'operational' costs.

The cost of operating a centre, either in the private or public sector, does include (for example) the cost of legal advice, of audit, and of engineering or repair services. It is fair to regard these as operating costs, whether they are charged to the parent department or another Council department. It is not fair however to regard as operational costs an arbitrary or over-loaded proportion of the authority's entire central management costs.

As a measure of the effectiveness of a manager in hitting targets (either year by year, or quarterly, or even weekly) it is helpful to recognise the distinction between "controllable" and "non-controllable" costs, so that a manager does not get the blame for costs outside his or her control. Equally, the manager should only get the credit for management-generated income.

RECOMMENDATIONS

1 Performance ratios should be used for the purpose of setting objectives and for the continued evaluation of the performance of a facility.

2 To this end, good data collection is essential.

3 From the wide range of ratios shown in this report, seven are recommended as 'key ratios' which will be of greatest use, especially in competitive tendering:

▶ Gross Recovery Rate

▶ Operational Recovery Rate

▶ Gross Subsidy

▶ Gross Subsidy per Attendance

▶ Operational Subsidy

▶ Operational Subsidy per Attendance

▶ Cost efficiency

4 These seven have been chosen in order to make clear the distinction between the overall cost of the service and the operational cost, a matter over which there has been confusion in the past.

5 Performance ratios are most effective when they are used "longitudinally" as an aid to management in assessing the performance of a facility over a unit of time such as a year, a quarter, or a week.

6 Ratios should be used with caution when comparing one facility with another, so as to compare like with like.

7 Known or published "standards" of performance should be used with care, especially when predicting the performance of a new facility.

8 Performance ratios should not be used without taking into account a number of variables which affect their result.

9 The results of analysing ratios should be matched against, and tempered by, the social and sporting objectives of the providing authority.

Chris Hespe
Alan Sillitoe
John Thorpe

Sports Council, Greater London & South East Regions, PO Box 480, Crystal Palace National Sports Centre, London SE19 2BQ

BIBLIOGRAPHY

Audit Inspectorate (1983)   — *Development and Operation of Leisure Centres (Selected Case Studies)* HMSO, London

Chartered Institute of Public Finance and Accountancy (1987)   — *Leisure and Recreation Statistics 1987-1988 Estimates* CIPFA Statistical Information Service, London

— *Charges for Leisure Services* Annual Sample Survey CIPFA Statistical Information Service, London

ECOTEC (1987)   — *The Sports Council's Standardised Approach to Sportshall Design — SASH Centres in Use: Design and Management* ECOTEC Research and Consulting Ltd, Priory House, Steelhouse Lane, Birmingham B4 6BJ

Sports Council (1981)   — *Making Better Use of Resources: Regional Recreation Strategy Subject Report* Greater London & South East Council for Sport and Recreation, London

Chapter Ten

Management buyouts

To many people involved in leisure management, there appears to be a natural logic in allowing leisure managers to operate their own facilities.

The theory is fine; the practice is somewhat different. The first consideration needs to be that of the views of the owners of the facility. Many local authorities jealously guard their leisure provisions. They are averse to the very thought of their facilities being handed over to the centre management. Other authorities are all too keen to transfer responsibility in the belief that more efficient operation will result.

BASIC PRINCIPLES

Any leisure management team considering a buyout needs to belong to an authority which will actively support, or at least permit, a buyout to take place. That basic premise has to be checked before any work begins. In a local authority (or for that matter with any contract), it is almost impossible for a buyout to be successfully achieved if the owner is not in full approval.

In commerce, when a management team declares it's bid; it can offer financial incentives to the owner of the company. But no adequate recompense can be made to a local authority where that authority is determined to retain control. In these circumstances, the local authority would undoubtedly prefer the agony of losing direct control of its amenities to an established company making a successful tender bid.

But given agreement between the local authority and its leisure management team, separate company status can be sought. It is a long and hard road. It is also risky, exacting, and exciting. The stakes are always high when people gamble with their life savings.

Definition

'Management buyout' is the wrong term for a leisure management contract bid. Although the management is involved, the buyout aspect of the deal is minimal or missing. Nevertheless, the term is widely used. It is generally understood to mean the transfer of responsibility from an existing employer to some or all of the employees. It is in this sense (strictly, incorrect), that the term is used in this book.

Nearly everyone who has taken part in a management buyout (or cooperative venture or other form of changed management) speaks of the months of agony involved. On top of their day to day workload, the management team must also find time to prepare a competently priced bid, and all this takes place in a strained atmosphere of uncertainty. The uncertainty stems from the fears about the ability, not to say wisdom, of going it alone.

Management buyouts do not proceed according to a preordained plan. Each is shaped according to the particular circumstances surrounding it. Each buyout is also greatly influenced by the personalities involved.

There are many features which need to be arranged: capital finance, insurance cover, financial bonds and guarantees. All this is to be accomplished before the company has had an oppportunity to establish its credibility in financial circles. As these difficulties are overcome, or not, so the hopes and aspirations of each individual rise and fall; soaring high with optimism one day, sinking low the next.

QUALIFYING CONDITIONS

If the first condition is prior council approval, then the second is absolute commitment by the leisure management team. This may include all the team or just the leading members, depending on circumstances. The team have to believe in themselves. Without that prerequisite, they are unlikely to command the confidence or respect of anyone else.

Third, a business plan is essential. Although there is no one perfect format for a business plan, the key essentials are;

- An evaluation of the operating environment.
- An indication of market trends.
- A financial forecast of income and expenditure.
- A detailed projection for the first two years.
- An indication of strengths and weaknesses.

Preparing a basic business plan will help build confidence and commitment. Once the business plan has been finalized, it then needs to be translated into projected balance sheets, income and expenditure forecasts and an exact analysis of estimated cash flow.

Most leisure managers involved in a buyout will not have the necessary skills to produce these financial forecasts. Even if they do have such expertise, they will not have the reputation necessary to influence banks and other financial institutions.

Therefore, the fourth condition is to secure a competent financial adviser.

Financial advice

Financial advisers come in all shapes and sizes, with vastly differing degrees of competency. Doormats throughout the nation are littered daily with financial offers from a huge range of companies. These vary from the best in the land to bogus businesses seeking ready cash from unwitting investors.

A sound financial adviser will take the basic business plan and produce reliable financial forecasts. Furthermore, the adviser will be able to deliver a professional account of the prospective company to interested financial backers.

There are, then, three principal requirements when seeking a financial adviser. The adviser must be professionally qualified as a chartered accountant, and operating within an established and reputable practice. The final requirement is that the adviser and the leisure management team are able to establish a good working relationship. Commitment is needed from the adviser as well as the team.

Working capital

To start a new company, financial capital is required. Quite obviously, sufficient cash reserves are necessary to operate the business during the initial few months. Expenditure will be needed for wages, stocks and supplies, marketing and publicity, and the cost of buying or leasing equipment.

With a leisure management contract from a local authority, there will be a significant income shortfall across the counter. As most local authority facilities are subsidized, a substantial monthly payment will be made by the authority to cover this shortfall. Thus, each month the new business will need to allow for this financial short-fall.

In fact, the business will need to prepare to operate for two months without receiving client subsidy, as most payments will be about one month in arrears. An overdraft from the bank might seem the most likely source of finance. It often is, but there are costs associated with this source of funds. A commercial rate of interest will be payable on the overdraft and, furthermore, no bank is likely to risk its money without some indication of confidence from the management team. The solution to both problems is equity capital.

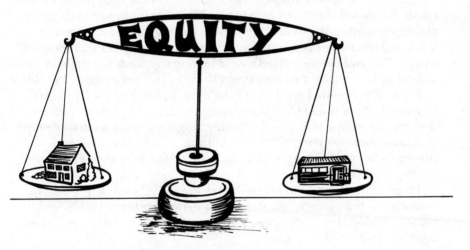

Fig. 10.1 The manager's house provides good equity.

Equity capital refers to the money put into the business by the members of the management team themselves. This may be added to by profits achieved over the years. There is normally no obligation to pay interest or dividends on equity capital, unlike borrowed money.

The provision of equity capital is the essential hallmark of a management team's commitment to, and confidence in, its own plans. With a competent financial adviser and sufficient equity capital, it should be possible for a viable business to seek a financial backer.

As there will be very few tangible assets in leisure management contracts, the financial institutions will be asked, in effect, to express total confidence in an unknown leisure management team to deliver profits. Thus the financial plan and the equity share will need to be very convincing to attract a financial institution in the first place.

In particular, financial advisers will wish to estimate the worst possible scenario. A competent and confident management team will naturally produce optimistic forecasts. A good adviser will look at the worst possible financial forecast for the worst possible month. The availability of finance to the company needs to take account of this situation. Many of these principles can be seen in action with actual management buyouts which have occurred.

THE WESTMINSTER 'BUYOUT'

One of the first leisure management buyouts in the country was that within the City of Westminster in the late 1980s. At the time, the council's majority political group was in favour of achieving greater economies and improved efficiency by means of submitting their services to competitive tender. This was before competitive tendering was made compulsory for all local authorities, by the amendment to the Local Government Act 1988.

The council invited tenders for the management of the five leisure facilities in Westminster. The assistant director of sports and recreation for the council, Roger Bottomley, together with a small group of fellow officers, considered submitting a bid. The first essential prerequisite for the group was to seek the approval of their employers for this course of action.

Their request was considered and granted. Such approval was essential. If the council had stipulated that the officers had to resign before making a bid, the personal risk would have increased to an unacceptable level.

Although the Council gave agreement, they did not give support. They stipulated that the work necessary to the buyout had to be undertaken in the employees' own time. The Council made one other, all-important, stipulation. The officers involved in the buyout bid were to be divorced entirely from all the client preparations. They had no responsibility for, or access to, the preparations and assessment of tenders.

A start-up company

Before submitting a bid, the officers had to form themselves into a company, a virtually unknown step for local government officers. Phil Reid, operations director for the new company explains:

> It was not a management buyout, in the true sense of the term. It was a start–up company. We were not buying anything. The buildings and plant remained in the ownership of the Council.

We started with four directors. We all contributed financially to the company, although Roger Bottomley paid for a 51 per cent majority of the shares. The Articles of Association of the company required any Director who wished to sell his shares to offer his shares back to the Company in the first instance. This was to decrease the likelihood of any unacceptable outside interest taking over.

Finance

To provide sufficient finance to operate the five centres involved in their tender submission the company set up with an authorized share capital of £100 000. The directors initially paid £50 000 with shares valued at £1 each. This equity capital of £50 000 put into the business by the directors, together with the strength of the business plan, gave the National Westminster Bank sufficient confidence to provide a loan facility if required.

The new company had difficulty in securing a performance bond as they had no track record. But, as performance bonds are part of a normal contract (an example is provided in Appendix A, at the end of the book) it had to be provided. The performance bond required as part of the contract amounted to a further £25 000. This proved to be not totally dead money. The bondsman paid interest on the £25 000, deposited. So although the company could not use the money on a week by week basis for operational purposes, at least the interest paid provided some small recompense. Phil Reid recalls:

> The financial side of the business took a great deal of arranging. For a company with no operational history, all the financial institutions had to be convinced on the basis of our financial statement of expenditure and income.
>
> Our success lay in seeking the very best financial adviser we could find. We evaluated a number of companies well known in financial circles. All were very helpful. But only with one did we feel totally at ease. He understood our aims and aspirations, and was able to translate this into a hard edged business plan which would carry weight with the financiers. A sense of real trust developed between us. The adviser was able to open doors.

Key elements for success

With sufficient financial backing in place, the start-up company was formed. The key elements to the company being formed were as follows:

1. Total commitment by those involved; including time, cash equity, and personal guarantees.
2. The approval of their employers.
3. The professionalism, competence and ability of the members of the company.
4. A clear business plan included;
   - a five-year indication of income growth
   - a more detailed analysis for the first 18 months
   - a clear statement of estimated income and expenditure
   - a clear indication of peaks and troughs in income during the year
5. Adequate financial backing to cover all likely situations.

All this ensured the presentation of a credible tender bid, detailed in Chapter 5.

THE ROCHFORD 'BUYOUT'

During the 1980s, Rochford District Council in Essex had also prided itself on being in the forefront of the drive to subject local authority services to competitive tender. However, virtually all the services (office cleaning, street cleansing, refuse collection and the like) had been lost to the private sector.

The leisure team at Rochford noticed all this with the greatest concern. Parks maintenance, which formed part of the department, was one of the last services to be subjected to tender. The parks went the same way as all the other services: into the private sector.

This was really rather too near home for the comfort of the leisure staff. They were well aware that the parks staff had, by general agreement, entered the competitive situation without any restructuring or change to their working methods.

At about the same time, in 1987, the government announced it was to consider adding leisure management to the list of services to be subject to compulsory competitive tendering. The time was right to act.

The company formation

Led by Peter Johnson, the director of leisure services, active consideration was given to the formation of a private company owned and managed by the employees, and in which the council would retain an interest for the first 12 months of operation. Both the council and the staff were agreed on the way forward. Plans for the company were well advanced by early 1988. The company was set to be operational from April 1, 1988.

Then a major disruption occurred. On February 10, 1988, the Secretary of State for the Environment announced in Parliament that; 'from midnight tonight, no council can award a contract to any company in which it has an interest in any of the defined services', in other words the services then subject to competitive tendering.

As catering (a defined activity) was included in the company being formed, the deal was dead.

A reappraisal was necessary. To the credit of both the council and the employees, the intention to form a company remained as strong as ever. There was one significant difference; from then on, the leisure staff had to form the company themselves. Yet among the staff there was 100 per cent support for continuing with the buyout. £50 000 capital was raised from the employees by the sale of £1 shares.

For their part, the council agreed that the company should continue to operate the facilities for one year. This would allow the council time to seek competitive tenders.

Circa Leisure

Without any support, but with tremendous commitment, the company was formed, and was indeed operational from April 1, 1988. The management agreement included all the indoor sports facilities (three sports centres and three halls), the sports development programme, and some ancillary leisure functions.

For the company to become a reality, major decisions and action had to be taken in those first few embryonic months.

Financial credibility

The company was greatly helped by their appointed bank manager. They had chosen to remain with the same bank as the council. The strength of the arrangement was that the bank already knew the business intimately; to them it was not a new business, just a change of management.

In addition, the company was successful in obtaining the services of an excellent financial adviser from one of the largest accountancy companies in the country. The advice given was free, on the condition that the company continued to use the financial company for accountancy services subsequently. The adviser provided the all-essential credibility needed in financial circles.

All the company had to offer was commitment, knowledge of the business built up over the previous five years and £50 000. Peter Johnson comments:

> We had nothing tangible on which to base any financial credibility. We did not own any assets, and would not be owning any assets. The buildings remained owned by the Council.
>
> Not much to impress a city financier: and yet we were determined to improve on the past performance. We considered that it was essential to raise sufficient capital to begin. We were concerned not just with funding the necessary cash flow to operate as a company, but also investing in marketing and facility improvements.

Freedom

The new company was able to implement many proposals which the council had been unable to fund. Peter Johnson explains:

> We had always believed that a proper marketing approach would pay for itself. However, the finance was never available from the council. There were always more pressing priorities within the council. Expenditure on marketing could never compete with the cash needed for say housing, or some other statutory function

Peter Johnson strikes a chord with many local authority leisure officers when he highlights the disadvantages of public management. These include:

- High central establishment charges;
- Time delays in decision making;
- Conditions of service which are really for office staff who work a 9 to 5 day;
- Delayed and inadequate financial information;
- Capital controls.

Freed of these controls and restrictions, the company was able to venture into a whole new and innovative style of management. This could only be achieved by securing the services of motivated staff.

Staff policies

Staff numbers reduced somewhat in the period leading up to the company formation. Due to the uncertainty, the council filled vacancies only on a temporary basis. However, the staff growth after the company formation was spectacular.

There was a small increase in full-time staff from 47 to 52; part-time staff increased from 40 to 61; and casual staff from 130 to 240. All the staff retained at least the same levels of pay as when employed by the council. In fact, the majority were earning more; and bonus was additional. Full pay was provided when staff were off sick for up to three months.

Within six months the company submitted their tender, along with four other tenderers. This particular part of the experience of Circa Leisure is detailed in Chapter 5. It is worth repeating here that they won the tender bid by the tightest of margins. So the faith and commitment made by the company were repaid. More important, use and income increased across a wide range of activities.

Capital injection

Subsequently, in order to improve their access to capital funds, Circa entered into agreement with a large property developer. Again it was a situation where the fledgling company considered it had no choice. They believed that to win tenders under competition, the new company needed a broader base of business experience and strong financial backing.

Fifty per cent of the shares were sold to the property company, who retained a non-controlling interest via a shareholder agreement. In addition to the non-controlling interest, the shareholder agreement had a pre-emption clause. Thus if the property company wished to sell their shares, they had to offer them back to Circa before offering them to anyone else.

Surprisingly, the property company itself went into receivership, despite its size. As far as Circa were concerned, this placed them in a strong position to seek other financial options and provided a wealth of additional experience about surviving in the commercial world.

THE AUDIT COMMISSION

The Audit Commission have lukewarm views about management

buyouts in local authorities. They fear that some buyouts may not be for the public good. Private gain may outweigh leisure benefits. Their checklist is reproduced in the addendum to this chapter.

Certainly there have been some spectacular buyouts which have gone sour, especially where computer buyouts are concerned. Caution is needed. The checklist should be studied, as should all the advice of the Audit Commission. The leisure facilities remain publicly owned even after the start of the contract. As the management operations will be subject to tender at regular intervals, it is important that these valuable community assets remain unfettered by externally imposed constraints.

SUMMARY

There was a sudden upsurge in local authority buyouts in the late 1980s, due to the major changes occurring in local government during those years. This may slow down in the 1990s. However, the principles relating to buyouts are instructive to anyone involved in leisure management. The experiences portrayed in this chapter contain many valuable pointers to a successful management operation whether by a buyout team, an in-house team, or an independent contractor. The key points are now summarized.

- 'Buyout' is the wrong term.
- In a leisure management contract bid, nothing is bought out at all.
- A 'start–up' company, or cooperative, is perhaps a better description.
- But 'buyout' is a common term, and is used to indicate the transfer of management from the owners (the local authority) to the employees.
- The local authority's prior approval is necessary before anyone contemplates a buyout.
- Many local authorities will never agree to buyouts.
- Such local authorities believe that only the local authority itself should operate, and be seen to operate, community facilities; even if by contract.
- Those who go down the buyout road, must be aware of the high personal risk factor.
- Commitment by the buyout team needs to be total for success.
- Expert financial advice is essential.
- It pays to shop around, before settling on an interested, qualified and committed adviser.

- A five-year business plan will have to be prepared, with special attention to the profiled estimated budget in the first 18 months.
- Working capital will be needed, with at least half coming from the buyout group.
- The two case studies in the chapter followed the same principles.
- However, they are very different in detail.
- Buyouts differ on account of the personalities involved and the prevailing climate.
- Staff must be treated as the valued asset which they are.
- Freedom from local authority restrictions allows flexibility for change.
- Both buyouts have been an outstanding success, and have grown quickly from their initial base.

Leisure management buyouts allow the creativity of the leisure officers in the authority to be released, and given expression in the most meaningful way: improved and better leisure opportunities for the local residents. Even by those officers and councils not in a buyout situation nothing less should be accepted. It will be harder to achieve the same results, and it will take longer, but there are substantially fewer risks. As a controller of the Audit Commission once said 'the best in local government is unassailable'.

ADDENDUM: THE ADVICE OF THE AUDIT COMMISSION.

The addendum to this chapter contains a checklist of advice given by the Audit Commission. Anyone seriously considering a buyout from a local authority should obtain a copy of the full document from Her Majesty's Stationery Office.

The extract in this addendum is reproduced from the Audit Commission Management Paper 'Management Buyouts: Public Interest or Private Gain?' Number 6, January 1990. It is reproduced with the permission of the Controller of Her Majesty's Stationery Office.

This checklist provides some of the key questions to be answered before contemplating a buyout. The checklist stresses the need for absolute propriety in all the considerations.

1. Has the authority let the contract to the MBO without external competition?
   * what do financial regulations/standing orders say on competition for contracts?
   * has the authority changed these requirements by using Director

of Finance/Chief Executive delegated powers, or committee/council resolution?
* what is the length of the contract? How does this compare with the lengths allowed under CCT? What is the justification for the period chosen?
* in the absence of open competition how has the authority satisfied itself that it has discharged its fiduciary duty?
* have the necessary post contract financial and performance monitoring procedures been put in place?
2. Will there still be an in-house bid for contracts?
3. Has the packaging of work been biased to allow the MBO company an advantage in competition?
4. Is the MBO company viable?
* has the authority taken financial references similar to those it would of any other private sector company?
5. Will there be redundancies in the authority?
* what redundancy costs (if any) will the authority have to pay to employees?
* have these matters been considered in awarding contracts to the MBO?
* have other costs been taken into consideration?
6. Is tender evaluation consistent with Audit Commission advice?

Table 10.1 Increase in value of MBOs

The value of some buy-out companies has increased significantly between buy-out and exit...

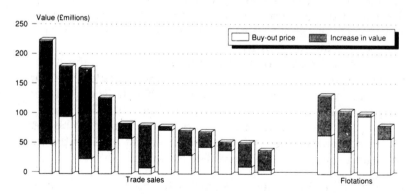

Source: CMBOR

Trade sales are particularly common with public sector MBOs...

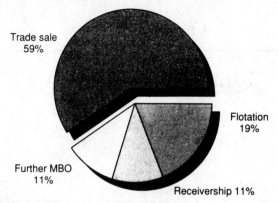

Trade sale
59%

Flotation
19%

Further MBO
11%

Receivership 11%

Source: CMBOR

Fig. 10.2 Exit routes of public sectors MBOs.

Chapter Eleven

Quality assurance

An effective system of monitoring is essential for the benefit of both parties to a contract.

The client will be particularly concerned to ensure that the contract is being operated entirely as stated in the specification. The contractor too will wish to ensure that the specification is met and, furthermore, that there is no impediment to maximizing the income from the facility.

To ensure a satisfactory operation from the point of view of both parties, many leisure management contracts will contain a quality assurance clause. Quality assurance is a relative newcomer to local authorities and service industries generally. It is a concept which originated in manufacturing industry and, indeed, evolved from quality control.

QUALITY CONTROL

Quality control is not to be confused with quality assurance. Quality control forms only a small, but important, part of a total quality assurance system.

In industry, quality controls were introduced to deal with products requiring specific accuracy. For example, the size and shape of nuts and bolts would need to conform to within a 0.5 per cent variation of the specification. If a sample showed that such conformity was not inherent in the production process, then the whole production batch would be discarded.

The quality control systems for soft contracts such as leisure management will differ slightly, because an exact technical measurement will not always be available. The addendum to Chapter 7 provides a good example of a quality control system where exact measurement is not possible; and the addendum to Chapter 6 provides an example of a quality control form for the Little London swimming pool.

In many operational aspects it will be essential for the full specification to be met (for example the quality of swimming pool water). The system shown in the addendum to Chapter 5 does allow for an easily understood method of control. However, leisure management is a complex area of operation which will require a multitude of forms if the contractor, and the client, are to retain control.

Client control

Many clients may willingly release control to the contractor, on the assumption that the contractor will wish to maximize the use (and therefore income) of the centre. There is too an assumption that the freedom given to the contractor will benefit the customers and users.

Assumptions can be very dangerous in business. The contractor (whether private or public sector) sees the operation of the leisure centre with very different eyes. Income and profit has to be the driving force. This motivation will, no doubt, ensure that the contractor performs at the best possible level for the customer for most of the time, but if financial difficulties arise the need to cut costs quickly override all other considerations.

In the last six months of the contract, control can also become very difficult. This is especially true when the contractor knows that a different contractor will be taking over when the contract terminates. In these circumstances, the need for client control increases radically.

With this in mind, perhaps, some clients demand close control of their facilities from the start of the contract. They will wish to satisfy themselves, for example, that all the loss-making social elements of the contract (swimming for people with disablilities, for example) are adequately provided. The multiplicity of forms will lead to innumerable meetings and continued attention being given to meeting the specification in all its exact detail.

Contract enforcement

Any control or monitoring system allows for some form of corrective action to be taken by the client. Yet formal corrective action is often an indication of failure by one or both parties. This can occur, for example, when a client officer is being officious, or when a profit maximizing contractor has overstepped the mark of permitted activities.

The use of control methods leads eventually to a number of corrective actions which can be taken by a client against a contractor. The actual methods of control will be determined by the provisions within the conditions of contract. Usually these will include at least some of the following;

- Oral warning.
- Written warning;
- Suspending part of the contract.
- Employing another contractor to carry out that part of the contract in which the original contractor has failed.
- Encouraging public complaints.
- Default (or penalty) points.
- Threatening poor references for future contracts.
- Threatening to terminate the contract.
- Terminating the contract.

It is all so depressingly negative.

When any of these formal control sanctions are taken, the good working relationship between client and contractor is being eroded. Furthermore, payments may be delayed to the contractor, while investigations are being carried out. This will lay a heavy burden on the contractor. Most leisure management contracts run on very tight cash flow schedules, so the contractors will be further weakened if they have to substitute borrowed money (at high interest rates) for part of the monthly pay cheque expected from the client.

The ultimate in any corrective system is termination of the contract. This can benefit no-one. Before termination, the formal relationship between client and contractor will have sunk to a very low level.

More importantly, the customers of the leisure facility will be suffering an inferior service in the period up to, and after, the termination. At worst, the facility will be closed for some time while the client appoints another contractor. When closure occurs in these circumstances, a number of technical and management difficulties will have to be overcome before a new contractor is operating smoothly. There is also a real loss of income. This is of importance to the client (and the local community charge payer, who has eventually to pay the bill).

In leisure management, therefore, a quality control system can only play a part in ensuring an adequate service to all users. It is much more important to establish the right working relationship between contractor and client, than seek to correct faults through a disciplinary or default system, although some sanctions are essential to every contract.

Fig. 11.1 Contract control is so burdensome.

There is a more positive aspect to contract management. It is summed up by comparing the two words: 'control' and 'assurance'.

Quality assurance provides a far better method of contract management with real benefits for the client, the contractor and the customer.

QUALITY ASSURANCE

Contained in many leisure management contracts will be a small clause requiring the contractor to seek and retain quality assurance. The clause will read something like this:

The contractor shall obtain certification for the services specified in the contract in accordance with the British Standard BS 5750: 1987, Part 2 (or any subsequent approved replacement or amendment), through a certifying body accredited by the National Accreditation Council for Certifying Bodies and approved by the authority, within two years from the date of commencement of this contract and shall retain certification for the remainder of the contract period.

This verbose clause will involve the contractor (and the client too) in considerable hard work and initial extra expense.

Quite simply, when a quality assurance system is in operation, the quality of the service is assured. Quality assurance demands that there are sufficient systems in place and working to ensure that the service specifications are met.

The benefit to the client and the contractor are very evident. They include:

- A reduced number of inspections;
- Reduced costs for both client and contractor;
- No need to withhold payments from the contractor;
- Increased satisfaction for everyone.

To be quality assured, the contractor needs to ensure that every single task and job is undertaken to a standard which conforms to the specification.

'Right first time' is the motto of a quality assured contractor.

Quality assurance demands a thorough and rigorous assessment of every aspect of the contractor's operation. Furthermore, once a contractor is quality assured, that contractor will be subject to continual assessment, to ensure standards are maintained.

The British Standard (BS 5750)

The basis for quality assurance lies within the British Standard BS 5750: 1987 and its international counterpart ISO 9000. It is Part 2 of the British Standard which is of particular relevance to local authority services operated by contract. It has been amended specifically to take account of those local authority services operated by contract, in accordance with a detailed specification.

This British Standard was initially instituted for use in manufacturing, where a contractor manufactured a product for a client. The client had first to provide a detailed specification of what was wanted, and then enter into a contract for the contractor to provide exactly what had been specified. The similarity to a contract for the provision of a service (say leisure management) is clearly evident. The requirement for an exact and detailed specification made it relatively easy to adapt this British Standard for service industries.

The addendum to this chapter details the key elements to the quality assurance scheme.

Definitions

A definition of quality assurance can be given as:

Quality is assured where the systems and procedures of an organization are sufficient to ensure that the service provided will always meet the specified standards of quality.

The 'Right First Time, Every Time' motto, is an equally good definition.

The benefits of a quality assured operation are evident to everyone involved: the client, the contractor, and most important of all – the customer. An inferior service is never provided. Complaints are eliminated. The need for strict supervision is greatly reduced.

KEY ELEMENTS

However, it is difficult to design the appropriate systems in the first place. Success in quality assurance relies on the provision and maintenance of appropriate systems and procedures.

Some of the key elements of a quality assurance system (listed in full in the addendum) need particular emphasis for a leisure management contract.

Management responsibility

There must be a clear and unambiguous statement of the responsibilities of the contractor and all management staff. This is often enshrined in an establishment chart or family tree which shows all personnel, from receptionist to manager, and their lines of accountability.

Contract review

This is particularly important in a leisure management contract. Trends in leisure are highly changeable. A sudden upsurge in interest takes place in a particular sport or activity and can just as quickly subside.

All leisure management contracts must allow for many minor (and some major) changes in the service delivery over the length of the contract. It is inconceivable that in an area of activity as dynamic as leisure the contract will remain unaltered for four to six years. Customer questionnaires, marketing and surveys will be of particular value in ensuring a leisure service which changes to meet the varying demands of the local population.

Document control

This aspect of the assurance system links most closely with the quality control discussed earlier in the chapter. To be effective, control documents should be prepared for each individual member of staff and completed by them. With effective delegation, this is relatively easy.

Purchasing

The purchasing of quality products is of paramount importance. Purchases for a leisure operation vary widely, from chemicals for swimming pool water sterilization to food provided for catering outlets. Inferior goods and purchases can never deliver a quality service.

Training

The importance of constant training has always been stressed within the hotel and catering trade.

Regrettably, the effort in these trades has rarely been transferred into other aspects of leisure management. Adequate and continual training of all staff is an essential ingredient in a quality assurance system.

Training is expensive in both staff time lost while undergoing training and the cost of providing trainers. This is true even when the trainers are already employed by the contractor in an operational capacity. But the cost of training does not compare with the hidden cost of customer dissatisfaction. Training will only be successful, however, if sufficient attention is given to detail. An example of receptionist training is given in the addendum to Chapter 7.

Auditing and control

Adequate internal and external auditing of standards is an essential part of a quality assurance system.

IMPLEMENTATION

Quality assurance systems vary from facility to facility. General principles can be applied across different facilities but, to succeed, a quality assurance system needs to be closely identified with the particular facility and service being provided.

Success will not stem from changing existing systems to correlate with the detailed points given in the addendum to this chapter. That will, at worst, warp existing systems for no apparent benefit and to everyone's annoyance.

Successful application of quality assurance to leisure management invariably requires the services of a specialist consultant. Someone experienced in the implementation of quality assurance will not simply try to impose the 18 conditions of a quality assurance system onto an existing contract or contractor.

The skilful application of quality assurance to a contract will start with the existing systems already in use. These can usually be adapted to provide the key elements required for quality assurance. It is far better to adapt and improve than impose anew.

AN OASIS

Swindon, Wilts is perhaps the most unlikely place to find an oasis. And yet, the Oasis leisure centre here has a long and proud history of providing high standards of service.

Opened originally in 1976, the centre continues to compete against new facilities being built by continually striving to improve. Awarded the Sports Council premier award for leisure management in the mid 1980s the centre again achieved national recognition in 1991 by becoming the first leisure centre to achieve registration to BS 5750 (Part 2).

It was only achieved after a lot of hard work and commitment. The staff worked on all aspects of the scheme for twelve months and were assisted by consultants.

The systems introduced include all the procedures and work instructions which are necessary to assure the quality of service provision to the centre customer. Reduced expenditure and increased income subsequently provide the long term benefit to the site.

Furthermore, with the experience and knowledge gained from this introduction Thamesdown Borough Council are seeking to introduce Quality Assurance to all their leisure facilities. The council see quality assurance complementing their forward thinking attitude to the provision of quality leisure facilities.

Validation

The British Standards Institute was selected as the certification body to assess the Oasis. They also undertake the regular monitoring of the system. The monitoring ensures that the management is providing a service consistent with the agreed standards. This being so, then the quality of service is assured.

The experience of the Oasis was closely followed by the British Quality Association Leisure Services Committee. They have produced specific advice, (together with an interpretation of BS 5750) for Leisure Services. Their publication, available from the Sports Council, is mentioned in Appendix E.

QUALITY CIRCLES

Quality circles approach the provision of quality services from a different angle. With quality circles, a group of equally ranked employees meets at regular intervals to consider improved practices. About one hour a week is allowed, and it is essential for success that only volunteers are allowed to join the circles. There should be no coercion or undue pressure brought to bear.

A case study

An interesting study has been made of the introduction of a quality circle to a hotel, (and detailed in *The Cornell H.R.A. Quarterly*).

The initial decision to introduce a quality circle into the hotel was due to a change in the market environment, a not dissimilar situation to that faced by leisure managers with the introduction of competitive tendering.

The hotel management was aware that its market position was threatened by new hotels being opened nearby. A market research study of customers and staff proved most uncomfortable. Departmental differences were leading directly to conflict and poor management systems. This adversely affected the customer. Employees generally believed that the management did not really care about them. Although the hotel had good occupancy figures, it was clear that all was not well.

Management commitment

The management appreciated that more was required than repainting signs or changing the uniforms of reception staff. As management commitment was essential to the success of the scheme, it was agreed to appoint a quality manager to act as a co-ordinator and, more importantly, to champion the quality cause within the top management team.

The first step of the manager was to seek representatives from every single sector within the hotel to join in preparing a quality scheme. This group included a receptionist, a chef, a member of the domestic department and union representatives, who acted as facilitators between the various departments of the hotel. Together they formed the quality team.

Resistance at all levels of the organization was initially apparent. However, this gradually gave way to more enthusiastic support as the team members systematically examined existing methods and suggested improved practices.

Everyone involved

The improved methods introduced proved popular. Furthermore, employees started to believe that they each had the ability to change existing practices for the better. Uncooperative employees found themselves open to the influence of peer pressure from their member of the quality circle.

Initially each proposal was individually examined by management before implementation. Top management were also able to take a 'sponsorship' role, one member of the management team being seconded to help the implementation of a particular proposal if invited by the quality team. Once confidence was established between the quality circle and the top management team in the hotel, then the circle was allowed to implement some changes directly. Management delegated, within certain limits.

There were very real rewards to all employees, including increased self-esteem and job satisfaction. The paraphernalia of certificates,

T-shirts and pens were also integrated into the scheme. Most important of all, for long lasting effect, there was a direct financial incentive.

The successes of the quality team were of two kinds: short term 'quick fixes' and longer term solutions to underlying organizational problems.

Some examples of quick fixes in the restaurant and kitchen included:

- Changing to nonslip tiles on all ramps,
- Changing the position of dining tables,
- Improving traffic flow for diners and staff,
- Automatic doors between kitchen and restaurant,

Examples of the longer term tasks undertaken by the office staff included:

- Improving the information flow to receptionists, (this required assistance from all departments).
- Reducing the time needed to prepare accounts.
- Increasing the number of telephone calls dealt with per hour.
- Standardizing service provision in the various food outlets.

As problems were solved, morale improved. This gave yet another added bonus to the whole exercise. Much better housekeeping became evident.

The hotel, which was in a vulnerable market position, maintained and improved its position through the total commitment of all the staff. Particularly important was the commitment of management, the quality manager, and each of the representatives.

The most difficult task was perhaps to dispel resistance during the problem solving stage, a time when tangible results were not evident. This was achieved by the continuing unity of purpose between the circle workers, supervisors and managers.

SUMMARY

Having given this example of the introduction and benefits of a quality circle, the other main aspects of this chapter are now highlighted.

- Regular inspection, monitoring and control is essential for any successful leisure operation.
- Contract management demands supervision by both the contractor and the client.
- The amount of supervision by the client will reflect the amount of control desired.

- Some client authorities wish to see maximum control retained over their facilities.
- Other clients will allow the contractor great latitude, in the belief that the demands of the customers will prevail.
- This will often be the case.
- However, the contractor's principal interest is cash and income motivated.
- Income maximization is fundamentally different from the client's social objectives.
- This is true whether the contractor is the public authority itself or an outside company.
- These differences are highlighted in difficult trading situations.
- Client control relies, sooner or later, on enforcing the terms of the contract.
- All contract control tends to be of a negative nature and sometimes punitive.
- There is real increased cost associated with increased control.
- Increased cost for the contractor as well as the client.
- Moreover all negative controls generate the wrong environment within a contract.
- Nevertheless, quality control is an important feature of most contracts.
- This is because quality control enforces the contract and ensures that the specification (as stipulated, and paid for by the client) is met.
- Quality assurance is a more positive approach.
- Quality assurance relies on the introduction of systems and procedures.
- These systems and procedures themselves then ensure that the level of quality stated in the contract is delivered.
- It is a lengthy and detailed process to introduce a quality assurance scheme.
- The initial outlay is recovered by reduced costs in operation.
- Quality assurance therefore offers real benefits to both the contractor and the client.
- Expert advice is invariably needed to implement a quality assurance scheme in a contract.
- More important, customers receive an assured quality service.
- It is all enshrined in the simple motto 'Right First Time, Every Time'.
- Quality circles provide a different method of assuring the provision of quality services.
- They rely on a group of volunteers examining better ways of working.
- Results can be impressive where there is real commitment by everyone.

Fig. 11.2 Assured quality is better for everyone.

- Extra attention is needed to ensure that the results are not short lived.

The provision of a quality service in all leisure facilities is an essential prerequisite to on-going success. When customers are satisfied with the service, they return.

Most leisure experiences are not easily repeatable. If the showers are cold, there is no immediate benefit to the squash player in knowing that they are going to be repaired next week. There can be no adequate recompense. If faults in service like this are regularly repeated, then the squash player will go and play elsewhere. When checked by the client, punitive action will follow.

For everyone involved in leisure provision, quality assurance is essential. This may be a formal assurance of quality as required by British Standard 5750; or a more local and informal method of delivery practised by the contractor or client, or both.

For adequate customer satisfaction, a quality leisure service has to be available each and every time the customer uses a facility.

ADDENDUM: QUALITY ASSURANCE GUIDELINES

This addendum provides the basic structure for a quality assurance scheme. It is reproduced with the permission of the Institute of Quality Assurance, from their publication; *Quality Assurance, Cleansing Services, Grounds Maintenance and Leisure Facilities* (1990).

FOREWORD

The British Quality Association acts as a focal point for quality matters at national level and provides a forum for examining the fundamentals of quality in every sector of the economy. The advent of the Local Government Bill stimulated much interest in Quality Assurance, and following informal discussions with senior local government officers the British Quality Association established a Local Authorities Sector Quality Committee to disseminate information on Quality Assurance, initially in the contexts of cleansing and grounds maintenance.

The Sector Committee first met in January 1988 and today with its sub-committees comprises over seventy individuals and representative organisations drawn from local government, the contracting industry, and Quality Assurance. Whilst much of the Committee's work was impelled by the Local Government Act 1988, the British Quality Association has no views as to the political context of the Act. It is also neutral regarding the use of contractors or direct labour, and has no views as to the structures authorities might use vis-a-vis the client function and DSOs. Quality Assurance is equally applicable to contractors and DSOs, and can be accommodated in a wide range of organisational structures.

This slightly revised guidance document is essentially a reprint of the now sold out edition that followed the consultative document published in May 1988. As before, this document's task is to illustrate how BS 5750: 1987; Part 2 can be applied to cleansing, grounds maintenance and leisure facilities. Little of substance has changed in this document which attests to the quality of advice received following the consultative document's publication. As soon as is practical – early to mid 1990 – advice regarding catering, vehicle maintenance, construction, education, social services, etc, will be produced – and work will be done on the monitoring implications of the impending environmental legislation. The advice and interpretations given in these guidance notes and any future such notes are, of course, those of the Committee and they may not necessarily correspond with the views of the individual bodies represented on it.

I would like to thank all those who have helped me to prepare this document, particularly the members of the technical working party of the Sector Committee, and not least George Jennings for his considerable help with proof-reading and technical advice. In addition, I know that we all share a sense of loss over the recent death of Freddie French the founder Chairman of the Local Authorities Committee. Without his contribution the Committee might never have been formed, and the impact of Quality Assurance in local government would not have been so timely or prominent.

Clive Bone.
Chairman: Local Authorities Sector Quality Committee.

Objectives
The purpose of this document is to outline how Quality
Assessment under BS 5750: 1987, can be implemented for the
services covered by the Local Government Act 1988; whether
they be undertaken by contractors or DSOs. In essence, BS
5750 is a codification of sound managerial practice. It specifies
the organisational criteria that must be met by a supplier's
system of management to assure consistent quality. These
criteria were developed mainly in manufacturing industry, but
they comprise organisational practices common to services and
production alike, and have been adopted world-wide through the
ISO 9000 series of specifications.

So far attention has been given to refuse collection, other
cleaning, the cleaning of buildings, grounds maintenance, and
very recently, leisure facilities. Each of these services is covered
in a separate Appendix, and it is expected that further
appendices covering catering, vehicle maintenance and highways
and construction will be added in due course. Since the first
drafting of these guidance notes sub-committees have been
formed to examine specific areas of importance – the application
of QA to education and social services, for example, is being
explored by such specialist sub-committees.

At the time this document was first drafted there was very little
practical experience available of quality assessment in respect of
local government services and these notes sought to synthesise
the collective experiences of those who were familiar with QA
and the services in question. The experience gained since the
first drafting suggests that these notes need little amendment.
The prime purpose of this document thus still remains – to
publish what is known in order to assist those seeking quality
assessment in local government, and to help those in the QA
world who may be unfamiliar with local authority services.

The ultimate objective of these guidance notes is to assist in the
improvement of the quality of services provided by local
government. To this end we must not forget the real customer –
the public who use the services local authorities provide. It is
their needs that must be paramount, not those of the supplier,
or the client organisation for that matter. Today's QA philosophy
is customer-centred, it embraces marketing and gives primacy to
the ultimate customer. This Total Quality Management approach

is not simply a question of techniques but a reflection of an organisation's underlying commitment to those it serves.

Client and contractor relations

In specifying that contractors must seek to be quality assessed and certified in accordance with BS 5750: 1987, authorities are making a commitment to quality that must be reflected at all levels. Quality is quite sensitive to good client/contractor relations, if they are bad quality will suffer. Nor is QA a remedy for poor management, the remedies for that must lie elsewhere. We should see BS 5750/ISO 9000 as a basic code of good practice, a starting point for sound management. If people cannot meet this minimal criteria then something is wrong.

In order to specify that a contractor seeks certification a contract clause is required to the effect that, ''The contractor must obtain certification for the specified services in accordance with BS 5750/ISO 9000: 1987, though a Certifying Body approved by the National Accreditation Council for Certifying Bodies (NACCB), within a specified period, and to retain certification thereafter.'' A minimum period of 12 to 18 months from the start of a contract is felt to be reasonable in most instances. Prior certification is not possible because it can only apply to existing services and not paper proposals.

The Local Government Act 1988 does not preclude questions regarding a tenderer's proposed management system, and client authorities should give firm guidance on the timetable required for gaining certification. Alternatively, the client could require prospective contractors to submit their own certification timetable, and take account of this when awarding the contract. It is not suggested that a failure to gain certification should, of itself, warrant contract termination. However, if the contractor lacks the commitment to introduce an adequate quality system it is most likely that the quality of service would be such so as to warrant termination in any event.

A contractor certified for a particular service in one local authority would, other things being equal, need only reproduce the same quality management system for a new authority to obtain another certificate. Government grants are available to help smaller firms obtain the consultancy help needed to get started with certification. Where the service is in-house the requirements for certification will be identical to those applied to a contractor. In any case, contractors and DSOs would be wise to have a quality system in accordance with BS 5750 as a matter of good practice even where this is not a contract requirement.

Any service that is Quality Assessed and duly certified will be subject to surveillance at least twice a year by the Certification Body that awarded the certificate. Nevertheless it is still the responsibility of the certificate holder to ensure that his system is being maintained, and to this end he should carry out his own programme of internal audits to ensure that his system is being implemented, and is efficient and effective.

Standards and monitoring
A clear and concise contract is vital to success in contracting-out. Work must clearly be specified, and there must be no room for dispute as to what the contractor is asked to do. The contractor can only be judged on what is in the contract. If he has been told to sweep a street once a week it is not his fault if, having done so properly, the street is dirty two days later. In such a case the specification was wrong, not the contractor. But how clean is clean? Attempts have been made to measure the cleanliness of floors; to photograph streets and count the items of litter, etc, but as yet no techniques are available that can be incorporated into a legal contract. Clients are thus reliant on visual inspection and the experienced eye to determine whether the work has been done to an agreed visual standard.

Fortunately BS 5701: 1980, on Number Defective Control Charts provides a sound sampling scheme for processes where only visual inspection is possible – whether a job has been done correctly or not. Experience to date suggests that it is quite possible to evolve consistent levels of visual consensus between council officers and the contractor's supervisory staff as to what constitutes an adequate standard. Quality certification requires that three factors, amongst others, be demonstrated. Firstly, that the quality level has been specified. Secondly, that the specified quality is then properly monitored and measured. Thirdly, that the people who do this monitoring and measuring are competent to do so.

To satisfy these requirements the factors that constitute the required standard must be written into the contract. The characteristics of a clean street, for example, should be included in the contract specification – clean gulleys, litter removed from footways, etc. It is then a matter of inspecting the work to an agreed visual standard on a day to day basis. Inspectors skilled in judging whether the standard has been reached are essential – working to either a 100% inspection system (the control of fly-tipping, vandalism, etc, might demand this) or a random sampling inspection regime based on BS 5701 or the BS 6000 series.

What is BS 5750: 1987?

This British Standard forms the basis for civilian consumer-orientated quality systems in Britain, and it is identical to the ISO 9000 series of standards used throughout the world. It has three parts. Part One is for organizations where there is a significant design responsibility. Part Two of BS 5750 covers organizations that produce goods or services to established specifications, and it is this part that is relevant to the services under discussion. Part Three covers systems for final inspections and tests.

It is worth stressing yet again that BS 5750 is best seen as the codification of sound management practice. It provides a framework of good practice that ensures consistent levels of product or service to the specified quality. It is for the client to specify the service quality: adherence to BS 5750 simply means that the client's specifications will be consistently met. It is for this reason that many sectors of the economy will only accept tenders from 'quality assessed' organisations. Whilst this does not remove a client's right to determine standards, it does in fact reduce the required amount of inspection and supervision.

The Appendices that follow on from here should be read with Part Two of BS 5750. The full title is:- "BS 5750: Part 2: 1987. Quality systems. Part 2. Specification for production and installation". The term, "production and installation," should simply be read as, "supply of service." Likewise, where the term "product," is used, "service" should be substituted. It is a fact of life that almost all of the management techniques used in local government have industrial origins and the language of British Standards in the field of Quality reflects this, but this in no way detracts from their usefulness in the service sector.

It is worth noting that the supporting document in the British Standard, "Guide to quality management and quality system elements. BS 5750: Part 0: Section 0.2: 1987 (ISO 9004: 1987),'' does include services throughout its terminology. In its introduction, for example, it says that, ''In order to be successful, a company must offer products or services that . . . .'' In due course it is hoped that all of BS 5750/ISO 9000 will be using the language of the services sector, and indeed the BQA has already taken some of the initiatives in this direction.

The interpretations of BS 5750 that follow are based on the Sector Committee's assessment of how the British Standard relates to refuse collection, building cleaning, other cleaning, grounds maintenance and leisure facilities. Many of the requirements are self-explanatory, but some are not and these notes are intended to help consultants, contractors, clients and Certifying Bodies alike. In order to follow these interpretations it is advised that they be read with a copy of BS 5750, Part 2, at hand.

Central Government, other authorities, and security.
These guidance notes are primarily addressed to the needs of local authorities operating in the ordinary course of their everyday duties. Nevertheless, Central Government and other authorities – Military, Civil Aviation, Health and other such bodies – will find these guidance notes of equal value when employing contractors for the services to which these notes relate. Further, any authority that has special requirements with respect to security – their contractor's employee vetting procedures, the monitoring of contractor's security arrangements, etc – may find that such requirements are more readily met within the disciplined framework of an audited quality system.

APPENDIX 5: interpreting BS 5750 for leisure facilities.

The Standard is in various parts thus:-

1 Scope and field of application
This clause starts with, "This International Standard specifies the quality system requirements for use where a contract between two parties requires demonstration of a supplier's capability to control processes that determine the acceptability of product supplied." The requirements specified in this Standard are aimed primarily at preventing and detecting any nonconformity in performing the services, and implementing the means to prevent the occurrence of nonconformities. It goes on to say that it, "is applicable in contractual situtations when

a) the specified requirements for product are stated in 'terms of an established design or specification;

b) confidence in product conformance can be attained by adequate demonstration of a certain supplier's capabilities in production and installation."

The Standard uses the word, "product," and the term, "production and installation." By substituting the word, "service," and the term, "operation and application," respectively the language becomes appropriate for leisure activities. Clauses 2 and 3 of the Standard refer to references and definitions and need not be examined here. Thus:-

4 Quality system requirements
This clause is the main clause in the Standard. It is divided into many sub-clauses and each outlines a specific requirement on the contractor's part. Thus:-

4.1 Management responsibility
Quality policy should be understood at all levels of the organisation. The documentation will include a quality manual – defining policy and objectives for, and commitment to, quality – with quality plans appropriate to the service, site and contract. The responsibilities of the supplier's head office and site staff should be clearly defined in the manual: identifying the in-built inspection system and standards employed, along with a method of system audit using staff not directly responsible for the work.

A management representative must be available, responsible for monitoring the implementation and upkeep of the quality system.

4.2 Quality system
This requires that the contractor should have a properly documented quality system. The notes in this sub-clause refer to the definition of quality objectives, allocation of responsibilities, written procedures, inspection and audit programmes. Items (b) (d) and (f) are thought not to apply, but the rest do.

4.3 Contract review
The client and contractor must understand and agree the scope and conditions of the contract prior to commencing the service. They must regularly review the working contract, to agree improvements and modifications in the light of experience, and to agree any work variations: new sports facilities to be provided, etc.

4.4 Document control
The key to good housekeeping. The records of facility use, and by whom, of coaching, pool attendant duties, pool plant operation procedures, pool plant maintenance records, etc, must be under control; updatings recorded, and they must be someone's particular responsibility. When records, work instructions, etc, are superseded, this should be clearly shown so as not to mislead through outdated information. A system to prove the issue of documents is a requirement. This requirement applies in particular to the Quality Manual, the Quality Plan, to all related quality records, and to all pool plant records.

4.5 Purchasing
This part relates to the purchase, by the contractor, of pool chemicals, pool plant items, catering services, sports equipment, etc. The specification of purchased items must be suitable for their purpose, a system of inspection employed, and adequate documentation used to monitor their service life and performance.

4.6 Purchaser supplied product
Where the local authority supplies the contractor with certain items; tennis nets, or turves, for example, the contractor must ensure that the materials supplied are fit for their purpose, store them in a suitable manner, and maintain records to monitor their service life and performance.

4.7 Product identification and traceability

For, ''product,'' substitute ''service.'' This requirement applies, as it stands. Who coached that child, or was in charge of that pool? Activities must be recorded so that the service can be identified and traced.

4.8 Process control

This covers the basic planning required by any leisure service, essentially this clause requires that the operational control be thought through and documented – the service profile, staff size, reporting procedures. However, 4.8.2. (Special processes) needs attention if the service includes the processes where the effects would not be noticed for some time. The use of chemicals for pool water, for example. The key here is to concentrate on getting the method right, ie, staff trained in the implementation of the procedure, and adequate call-back facilities, etc.

4.9 Inspection and testing

Generally the service will be 'final inspection' only with visual standards agreed between the local authority and the supplier. Records of the inspections carried out each day must be kept.

4.10 Inspection, measuring and test equipment.

This clause is not thought to apply to leisure facilities. (Since the first edition of this document, this view has been questioned in relation to test equipment used for pool water, etc, but at this point no definitive view has been established).

4.11 Inspection and test status

Not applicable. The status of inspection of any area of work is by reference to the inspection records.

4.12 Control of nonconforming product

It applies to facilities, coaching, etc, that are below standard. The procedures required here relate to service failure: ensuring that such failures are properly recorded and are acted upon without delay.

4.13 Corrective action

The need to have procedures for determining the cause of sub-standard or non-conforming services, complaints, etc, and the need to take appropriate action to prevent its re-occurance.

4.14 Handling, storage, packaging and delivery
Procedures for handling, storage and disposal of chemicals, foodstuffs and other materials used in the execution of the service shall accord with the contract's requirements and statutory regulations and bye laws.

4.15 Quality records
This part of the Standard identifies the factors that should be reflected in sound quality record practice. It includes the results of random surveys, the keeping of control charts, etc.

4.16 Internal quality audits
The service supplier must audit the effectiveness of the quality system in accordance with a written procedure and schedule, using someone without direct responsibility for the service. On large sites this could be done by a member of the site's management team, but on smaller sites with fewer personnel a representative from head office or from another site might be more appropriate.

4.17 Training
This relates to people being trained in the procedures documented by the contractor, which will include safe working methods. Staff must be trained to do the job in hand, and the work must be adequately documented so as to permit new staff to understand procedures. (NB. It has been suggested that this might conflict with the 'non-commercial' clauses of the Local Government Act 1988. It is thought not to, but in any event it is the Certification Body that will make any inquiries in this context).

4.18 Statistical techniques
This covers the methods used for inspection and work sampling. BS 5701: 1980 and the BS 6000 series would cover the services in this Appendix, but that does not exclude other sampling plans.

Chapter Twelve

Promotions and Marketing

The operational leisure facility manager invariably approaches marketing from a sales and advertizing viewpoint. The manager's principal objective is, after all, to increase income and increase use.

To approach marketing from a sales and promotions angle is, however, as limited as approaching quality assurance via quality control. Quality control is but a small part of quality assurance. Advertizing and promotions are similarly but a small part of marketing.

However, under intense pressure to achieve results from the first day of the contract, the leisure facility manager invariably has to take a sales and promotional stance. Market research and a fuller analysis of the marketing requirements are left until later.

Also, the traditional ingredients of a marketing mix are largely determined by the client. Namely:

- product
- place
- price

The product (the recreational activities on offer) and the place are both set in the contract, and even the prices are determined by the client authority. So what hope has an incoming leisure manager of taking a marketing view? The answer to that question will be left to later in the chapter. First we look at advertizing and promotions from an operational manager's viewpoint.

ADVERTIZING

Any manager embarking on the management of a leisure facility by contract can make a quick impact by improved advertizing. This obviously requires no change of programmes or client approval. It is worth paying £90 extra on advertizing for every additional £100 net income. That is elementary salesmanship.

Local authority attitudes.

Regrettably, too many local authorities see increasing the spending on advertizing as mere speculation. There can be no guarantee that the subsequent income will be forthcoming, even to the extent of recouping the additional costs of advertizing.

This highlights, in a very basic way, the difference in approach between a local authority contractor and a private sector contractor. The local authority viewpoint is understandable, given that their principal purpose for existence is to provide anything and everything necessary for the benefit of the local community. They have no remit to undertake risky ventures. However, the implications for the local authority leisure management contractor are alarming.

The cash allocated for leisure advertizing generally by local authorities is grossly inadequate. Even if most local authority budgets were to be doubled or tripled, they would not reach the level of commercial operators.

Some commercial operators allocate as much as 10 per cent of their total expenditure to advertizing, but there is no magical norm. The percentage allocations by other operators are important only as an interesting comparison. What is far more important is to achieve the expenditure allocation appropriate to a specific facility.

Advertizing to a budget

The simple truth is that advertizing is indeed speculative. Like so much in leisure management, the direct financial benefit of advertizing is difficult to measure. If the value of advertizing has to be quantified, then the only way is to set a budget of projected income and expenditure.

A campaign aimed at increasing the number of young swimmers, for example, should be easy to identify in the resulting income and usage figures achieved. This is also true of an all-female fitness session or any other easily identifiable course or programme. As with all business management, clear results are essential. Advertizing specifically related to a particular activity is easy to monitor and a good quick indicator of commercial success, or otherwise. That is of value to any contractor, public or private.

Posters

Posters can provide cheap and effective advertizing. They are inexpensive to produce and have a relatively long life.

Quick telephone calls to a dozen local printers will discover a number who would be willing and able to design and print posters. Even a colour copier can produce dramatic results. Having identified a few interested printers, a quotation should be sought from them all. Seeking a quotation requires that the manager decides at least certain key essentials. These include:

- Size of poster;
- Display locations, and thus quantity needed;
- Target groups to be attracted;
- Corporate logo to be used;

A good graphic design artist is essential for best impact, provided by clear drawings and a minimum of words. As a matter of interest, the artist who has provided the illustrations and cartoons for this book also provides posters for her local leisure centre.

Fig. 12.1 Posters with good artwork are effective.

The poster has succeeded if it attracts interest and enquiries. By the way, it is always helpful to place in the small print at the base of the poster the date for removal.

The leisure facility itself is an obvious place to display posters, but they will only be seen by existing customers. Other locations must be identified. Many local authorities have their own noticeboards at various locations around the district. They may be more than willing to allow posters to be placed on these noticeboards, especially to advertize their own facilities.

The media

Local newspapers reach every home in the neighbourhood. Advertizing in them may be essential to attract more users, announce a change of management direction and create a new image.

But caution is needed. Newspaper advertizing is expensive and of very short duration. Repeated advertizing in the same newspaper is necessary to obtain the readers' attention, but the cost may outweigh the benefits. The cost can be reduced somewhat, by negotiation. No self respecting manager will ever pay the stated rate. Negotiation and discussion always reduces the rate. Try it.

There is little point in placing an advert in every single newspaper; it is better to select the most popular one or two for best value. If it should be difficult to decide which newspapers to use, a simple cut-off coupon to be redeemed at the reception desk will establish the newspaper with the largest drawing power. This is much more accurate than accepting the newspapers' own distribution figures. Delivery to a household does not ensure that the paper is actually read.

A new manager does not need to rely on sophisticated advertizing techniques. It is more important to know the type and range of customers to be attracted to use the leisure facility and the times of week which will suit these target groups best.

Attention to eyecatching artwork is also essential. Perhaps a picture does not actually convey as much as a thousand words but in this televisual age, snapshot images are what the customer responds to. They have quick impact.

UNDER NEW MANAGEMENT

There are many ways in which a new management team can make

an immediate impact. Some key areas for attention include new and appropriate clothing for receptionists and other staff.

This need not be too expensive. A simple sweatshirt with a skirt or shorts will accommodate most shapes and sizes. It is best to find a style and colour which is distinctive and yet contrasts with the background colour scheme.

An improved entrance area is also an excellent way to establish a new identity. Again, this does not need to involve a large outlay. Smart signs, new curtain drapes, a coat of paint and even a few new doormats can quickly alert customers to the fact that something is changing.

Membership schemes can be introduced. If this involves a change in council policy, client approval will be needed. But many membership schemes can be introduced solely for promotional reasons. A list of names and addresses of customers is always useful for sending details of forthcoming special events such as holiday play schemes or short courses.

SPONSORSHIP

Sponsorship of activities has much to commend it. However, as a means to an end sponsorship is often greatly overrated. To achieve any worthwhile results, securing sponsorship is long, hard work. A national advertizing company may, if the client allows, be contracted to supply adverts, but this cannot be regarded as sponsorship.

The best sponsorship is that from a local business. A good example is when a local sports shop or newspaper sponsors a local league or inter-centre competition.

Value for money

To be successful, the manager must approach sponsorship from the sponsor's viewpoint. Sponsors are looking for sufficient publicity to justify the financial outlay of prizes and the rest of the sponsorship package. Sponsorship has to be a mutually beneficial relationship between the sponsor and the leisure centre.

The sponsor may agree to assist with advertizing and publicity, organizing leagues and taking an active role in a particular activity. Relieved of these tasks, the manager must then ensure that the sponsor is satisfied with the increased exposure that his business gains through the sponsorship. The least that should be expected is a photograph in the local newspaper of the sponsor giving the prizes. Suitable displays in the leisure centre, after the event, will also help. The success of sponsorship rests with the willing commitment of the two parties. Although all sponsors are usually hesitant when first approached, some quickly warm to the idea of a particular sponsorship package. The secret is to speak to a known contact (Dear Sir letters are absolutely useless) and emphasize the benefits from sponsorship. Sermonizing about putting something back into the community is best left out.

The success of an advertizing or promotion campaign depends on attracting the right customers into the centre. This presupposes that the manager is aware of the particular group of potential customers to be attracted. For this, marketplace information is required. A customer survey is often the place to start.

CUSTOMER ASSESSMENTS

The success of a leisure facility rests on maximizing use and income. In a local authority leisure facility there will be as much emphasis on increasing use as on increasing income, unless the client has abdicated responsibility to an income maximizing contractor.

Both client and contractor need an accurate knowledge of existing customers and of potential customers. This can be achieved through competent market research. There tends to be a misconception that market research has to be expensive, sophisticated and done by specialists. No doubt for the best market research, this is true. The benefits for Circa Leisure of a complete and professional market research survey were more than repaid.

But most local leisure centres are unable to afford the services of a specialist market research company. It is therefore necessary initially to draw on home resources.

There is no better, or easier, place to start, than with a customer satisfaction survey. Managers who think that they know the views of customers because they see them daily know nothing. A customer's perceptions survey often produces a complete surprise to the manager of the facility.

It can be equally eye-opening and painful for the client. Customers do not generally differentiate between the two. If the water in the showers is not hot enough it could be the fault of the client or the operator, (depending on the exact nature of the problem) and the terms of the contract. The customer cares not a jot who is responsible; what is important is to order the repair.

QUESTIONNAIRES

A simple questionnaire, targetted at existing customers, provides much valuable information. Correctly set out, a questionnaire can provide a measure of:

- The most popular activities;
- Satisfactory aspects of the facility;
- Unsatisfactory aspects of the facility;
- Staff courtesy and friendliness;
- New activity demands and desires.

It can also provide a list of names and addresses for future contact.

Thus, a questionnaire can be the source of much worthwhile information about improvements to be made. Of course, such questionnaires do tend to be completed only by those users who have the time and ability to do so. Unfortunately, many leisure centres attract solely that type of person. A quick comparison between customers of a leisure centre and local shoppers would soon prove this point.

Nevertheless, an in-house questionnaire is an effortless and inexpensive way to start a market oriented approach to leisure management.

Market orientation

The name and address of the customer completing the questionnaire is particularly important. This must be the last question on the form, so that it does not deter anyone completing it. The manager will then be in a position to place on the office wall a large map of the locality showing precisely the catchment area from which customers are drawn. Different coloured pins can be used to denote different activities or different age groups.

Attention can be then given to attracting specific interest groups. The information base should be continually augmented.

For example, a fun session in the swimming pool can be promoted through the local schools. A questionnaire at the end of the session (together with a suitable prize) will provide invaluable information for future targeted events. The same is true for an orchestral concert in the sports hall. The more names and addresses obtained by various surveys the better.

This asset can even be extended by customers who are prepared to pay a nominal sum, say £1, to be put on a mailing list. If the payment only covers the cost of a quarterly mailing, there can be no cheaper or more targetted method of advertizing.

Customers' postcodes are important too, as the map on the office wall should be segmented into postcode areas. The local telephone book can be used to identify the postcodes for individual streets. The postcode provides key information in respect to the location of customers with interests in different activities. The theory is, and the practice too, that similar people live in similar localities. Targetting publicity is therefore made easier.

This type of socio-economic analysis of an area is enshrined in the ACORN method of market research which looks at residential location. A more traditional method of classification is by socio-economic groups (A, B, C1, C2, D, E).

Time gap analysis

In addition to a market research survey across a section of society, a time gap analysis also has much to offer. This is where the same survey is carried out, often with the same people constituting a panel, at regular intervals. The key requirement is to ensure that the information obtained is consistent. An example in the addendum to this chapter shows how one survey, undertaken on a random basis annually, provides a consistent and accurate flow of information.

CONTRACT MONITORING

Customer surveys are an excellent start, for both the client and the contractor, to providing a more customer friendly service. The questionnaire can go further and seek out specific information for both the contractor and the client. Both should be prepared to contribute towards the survey.

The client needs to know such things as:

- Do customers feel well treated by the contractor's staff?
- Is there a high satisfaction rating?

The contractor is more interested in:

- If changes were made, would they attract more use?
- What aspects of the facility should be improved to increase income potential?

Both parties are interested to know:

- What new sports and recreations are not catered for?
- What type of people are being attracted to the facility and where do they live?

In a contract situation, the contractor has to rely on directions from the client.

However, where an unmet need is apparent, a client will usually grant permission for changes to be made. This is especially true where increased usage from the local community is to be expected and where a net community gain will result. At the same time, of course, the contractor will be able to increase income levels.

TARGETTED MARKETING

Traditionally, publicity about local authority leisure facilities has been grossly inadequate. The inadequate provision has been further aggravated by blanket coverage of whole populations; an often wasteful and highly ineffective activity.

Fig. 12.2 Know your target markets.

If a promotion is intended to increase usage within specific groups of people (for social or income reasons), then it naturally follows that publicity should be aimed at these specific individuals.

This is achieved by using the basic data bank which has been built up listing customer preferences, desires and demands – together with their addresses. This is far better than scattering glossy coloured leaflets everywhere. The blunderbuss approach to publicity is unlikely to make good commercial sense for a cost conscious contractor.

DELEGATION

The major issue to be addressed by the leisure business manager is whether the marketing and publicity function is seen to be separate from the sports, recreation, catering and other business ventures.

There is a view that marketing and publicity should form an integral part of each unit manager's brief. Incentive is maximized and there is no elaborate chain of command to sap energy and reduce interest.

The alternative argument is that the complex nature of marketing and publicity requires specialist staff. The use of agencies offers a third option to be considered.

Different centres warrant different approaches. No one option is to be recommended more than another.

MARKETING

In the context of this chapter, the term marketing can be taken to mean the continual change of facilities and services to meet the changing desires and demands of customers. Marketing means evolving a product or service to suit the needs of the customer or consumer.

It is the exact opposite of salesmanship.

Salesmen sell what they have to offer, as it stands. A marketing manager tailors what the centre has to offer according to what is required or demanded. Equally important, the marketing manager will seek to alter the current facility and programme to match current demands more exactly.

A positive approach to marketing will lead to continual changes to the contract and no doubt a major change when the time comes to relet the contract.

If attention is initially given to advertizing and promotion at the start of a new contract, then a proper marketing approach should be adopted later to underpin longer term success. Furthermore, if the customer surveys have proved their worth, it will be much easier to fund a full, professionally produced market research programme.

An outline approach

A marketing approach demands time and thought, and will not succeed with a quick fix. A possible marketing approach for a leisure facility is now outlined.

1. Define the catchment area.
   The key essentials include: the more obvious boundaries (a town or district boundary), the travel distance by bus and car, the postcode areas mostly served.
2. Assess the population profile.
   The 1990s are seeing a significant reduction in the number of young adults within the population, yet an increasing number of young children. This has obvious implications for a leisure facility. However, this national trend needs to be checked against the specific catchment area of the leisure facility. The local council or county council planning department should be able to provide a vast range of demographic information. Local libraries also keep details of the most recent census.
3. Assess demands and desires.
   The questionnaire surveys are particularly valuable here. Surveys should also be made of non-users. A survey in the High Street will yield quite different information from one taken in the leisure centre, and different again from one taken in the local street market.
4. Reassess the leisure facility.
   Build on past success and current strengths by further improving or adapting to serve a wider cross section of use.
5. Reassess the competition.
   Each leisure facility has specialisms and strengths. It is not necessarily wise to compete with a neighbouring centre for the same slice of the market. While both should provide for a wide range of activities, each should also have special market niches. This will attract more people.
6. Change.
   With client and contractor approval where necessary, change the existing features, or the time allocations for different activities to more adequately provide for customers' demands.
7. Be a customer.
   It is very difficult for a manager to visualize the leisure facility through a customer's eyes. Of course the questionnaires taken within the facility will be of help here, as will brief informal discussions with customers as they leave the building. But, best of all, the leisure facility staff should use it themselves – at a discount, of course.

8. Market differentiation.
   Constantly redetermine peak and off-peak times and the differing groups of people who could be attracted into the centre. Senior citizens' coffee mornings and afternoon tea dances are just two ways to increase off-peak usage.
9. Constantly analyse trends.
   The successful manager needs to know which sports and activities are increasing in popularity and those which are diminishing. Although figures for the last 12 months are helpful, these need to be contrasted and compared with figures from the last month.
10. Go for it.
    Having completed the analysis and decided the way forward, do not hesitate – go for it. Improve and change the leisure facility, and alter the programme of activities. This will need honest and open discussion between client and contractor. Both are committed to providing the fullest use of the leisure facility by the local population. Nothing should impede that objective.

Leisure provision is a volatile business. Any number of major changes take place within a four to six year period. In the early 1990s fitness suites were attracting record usage, and the demand for golf, multiplex cinemas and ten pin bowling appeared insatiable. On the other hand, the game of squash was reducing in popularity, except among younger females. The pattern of leisure demands is constantly changing.

Whereas major changes to buildings are restricted in the contract situation, there is no reason why individual rooms cannot be changed to suit different activities.

This chapter has looked at a marketing approach from a leisure facility manager's point of view. Initially, in a contract situation, attention has to be concentrated in advertizing and publicity. For long term success however, a proper marketing approach must be employed. A brief synopsis of this chapter is now given.

SUMMARY

Marketing is providing for customers' demands, not just packaging what is currently available. In a contract situation however, the first and overriding objective will be to advertize, promote and establish an image, all with a view to increasing income and use.

- Local authorities are not traditionally organized to these ends. Local authority contractors will work much harder to achieve the same results as the private sector.

- Advertizing needs to be cost-effective.
- Some form of assessment is necessary, such as tear off coupons or an advertizing budget linked directly to a specific course or promotion.
- Posters offer a cheap and effective form of advertizing for a quite long period.
- Local newspapers cover the whole area, but are expensive, and have a limited impact.
- Impact comes from the image created; by creative artwork, distinctive staff clothing and the like.
- High initial expense is not necessary.
- Sponsorship is hard work, and needs personal contacts for success.
- Customer surveys are essential to check real success.
- These can be organized by the contractor (or the client or the local college for that matter), at relatively little cost.
- Constant attention should be paid to identifying customers' work and home locations – for targetted promotion campaigns.
- Targetted marketing is the most effective.
- The best approach is to afford a full professional market research survey, followed by a marketing policy and plan for action.
- A fulltime marketing manager will greatly increase income in many centres.
- The alternative is to leave the responsibility with each individual activity manager.

Leisure management contractors who are subject to competition must constantly research their market and change the programme and activities to suit current demands. More importantly, they need to promote an image of their centre, based on its special features, so that the customer takes pride in using that centre and not the competitors. In this way the competitive leisure manager is able to secure a valuable market niche.

ADDENDUM: TARGET GROUPS

The Target Group Index published annually by the British Market Research Bureau (BMRB) provides a valuable source of national data about leisure trends and people's preferences.

Their survey has been undertaken for over 20 years, ever since leisure time started to expand. Leisure is still a growth industry and will remain so, as long as an increasing amount of free time and the necessary disposable income are available. This area of expansion crosses all socio-economic groups and continues despite swings in the national economy.

The annual survey involves over 20 000 households per year. Exact instructions are given to establish a totally representative base of the population as a whole. The results are widely used by many companies to target their products more accurately.

Extracts from the British Market Research Bureau's questionnaire on leisure activities, from their booklet *What do you buy?*, are reproduced, with permission. This addendum also includes a small insight into customer 'cluster' groupings, taken from BRMB's *The Target Group Index*.

214 Promotions and marketing

SPORTS AND LEISURE ACTIVITIES

1. Here is a list of sports and games.

Which of them do you take part in or play <u>yourself</u> these days?

Betting on horse racing	32 y	Water Skiing	8
Bingo (in a club where a charge is made for admission)	x	Wind Surfing	9
		Weight Training	33 y
Camping	0	Sailing	x
Climbing	1	Shooting – Game	0
Dancing (in a club, hall, disco or palais where a charge is made for admission)	2	Rough	1
		Clay	2
Football Pools	3	Target	3
Horse Riding	4	Ten–pin Bowling	4
Jogging/Training	5	Yoga	5
Keep Fit/Dancing Classes	6		
Rambling/Hiking	7		

2. Which of these:
(a) do you take part in or play <u>yourself</u> these days?
(b) have you paid to watch in the last 12 months?
(c) do you like to watch on TV, if it's shown?
(d) do you like to read about in the papers, if there's a report?

	I play or do myself these days	I have paid to watch	I like to watch on TV	I like to read about in the papers
Association Football	34	35	36	37 y
American Football				x
Athletics				0
Badminton				1
Basketball				2
Billiards				3
Bowls				4
Boxing				5
Bridge				6
Chess				7
Cricket				8
Darts				9
Fishing – Trout	38	39	40	41 y
– Coarse				x
– Sea				0
Golf				1
Greyhound Racing				2
Horse Racing				3
Ice Hockey				4
Motor-cycle Racing				5
Motor Racing				6
Motor Rallying	42	43	44	45 8
Rugby League	38	39	40	41 7
Rugby Union				8
Skating				9
Skiing	42	43	44	45 y
Show Jumping				x
Snooker				0
Speedway Racing				1
Squash				2
Stock–car Racing				3
Swimming				4
Table Tennis				5
Tennis				6
Wrestling				7

SPORTS CLOTHING AND EQUIPMENT

Which of these items of sports clothing and equipment have you bought in the last 12 months?

Swimwear	46 y
Leotards and Dancewear	x
Sports Shoes	0
Tracksuit/Jogging Suit	1
Ski Clothing	2
Other Sports Clothing	3
Rackets	4
Golf Clubs	5
Other sporting equipment	6

FILM FOR STILL PHOTOGRAPHS

1. Do you ever use it?   Yes 47 1   No 2

IF YOU DO

2. About how many films have you used in the last TWELVE MONTHS?

20 or more	3
10 - 19	4
6 - 9	5
4 or 5	6
3	7
2	8
1 or less	9

3. Which kinds of film do you use?

Black and White	0
Colour for <u>prints</u>	x
Colour for <u>slides</u>	y

4. Which outlet do you use most often to buy or to process your films?

	Buy	Process
Boots	48	49 y
Other Chemist		x
Photographic Equipment Outlet		0
Specialist Processing Shop		1
Mail Order/Post		2
Other Outlets		3

5. Which brands do you use?

	Most Often	Others
Agfa Gevaert	65	66 y
Asda		x
Bonus Print/Bonus Photo		0
Boots		1
Fuji		2
Ilford		3
Kodak		4
Polaroid		5
Prinzcolor		6
Supa-Snaps		7
Truprint		8
Tudorcolor		9
OTHER BRANDS	67	68 9

PLEASE USE PENCIL ONLY

ENTERTAINING

1. Do you ever have friends or relations in for a meal these days?

Yes   51 ▭ y
No   ▭ x

IF YES
2. How often?

More than once a WEEK	▭ 0
Once a WEEK	▭ 1
2 or 3 times a MONTH	▭ 2
Once a MONTH	▭ 3
Less than once a MONTH	▭ 4

PUBS AND CLUBS

How often do you visit them?

	Pubs	Licensed Clubs
Never	52 ▭	53 ▭ y
Less than once a MONTH	▭	▭ x
Once a MONTH	▭	▭ 0
2 or 3 times a MONTH	▭	▭ 1
Once a WEEK	▭	▭ 2
2 or 3 times a WEEK	▭	▭ 3
Once a DAY or more	▭	▭ 4

WINE BARS

How often do you visit them?

Never	54 ▭ y
Less than once a MONTH	▭ x
Once a MONTH	▭ 0
2 or 3 times a MONTH	▭ 1
Once a WEEK	▭ 2
More than once a WEEK	▭ 3

EXHIBITIONS AND OUTINGS

Have you been to any of the following in the last 12 months?

Camping and Outdoor Life Exhibition	55 ▭ y
Ideal Home Exhibition	▭ x
International Boat Show	▭ 0
International Handicrafts and D.I.Y. Exhibition	▭ 1
International Motor Exhibition (Motor Show)	▭ 2
Archaeological sites (e.g. Stonehenge)	▭ 3
Beauty Spots/Gardens	▭ 4
Museums	▭ 5
Safari Parks	▭ 6
Stately Homes/Castles	▭ 7
Theme Parks	▭ 8
Zoos	▭ 9
Other Places of Historic Interest	56 ▭ y
Other Places of Natural Interest	▭ x

TAKE–AWAY FOODS AND FAST FOODS

1. Do you ever buy 'Take-Away' foods or eat-in at a Fast-Food restaurant?

	Take-Away	Eat-In
Yes	57 ▭	58 ▭ y
No	▭	▭ x

IF YOU DO
2. Which ones have you used in the last 3 months?

	Take-Away	Eat-In
Burger King	▭	▭ 0
Casey Jones	▭	▭ 1
Kentucky Fried Chicken	▭	▭ 2
McDonald's	▭	▭ 3
Pizza Express	▭	▭ 4
Pizza Hut	▭	▭ 5
Pizzaland	▭	▭ 6
Quick Burger	▭	▭ 7
Spud-U-Like	▭	▭ 8
Wimpy	▭	▭ 9
Other Hamburger Bars	59 ▭	60 ▭ y
Other Pizza Bars	▭	▭ x
Fish and Chip Shop	▭	▭ 0
Chinese (Take-Away)	▭	
Indian (Take-Away)	▭	
Others	▭	▭ 9

EATING OUT IN RESTAURANTS

1. Do you ever go out for a meal in a restaurant these days?

	Restaurants (in the day)	Restaurants (in the evening)
Yes	61 ▭	62 ▭ y
No	▭	▭ x

IF YOU DO
2. How often do you visit them?

More than once a WEEK	▭ 0
Once a WEEK	▭ 1
2 or 3 times a MONTH	▭ 2
Once a MONTH	▭ 3
Less than once a MONTH	▭ 4

3. Which types of restaurants have you visited in the last 3 MONTHS?

	Restaurants (in the day)	Restaurants (in the evening)
Hamburger Bars	63 ▭	64 ▭ y
Steak Houses	▭	▭ x
Chinese	▭	▭ 0
English	▭	▭ 1
French	▭	▭ 2
Greek/Turkish	▭	▭ 3
Indian	▭	▭ 4
Italian	▭	▭ 5
Others	▭	▭ 9

▲4

BOOKS

1. Have you yourself bought any hardback or paperback books in the last 12 months?

	Hard-back	Paper-back
Yes	1 ▭	2 ▭ y
No	▭	▭ x

IF YES
2. About how many books with hardback and paperback would you say that you personally bought for yourself in the last 12 months?

	Hard-back	Paper-back
None	▭	▭ 0
1	▭	▭ 1
2	▭	▭ 2
3	▭	▭ 3
4	▭	▭ 4
5 – 9	▭	▭ 5
10 or more	▭	▭ 6

3. What type of books do you buy?

	Hard-back	Paper-back
Fiction	3 ▭	4 ▭ y
Non–Fiction	▭	▭ x

4. Which of these sources have you used to buy your hardback and paperback books in the last 12 months?

	Hard-back	Paper-back
Stationers	▭	▭ 0
Book Clubs	▭	▭ 1
Reader's Digest – by post	▭	▭ 2
Other Stores/Shops	▭	▭ 3

MAGAZINES

1. Does your household have a subscription to Reader's Digest magazine which is delivered by post?

Yes   5 ▭ y
No   ▭ x

2. Do you have other magazines that are paid for, delivered to your home these days?

Yes   ▭ 0
No   ▭ 1

IF YES
3. How many weekly or monthly magazines do you have delivered?

	Weekly Magazines	Monthly Magazines
1	▭	▭ 5
2	▭	▭ 6
3 or more	▭	▭ 7

RECORDS AND TAPES

1. Have you yourself bought any records or tapes through the post in the last two years?

Records - Yes 7 ▭ y
Tapes - Yes ▭ x
Neither ▭ 0

IF YES
2. From which firms have you bought them in the last two years?

Brittannia Music	▭ 1
Reader's Digest	▭ 2
World Record Club	▭ 3
Others	▭ 4

MAGAZINES   71

Please continue filling in, as for Monthly Magazines, but note that question B is different

A I LOOK AT THIS MAGAZINE   **B** I LAST LOOKED AT ANY COPY:

Weekly Magazines	Almost Always (at least 3 out of 4)	Quite Often (at least 1 out of 4)	Only Occasionally (less than 1 out of 4)	Not in Past Year	Within past 7 days	Longer ago
TV Guide	6 ☐ 1	☐ 2	☐ 3	☐ 4	☐ 8	☐ 9
TV Times	45 ☐	☐	☐	☐	☐	☐
Radio Times	46 ☐	☐	☐	☐	☐	☐
The Listener	47 ☐	☐	☐	☐	☐	☐
Hello!	48 ☐ 1	☐ 2	☐ 3	☐ 4	☐ 8	☐ 9
Weekend	49 ☐ 1	☐ 2	☐ 3	☐ 4	☐ 8	☐ 9
Weekly News	50 ☐	☐	☐	☐	☐	☐
Exchange & Mart	51 ☐	☐	☐	☐	☐	☐
Woman	52 ☐ 1	☐ 2	☐ 3	☐ 4	☐ 8	☐ 9
Woman's Own	53 ☐	☐	☐	☐	☐	☐
Woman's Realm	54 ☐	☐	☐	☐	☐	☐
Woman's Weekly	55 ☐	☐	☐	☐	☐	☐
My Weekly	56 ☐	☐	☐	☐	☐	☐
People's Friend	57 ☐	☐	☐	☐	☐	☐
Bella	58 ☐ 1	☐ 2	☐ 3	☐ 4	☐ 8	☐ 9
Best	59 ☐	☐	☐	☐	☐	☐
Chat	60 ☐	☐	☐	☐	☐	☐
Me	68 ☐	☐	☐	☐	☐	☐
Girl About Town	61 ☐	☐	☐	☐	☐	☐
Midweek	32 ☐	☐	☐	☐	☐	☐
Ms London	69 ☐	☐	☐	☐	☐	☐
Punch	62 ☐ 1	☐ 2	☐ 3	☐ 4	☐ 8	☐ 9
The Economist	63 ☐	☐	☐	☐	☐	☐
Investors Chronicle	64 ☐	☐	☐	☐	☐	☐
New Scientist	65 ☐	☐	☐	☐	☐	☐
New Statesman & Society	66 ☐	☐	☐	☐	☐	☐
Country Life	67 ☐ 1	☐ 2	☐ 3	☐ 4	☐ 8	☐ 9

△34

Notice B is different from the weekly magazines   ▽28

Other Magazines					Within past 2 months	Longer ago
Under 5	6 ☐ 1	☐ 2	☐ 3	☐ 4	☐ 8	☐ 9
Brides & Setting Up Home	1 ☐ 1	☐ 2	☐ 3	☐ 4	☐ 8	☐ 9
Wedding & Home	2 ☐	☐	☐	☐	☐	☐
Slimming	3 ☐	☐	☐	☐	☐	☐
Successful Slimming	4 ☐	☐	☐	☐	☐	☐
Weight Watchers	5 ☐	☐	☐	☐	☐	☐
Illustrated London News	7 ☐ 1	☐ 2	☐ 3	☐ 4	☐ 8	☐ 9
Expression (the American Express Mag)	8 ☐	☐	☐	☐	☐	☐
Giroscope (Girobank Magazine)	9 ☐	☐	☐	☐	☐	☐

					Within past 3 months	Longer ago
Childsplay/Parentcare	12 ☐ 1	☐ 2	☐ 3	☐ 4	☐ 8	☐ 9
House Beautiful	11 ☐	☐	☐	☐	☐	☐
Moneycare (The Nat West Bank Magazine)	13 ☐	☐	☐	☐	☐	☐

△26

PLEASE USE PENCIL ONLY

88

And now, the last set of questions on your attitudes, opinions and interests.

	Definitely Agree	Tend to Agree	Neither Agree Nor Disagree	Tend to Disagree	Definitely Disagree	Not Applicable
I am always on the look out for sales and special offers	23 ☐ 1	☐ 2	☐ 3	☐ 4	☐ 5	☐ 6
I rarely notice poster advertisements	24 ☐	☐	☐	☐	☐	☐
I think children should eat what they are given	25 ☐	☐	☐	☐	☐	☐
I don't like the idea of being in debt	26 ☐	☐	☐	☐	☐	☐
I don't normally nibble between meals	27 ☐	☐	☐	☐	☐	☐
I drink lager rather than beer these days	28 ☐ 1	☐ 2	☐ 3	☐ 4	☐ 5	☐ 6
I am not interested in what goes on under the bonnet of a car	29 ☐	☐	☐	☐	☐	☐
I enjoy entertaining people at home	30 ☐	☐	☐	☐	☐	☐
I like to try new drinks	31 ☐	☐	☐	☐	☐	☐
I try to give my family as few sweets and cakes as possible	32 ☐	☐	☐	☐	☐	☐
I don't go to the pub as often as I used to	33 ☐ 1	☐ 2	☐ 3	☐ 4	☐ 5	☐ 6
When people come to my home they have to take me as they find me	34 ☐	☐	☐	☐	☐	☐
I make sure I take regular exercise	35 ☐	☐	☐	☐	☐	☐
I really do enjoy my food	36 ☐	☐	☐	☐	☐	☐
We drink more wine at home these days	37 ☐	☐	☐	☐	☐	☐
I prefer to get all my shopping done in one large shop/supermarket	38 ☐ 1	☐ 2	☐ 3	☐ 4	☐ 5	☐ 6
My family is more important to me than my career	39 ☐	☐	☐	☐	☐	☐
I usually take the car when holidaying abroad	40 ☐	☐	☐	☐	☐	☐
I really enjoy a night out at the pub	41 ☐	☐	☐	☐	☐	☐
I am very good at managing money	42 ☐	☐	☐	☐	☐	☐
Jogging doesn't do you any good	43 ☐ 1	☐ 2	☐ 3	☐ 4	☐ 5	☐ 6
I only give flowers when I can't think of any other present	44 ☐	☐	☐	☐	☐	☐
I often do things on the spur of the moment	45 ☐	☐	☐	☐	☐	☐
I'd rather have a boring job than no job at all	46 ☐	☐	☐	☐	☐	☐
I often buy foods because I have seen them advertised	47 ☐	☐	☐	☐	☐	☐
I love travelling abroad	48 ☐ 1	☐ 2	☐ 3	☐ 4	☐ 5	☐ 6
I like to enjoy life and don't worry about the future	49 ☐	☐	☐	☐	☐	
I like to pay cash for everything I buy	50 ☐	☐	☐	☐	☐	
I like savoury things more than sweet things	51 ☐	☐	☐	☐	☐	
I sometimes respond to direct mail from companies offering goods or services	52 ☐	☐	☐	☐	☐	
By this time next year, I expect to be watching Satellite TV at home, on at least two days a week	53 ☐	☐	☐	☐	☐	
Irradiation is the best way to keep food fresh	5 ☐ 1	☐ 2	☐ 3	☐ 4	☐ 5	☐ 6
I would never buy toiletries & cosmetics that have been tested on animals	6 ☐	☐	☐	☐	☐	
I would be prepared to pay as much for unleaded petrol as leaded	7 ☐	☐	☐	☐	☐	

CLUSTER GROUPINGS

Base - Women aged 15-44
6 Cluster Solution

Cluster		% of Base —
1	SELF AWARE	15.2
2	UNCONCERNED	19.4
3	FASHION - DIRECTED	17.7
4	DOWDIES	11.7
5	GREEN GODDESS	17.4
6	THE CONSCIENCE - - STRICKEN	18.7

(CLUSTER 1)

SELF – AWARE

ATTITUDINAL BIASES-

- Positive on all statements concerned with appearance.
- Concern with fashion and style.
- Interest in exercise.
- Can't resist buying magazines.

DEMOGRAPHIC BIASES-

- Younger (Aged 15-24)
- No strong class bias.
- Single or engaged.
- More likely to be studying.
- Live alone.

(CLUSTER TWO)

UN-CONCERNED

ATTITUDINAL BIASES-

- Agreed more than average with statements like
  "I am not too concerned about my appearance."
- Disagreed with
  "It is important to me to look well dressed."
  Neutral on exercise statements.

DEMOGRAPHIC BIASES

- Younger (15-19)
- Downmarket (DE)
- Rent their accomodation.

(CLUSTER THREE)

FASHION DIRECTED

ATTITUDINAL BIASES-

- Group were very concerned with appearance, with strong agreement on statements like

"I like to keep up with the latest fashions"

- Negative on statements concerned with exercise or sport.

DEMOGRAPHIC BIASES-

- Young /AB.
- Single /Working full time.
- High household income.

(CLUSTER FOUR)

DOWDIES

ATTITUDINAL BIASES-

-"I buy clothes for comfort, not for style".

- Negative on statements concerned with appearance.

"It is important to me to look well dressed".

"I like to keep up with the latest fashions."

DEMOGRAPHIC BIASES-

- Age 25-44
- Slightly downmarket
- Married with children

(CLUSTER FIVE)

GREEN GODDESSES

ATTITUDINAL BIASES-

- Very positive attitude towards sport & exercise.

    "I make sure I take regular exercise."

    "I do some form of sport or exercise at least once
    a week.

- More concerned than average over their appearance

DEMOGRAPHIC BIASES

- Slightly older /AB.

(CLUSTER SIX)

THE CONSCIENCE STRICKEN

ATTITUDINAL BIASES

-"I know I should exercise more than I do"

- Disagreement with:

 "I am not too concerned about my appearance".

- Not impulsive buyers, not treating themselves to items not needed/expensive perfume/designer clothes or magazines.

DEMOGRAPHIC BIASES-

- Older /Housewives

- C1

- Married (5 years+)

DRINK

"HEAVY"	Self Aware	Un-concerned	Fashion Directed	Dowdies	Green Goddess	The Conscience Stricken
Fruit & Vegetable Juice	128	87	99	84	118	82
Cola	147	148	113	71	50	68
Cider	110	114	112	90	92	78
Sherry	101	82	105	74	143	81
Gin	119	66	124	70	116	93
Vodka	130	73	156	51	82	90
Wine	152	61	125	84	100	77
Aperitifs	137	102	145	63	71	75
Home Brewing	57	99	75	203	69	130

Base= Women 15-44	Self Aware	Un- Concerned	Fashion Directed	Dowdies	Green Goddesses	The Conscience Stricken
Jogging	187	83	57	70	185	27
Badminton	128	104	73	64	183	44
Dancing	149	96	135	44	97	70
Camping	78	94	81	134	134	89
Yoga	144	108	62	93	149	51
Rambling	59	73	76	186	189	48
Keep Fit	202	81	61	53	180	30

100 = Average Likelihood

Chapter Thirteen

Conclusions

By the start of the new century, client and contractor management of local authority leisure facilities will ensure many changes from the conditions prevailing before 1990.

The client will seek to provide the best for the local community. This will include the best financial deal to be achieved by competitive tender, as well as the widest uptake of leisure activities by the population as a whole. The contractor will seek to maximize income and usage within the constraints laid down by the client.

The contract documentation will determine precisely how the facility is to be operated. Tenders will be let at regular intervals, between four to six years where a local authority continues to operate a leisure facility. A somewhat longer period is likely where a private sector contractor is managing the facility. The Act requires retendering only where direct management is a feature.

The number of specialist contractors will increase over the years. There are three principal types of contractor who undertake the management of public leisure facilities:

- Local authorities using directly employed staff.
- Management buy-out groups or similar.
- Private sector companies.

The actual contractor appointed to operate a particular facility will be the one who is awarded the contract after submitting a successful tender bid.

In earlier chapters reference has been made to local authority contractors and management buyout teams; no detailed mention has yet been made of leisure management in the private sector.

Although leisure management contracts are small, they will increasingly attract the interest of the private sector, once the private sector fully appreciates that all leisure management contracts are profitable (because the client subsidy stated in the tender covers

the anticipated losses). A final interesting case study is now given of
a private sector company.

CIVIC LEISURE

In the early 1980s, a Dutch squash enthusiast, Harm Tegelaars,
opened his own squash and health club in West London, and the
Metropolitan Clubs were born. During the 1980s his company,
Latchmere Leisure, expanded into a wide range of health and fitness
clubs branded under the Metropolitan banner in and around the
London area. The clubs established an excellent reputation for high
quality leisure provision.

In 1988, Westminster City Council put out to competitive tender
the management of its five leisure centres in advance of the impending
legislation on compulsory competitive tendering. Civic Leisure was
formed to submit a bid for the management of the centres and Harm
Tegelaars was joined by Malcolm Chamberlain, a local authority leisure
manager, to head up this bid. Civic Leisure Ltd was successful in
securing the contract to manage three of the centres within the City
of Westminster.

Both Civic Leisure Ltd and Latchmere Leisure Ltd trade as
subsidiaries of their holding company Archer Securities Ltd. A third
company under the umbrella is Centre Court Tennis, set up to develop
low-cost tennis centres around the country, an initiative being
promoted in conjunction with the Lawn Tennis Association.

At this time, Queens Moat Houses, a major international hotel chain,
was seeking to introduce health and fitness into its portfolio. They
researched the market and chose Archer Securities, which, in due
course was purchased, to become a wholly owned subsidiary of
Queens Moat Houses. Civic Leisure Ltd thereby became part of a large
international company, with the advantages this brings in terms of
financial stability.

Development strategy

In 1988 Civic was also successful in being awarded a contract for the
management of Grundy Park Leisure Centre in Broxbourne,
Hertfordshire.

The company's strategy is to tender selectively only for business
which can provide a good return for the company and the local authority. They see no point in submitting tenders where there is a

hostile environment. Like many other companies, they feel that the compulsory element, although probably the only way to achieve local authority evaluation of the quality and cost effectiveness of its services, results in the exercise being looked at by many authorities as negative rather than positive.

Capital developments

Once a contract has been awarded to Civic Leisure, the company seeks to improve the facilities where possible. Being part of a large national conglomerate, the funds for capital investment in facilities are readily available, provided there is the mechanism for a commercial rate of return on the investment.

With this in mind, the company has invested around £500 000 in the City of Westminster and £250 000 at Broxbourne. This investment has been in such areas as health and fitness suites, including state of the art weights and cardiovascular equipment, spa baths saunas, beauty therapy facilities and so on. Perhaps one of the most striking examples of innovation is the turning of a disused spectator area into a steam and sauna suite at the Marshall Street Leisure Centre.

Increasing usage

The company's aim is to provide a quality leisure experience for every single customer, which has resulted in huge increases of usage in the Westminster centres. Different groups are targetted throughout the day, with a view to achieving a high level of usage at all times.

The company looks to the future with confidence. With the resources, drive and commitment to be successful, they can be sure that where there is a willing partner, anything is possible. A wide variety of further contracts, within both the private and public sectors, awaits them.

Similarly, all future contractors, whether public or private sector, will be looking to continued success. This is only possible by constant attention and continual assessment of management information.

COMPETITIVE MANAGEMENT

In a competitive environment, the contractor has two critical performance indicators.

1. Total profit or loss.
   This is the principal performance indicator used. The contractor's estimated income and expenditure (as expressed in the tender bid), has to be achieved each and every year (after allowing for inflation) otherwise a loss is made. Then the contractor ceases to trade (even in the public sector).
2. Activity profit or loss.
   For total profit to be achieved, each and every expenditure and income item has to be constantly checked against the estimated target. This is best achieved by all the staff working as a coherent delegated team.

Compete to win

By proper delegation, the facility manager is released to further reduce cost, and increase income. An aggressive leisure manager will compete to win. Key elements to the winning strategy include:

- An all-out drive to increase use by everyone;
- Targetted publicity and promotions;
- Adopting a high profile;
- Special discount rates at off peak times;
- High rates at peak times (with client approval);
- Encouraging senior citizens during the daytime;
- Waging war on overheads and unnecessary costs;
- Paying real bonus payments to staff who perform;
- Researching the market regularly;
- Providing what is requested, rather than what is there already;
- Being attentive to all users at all times.

Leisure managers will delight in the decisiveness provided by the new environment. There is nothing more satisfying than breaking through barriers. Indeed that is what management is all about; turning problems and opportunities into tangible benefits for others.

A SUMMARY OF MANAGEMENT

Management is also all about 'one-offs'. There are no two identical management problems and so no two identical solutions. There is no looseleaf management manual giving an A – Z of ready answers to likely problems. Management is just not like that, as any manager will testify.

This book has therefore emphasized the principles of management and indicated some sources for further information. By and large, these sources have not been other books but rather case studies. Also relevant current examples of good and poor management can be seen in leisure facilities in every locality.

The key criteria for successful leisure management in the 1990s and beyond are encapsulated in the chapter titles of this book. They provide a clear indication of the way forward to successful leisure management for client or contractor.

THE WAY FORWARD

Every leisure facility can be improved. Basic attention to key essentials such as customer satisfaction, financial incentives to staff, targetted marketing, precise comparisons of income and expenditure will all improve leisure facilities and their use.

Leisure has always offered a worthwhile career for dynamic people. To be purposeful now, that energy has to be directed at the management of facilities and situations, as well as at the improved pursuit of a particular sport or activity.

Strategy, tactics and a visible goal are what a team needs to succeed in any sport. Champions are bred on these three key ingredients.

Strategy, tactics and a view of the goal are equally essential for leisure managers. Every leisure manager and practitioner needs to harness the opportunities of the growing competitive environment to ensure a healthy future.

The 1990s will be a difficult and demanding decade for leisure. There will be more change in public sector management than there has been in the last 150 years. The full effects of a competitive environment will be brought to bear at regular intervals on local authority leisure facilities. This will greatly increase the profit maximizing practices of the contractor. The client authority will either abdicate responsibility and enjoy greater financial returns, or take a positive attitude towards ensuring the provision of a wide range of leisure activities within every leisure centre and every leisure facility.

WHO BENEFITS?

Finally, a word of warning: if public leisure centres become the exclusive preserve of the middle class families, then leisure management has failed.

The drive for income maximization can never be justified on these terms. The widest cross section of the community should be attracted into local leisure centres. Activities need to include coffee mornings, luncheon clubs and tea dances. Local authority leisure facilities were built for, and should remain for, everyone.

If competition means reduced costs and increased participation by a wide cross section of the community, who then can complain?

Appendix A: Outline contract documents

This appendix provides an outline of the main parts to be expected in most tender and contract documents. In addition to the outline, a few example clauses are given on the pages which follow.

1. *Instructions for Tendering*
   A formal statement of how to go about submitting the tender.
2. *Form of tender*
   Quite brief; this is the actual tender, the formal offer.
3. *Financial Summaries*
   This is the summary of anticipated income and expenditure.
4. *Draft Form of Contract*
   Brief; this is the actual written contract, when signed.
5. *Conditions of Contract*
   The rules or conditions by which the contract will be operated.
6. *Form of Bond*
   This is a guarantee from a third party to honour the contract if the appointed contractor should fail.
7. *Form of Insurance*
   Covers the contractor for normal risks.
8. *Specifications and Activity programmes*
   Many pages of specific work instructions, and activity scheduling to be provided eg. school swimming 9.30–11.30.
9. *Schedule of Rates*
   These are provided to help price events, or works, of a 'one-off' nature.
10. *Parent Company Indemnity*
    Where a small subsidiary company wins a contract this form will ensure that the parent company is responsible for any costs arising through the failure of that smaller company.

In addition there are appendices. These will include plans and maps; some demographic information about the area; recent income trends; current fees and charges; samples of forms in use etc.

A1 INSTRUCTIONS FOR TENDERING

These instructions give a formal guide to the tenderer on how to complete the tender document.

1   Preparations by the tenderer.

1.1 The tenderer will be responsible, entirely at his own expense, for obtaining all the information required to complete the tender.

1.2 When completed, the tender document will be returned in its entirety to the client. Hence two copies of the tender document are normally supplied to the contractor, so that he may retain one.

1.3 The tenderer will be required to meet the client and discuss details.

1.4 Pricing will be in pounds sterling, and two decimal places.

2   Variations

2.1 Any enquiries relating to any part of the documents are to be made in writing to the client. At his absolute discretion, the client may amend or alter any document, by giving written notification to all the tenderers.

3   Additional information to be provided.

3.1 The tenderer will enclose a copy of his current Health and Safety policy with the tender.

3.2 The tenderer is to supply an outline of working methods for two parts of the contract e.g. plant operation and catering management. This is to provide a clear demonstration of his ability to perform the contract.

4   Submission.

4.1 The completed tender is to be submitted by or before 12 noon on the stated date.

5   Acceptance and publication.

5.1 The authority does not bind itself to accept the lowest – or indeed any – tender.

5.2 The authority will publish the value of all tenders and the names of all tenderers.

A2 FORM OF TENDER

The following is the actual formal offer (or tender) from the tenderer to the client.

PUBLIC AUTHORITY XYZ
LEISURE MANAGEMENT TENDER

To the members of Public Authority XYZ
Address:

Ladies and Gentlemen

Having examined all the documents contained herein, we offer to undertake the contract for the management, maintenance, and operation of the Little London Swimming Pool entirely in accordance with these documents for the fixed price in the first year of £_____ and thereafter at a variation of that price as provided in the Conditions of Contract for a further three years.

We agree that within one calendar month of the acceptance of this tender, we will:
- enter into a formal Agreement which will bind us contractually to undertake the priced contract;
- enter into a formal performance bond;
- provide all financial information requested.

We accept that you are not bound to accept the lowest or any tender.

We are, Ladies and Gentlemen

Name of Company: _____
Authorized signatures: _____

_____

(authorized to sign on behalf of the Company)

PRINT NAMES IN FULL _____

_____

Address:
Date:

Your attention is particularly drawn to the 'Instructions for Tendering'. The tender is to be returned, sealed in the envelope provided, to the Authority's office, at the address stated above, before noon on _____. Tenders received after this time WILL NOT be considered.

A3 FINANCIAL SUMMARIES

The information stated on this page will detail the income and expenditure anticipated by the tenderer. The final total will then be transferred to the previous page as the tendered sum. As with all other sections of the documents, the size of this section varies from authority to authority. It may be just one page in length, or extend to many pages, profiled across the four years of the contract.

LITTLE LONDON SWIMMING POOL

Expenditure for Year 1 of the contract

On these pages, the tenderer is to detail all expenditure and income anticipated in the first year of the contract.

EXPENDITURE ITEMS   £

Manpower

Management and office staff
Operational staff
Other (state)

Supplies and Services

Utilities; heat, water, and power
Specialist services
Supplies, materials and chemicals
Other (state)

Other costs

Central establishment charges
(head office)
Business rates, insurances
Leasing and debt charges
Other (state)   _____

Expenditure Total   £

_____

LITTLE LONDON SWIMMING POOL

Income for Year 1 of the contract

INCOME ITEMS   £

Entrance fees

Adult
Youth
Unwaged

Special sessions

Women
Ethnic
Fun sessions
Learn to swim
Club
Other (state)

Vending (net)

Food
Drink
Other (state)

Sales

Swim wear
Booklets
Other (state)   _____

Income total   £
                                   _____

LITTLE LONDON SWIMMING POOL

TOTALS   £

Expenditure
Income   _____

Therefore: TENDER BID   £
                                   _____

(transfer to Form of Tender)

A4 DRAFT FORM OF CONTRACT

The example given below provides a summary guideline to the type
of contract which will be signed by both parties (client and contractor).

LITTLE LONDON SWIMMING POOL

This agreement is made this day of _____ between
Public Authority XYZ (referred to subsequently as 'the client') and
Contractor ABC (referred to subsequently as the 'contractor').

The client has accepted the tender submitted by the contractor, for
the management, maintenance and operation of the Little London
Swimming Pool entirely in accordance with these documents for the
fixed price in the first year of £_____ and thereafter at a
variation of that price as provided in the Conditions of Contract for
a further three years from _____ (date), to the continued
satisfaction of the client.

All the documents contained within the tender numbered 1 to 10,
together with all other documents/letters stated, will now form part
of this Agreement.

The client hereby undertakes to pay the contractor the agreed
payments, at the frequency, and in the manner, stated in the
conditions.

Signed:
(for the client)

Mayor: _____
Witness: _____

(for the contractor)

Director: _____
Witness   _____

A5 CONDITIONS OF CONTRACT

The conditions stated here only cover, in brief outline, an example of some of the more important conditions of contract, which will frequently occur.

1. Definitions
(a) Client: the Public Authority XYZ
(b) Contractor: the company or individual who submitted the tender which has been accepted.
(c) Supervising Officer: the officer of the client who has been formally introduced to the contractor as the Supervising Officer.
(d) (All other important, frequently occurring terms will be defined.)

2. Contract period
Four years, with an option to extend for an additional two years.

3. The Facility and premises are as stated in the documents and shown on the accompanying plans, which identify each room included in the contract and the outside curtilage.

4. Use of the Authority's Premises
The Authority shall during the contract period permit the Contractor to use the premises only for the provision of the services stated in this contract, and the contractor will only use the premises for these stated services. The permission given is personal to the contractor and staff and shall cease immediately the contract terminates. The permission to enter and use the premises is not the grant of a tenancy of any part of the premises.

5. Quality of service
The quality of service is to be entirely in accordance with the contract documents, and to the satisfaction of the client and his Supervising Officer. A requirement to attain BS 5750 Quality Assurance certification is included.

6. Payments
The contractor will submit to the client, at the end of each month, a detailed financial statement of all income and expenditure (and usage figures) from the previous month in the format stated by the client, together with an invoice, stating the sums to which the contractor considers himself entitled (including any variation agreed in writing by the client). The client will pay all agreed invoices within one calendar month thereafter.

7. Staff
(a) Only able and competent staff will be employed

(b) . . . race relations.
(c) . . . health and safety at work.
(d) . . . identification of staff.

8. Supervision

9. British Standards

10. Opening hours

11. Indemnity and insurance

12. Annual price increases allowed for inflation

13. Assignment
Assignment of this contract, in part or in full, will not be allowed unless specific prior written permission has been given by the client to another named contractor approved by the client.

14. Termination
The client may terminate the contract if:
(a) the contractor has offered or accepted any inducement in attempting to secure the contract;
(b) the contractor commits any breach of obligation as stated in this contract;
(c) the contractor becomes bankrupt, or insolvent, or goes into receivership; and if the contract is terminated, then:
(d) the client is permitted to employ other contractors to undertake the works, entirely at the expense of the original contractor; this expense to form a debt on that contractor.

15. Arbitration
Where a dispute exists between the client and contractor, and it cannot be satisfactorily settled by negotiation between the two parties, the matter will be referred to an independent arbitrator to obtain a decision.

A6 FORM OF BOND

The bond will literally bond a third party to cover any costs resulting from poor performance by the contractor, where the contractor is unable to meet these costs himself. Again, only an outline bond is given here.

By this bond, we the contractor whose registered office is at___ _____ together with the financial company/bank/ insurance company, whose registered office is at _____ are bound to the Public Authority XYZ to the value of £

It be hereby understood by both parties that the Contractor has entered into a contract with Public Authority XYZ for the management, maintenance and operation of the Little London Swimming Pool entirely in accordance with the contract documents.

The Conditions of the Bond are that if the Contractor does not satisfy all or part of the contract, then the financial company/bank/insurance company will meet the costs incurred by Public Authority XYZ in carrying out the management, maintenance and operation of the Little London Swimming Pool to the full amount of this Bond.

Signed:
(for the financial company)

Director: _____
Witness: _____
Date: _____

Signed:
(for the contractor)

Director: _____
Witness: _____
Date: _____

A7 FORM OF INSURANCE

This form, when duly completed, provides evidence to the client as to the exact insurance cover being provided to the contractor. In the event of any claim resulting during the operation of the contract, all costs are to be fully covered. The indemnity ensures that the responsibility rests entirely with the contractor, and not the client.

To the Members of Public Authority XYZ
Address:

This is to certify that

Contractor: _____

who is to undertake the management, maintenance and operation of the Little London Swimming Pool entirely in accordance with the contract documents for Public Authority XYZ, is covered in respect of all risks referred to within the Conditions of Contract.

The Policy number is: _____
and expiry date is: _____

The limit of liability for any one accident is £5 000 000.

Insurers: _____

Address: _____

Authorized signature: _____
(authorized by the Insurance
Company to sign on behalf
of the Company)

PRINT NAME IN FULL _____

Witness: _____

Date: _____

A8 SPECIFICATIONS

There will be many pages of detailed instructions specifying exactly how to carry out all the works. In addition, there will be detailed programmes of use; eg. synchronized swimming on Thursday evenings.

AN EXAMPLE CLEANING SPECIFICATION

1. The Contractor will enter into an agreement with the Authority paying the appropriate charge to provide a bulk refuse disposal service for all waste, litter etc., emanating from the facility.

2. The Contractor will:
   a) supply and fit suitable toilet tissue dispensers in each w.c. compartment – daily;
   b) fill liquid soap dispensers above each wash hand basin – daily;
   c) clean and fill tissue dispensers for hand drying – daily;
   d) empty and clean the sanitary towel disposal bin in each female w.c. compartment – daily;
   e) empty and clean all litter bins, ash trays and containers and used hand-drying tissues.

3. The Contractor will ensure that all soaps, chemicals, cleaning materials and all other materials are approved in writing by the client prior to use and are properly labelled, securely stored and used only in accordance with the manufacturer's instructions.

4. The Contractor will clean the building in the manner and to the frequencies and schedules as now stated;

   a) the Contractor will, every 28 days . . . .
   b)
   c)

Appendix B provides a fuller insight into specification writing.

A9 SCHEDULE OF RATES

A schedule of the contractor's rates (or prices) will often be required in addition to the Financial Summaries. This will provide an accurate base from which to price 'one – off' events; or to price additional works where needed; or to determine the contractor's financial liability in a default situation.

Item no.	Brief description	Unit of measure- ment	Rate £.p
R.1	Provision of the manager	per hour	
R.2	Provision of a supervisor	per hour	
R.3	Provision of a lifeguard or receptionist	per hour	
R.4	Provision of the pool, without personnel; 00.00 – 06.00 06.00 – 09.00 09.00 – 12.00 12.00 – 18.00 18.00 – 22.00 22.00 – 00.00	per hour	
R.5	Any additional supplement to R.4 for; Bank Holidays Saturdays Sundays	per hour	
R.6	To raise air temperatures	per 1%C	
R.7	To raise water temperatures	per 1%C	
R.8	To lower air temperatures	per 1%C	
R.9	To lower water temperatures	per 1%C	
R.10	To gloss paint woodwork, entirely as stated in Specification P. 261	per $10m^2$	

The tenderer will complete the final column and return to the Authority with the tender.

A10 PARENT COMPANY INDEMNITY

Where a subsidiary company is to undertake a contract, the client will wish to ensure that it has sufficient capability and financial resources to fulfil its obligations. There is no better method open to the client than to require a formal and binding statement from the parent company (although the Bond will provide similar protection).

This Agreement is made this day of _____
between Public Authority XYZ (referred to subsequently as 'the client') and the parent company of the contractor ABC (referred to subsequently as the 'parent company').

Whereas the client has entered into a contract with contractor ABC, the parent company has now agreed to indemnify the client in the event of any failure of due performance by contractor ABC, howsoever caused.

The indemnity is to cover any and all losses, claims, costs, expenses or damages, howsoever arising – being due to the breach of any part of the contract between the client and contractor, and entirely in accordance with the contract between the client and contractor ABC.

Should this indemnity come into operation, the parent company will be bound entirely by the totality of the contract, without variation, between the client and contractor ABC.

Signed:
(for the client)

Mayor: _____

Witness: _____

Signed:
(for the parent company)

Director: _____

Witness: _____

Appendix B: Preparing specifications

INTRODUCTION

Due to the importance of specifications this appendix provides a method by which to start preparing these all important documents.

Although normally associated with the contract documents themselves specifications can also be provided as part of:

* job description for each individual employee
* the documentation necessary to ensure consistent quality

Only by providing detailed specifications can the contractor (or the client) ensure an adequate and consistent service delivery. The days of 'management by assumption' have gone. Each employee's work needs to be in harmony with everyone else.

Staff uniforms are a good example. With distinctive clothing, contrasting with the background decor, a very distinctive impression of a facility is made possible. For this to be achieved, someone needs to sit down and specify the type and style of clothing and then make arrangements to purchase it.

Similarly, specifications are needed for all the other many requirements of a successful leisure operation. Consistent performance is only achieved as a result of the continual application of consistent practices.

In a contract situation, as well as consistent service delivery, critical attention is needed to the contractor/client division. Specifications need to clearly differentiate between client and contractor responsibilities.

Again a simple example will bring all these aspects into high relief.

If during a contract, a heating boiler ceases to function, who is responsible? Furthermore, can the contractor justify a claim for loss of income from the client?

This simple example has many ramifications. The impact is clear to see.

As with most leisure management specifications, there is no one right answer. The particular arrangements for one centre (with one age and type of boiler) will be different to another.

All industries which have been operating by contract for many years (eg. building maintenance) have learnt one lesson the hard way. That is; how essential it is to have detailed specifications. The aim of this appendix is therefore to assist in addressing the problems and requirements in preparing specifications for a leisure facility.

However, a complex leisure centre could take more than 50 man weeks of work to prepare comprehensive specifications. Clearly, no one person could undertake this task. Indeed it is doubtful that any one person would have sufficient expertise to undertake all the necessary writing.

A team effort is essential.

There is no better method than involving everyone in the provision of the specifications. The example form provided next gives a method by which a start can be made on preparing specifications by the staff themselves.

And the right time to start is NOW. No matter how detailed the specifications provided as part of the original contract, omissions will have been made. Also, as time passes, additions and changes will be necessary.

Specification writing is not just a 'once every 4 year' task. Good specifications should continually be evolved and put into practice.

B1 A TEAM EFFORT

This form is for completion by everyone employed in a leisure facility
– to provide a detailed summary of all tasks currently being undertaken. The key requirements in completing the form include:

* one form per day or per shift
* each person to complete the form every half hour
* state all the tasks carried out
* when repeating a task, a brief note will suffice
* especial attention to any unusual or "one off" tasks carried out
* continue for one week, or one month

It is important to stress to participants that the time they take doing
each task is unimportant. The half hour "slots" are to act as a prompt,
not as a time study.

Name _____ Day/Date _____ Job _____

Time	*Work Area*	*Tasks Undertaken*	*Comments*
.00			
.30			
.00			
.30			
.00			
.30			
.00			
.30			
.00			
.30			
.00			
.30			
.00			
.30			
.00			
.30			
.00			
.30			
.00			
.30			
.00			
.30			
.00			
.30			

Any general comments?

_____
_____
_____

B2 MAINTENANCE REQUIREMENTS

This next form provides a basis for the maintenance requirements of a centre to be listed. It can be adapted for use in any room. Start at the ceiling and list all the elements, fixtures and fittings, which will need to be adequately maintained and managed for adequate service delivery.

For example.

Room Name Number and Function	Item	Maintenance Detail	Frequency	Specification Applicable
Reception Room 1	Ceiling	Repaint	3rd year	ABC 123
	Lights 2x 6ft fluor.	Wash diffuser	6 monthly	DEF 456
		Replace tube when flickering or out	Immediately	GHI 789
	Ventilator (extract)	Wash	6 monthly	DEF 456
		Replace Filter	Annually	JKL 101

Date room surveyed _____ Surveyor _____

Agreed for the Contractor ____ Name _____ Date _____

Agreed for the Client _____ Name _____ Date _____

This is a relatively simple system to adopt. The sheer size of the task is the only difficulty. That is why a team effort is essential. The task needs to be repeated for each and every room in each and every leisure facility. There is no other way to ensure adequate contract management and maintenance. Photographs of every room taken just before contract commencement and termination, with both contractor and client representatives present, are an invaluable reference source.

B3 SOME SPECIFICATIONS

An index of some of the more important specifications in a leisure management contract will include:

Durable equipment.
Renewable equipment.
Consumable equipment.
Approved chemicals; cleaning materials.
Maintenance and repair.
Staff qualifications and ongoing training.
Staff levels.
Sponsorship.
Advertising; publicity.
Stationery.
Opening hours.
Programming.
Booking systems; procedures.
Marketing.
Use of sub–contractors e.g. physiotherapy.
Pool maintenance.
Pool management.
Reception.
Cleaning.
Licences.
The list goes on seemingly endlessly.

Provided on the following pages are examples of how to start preparing specifications for a comprehensive leisure management contract document. If desired, the format can be changed to that necessary for job descriptions.

B4 DURABLE EQUIPMENT

1. Fundamental Requirements
   What specific and particular requirements are needed in relation
   to the provision and replacement of durable equipment to ensure
   a satisfactory service delivery?
   Make a list: eg. boilers, toilets

2. Then adapt to a specification format.
   Adapt the list into single sentences, which clearly state exactly
   what the contractor (or member of staff) has to do.

3. Write the specification
   The contractor shall,

   1.
   2.
   3.
   4.
   5.
   6.
   7.
   8.
   9.
   10.

B5 RENEWABLE EQUIPMENT

1. Fundamental Requirements
   What specific and particular requirements are needed to ensure a satisfactory service delivery from equipment which will need renewing during the life of the contract?

   Make a list: eg. nets, curtains

2. Adapt to a specification format
   Adapt the list into single sentences, which clearly state exactly what the contractor (or member of staff) has to do.

3. Write the specification
   The contractor shall,
   1.
   2.
   3.
   4.
   5.
   6.
   7.
   8.
   9.
   10.

   This format can be adapted to use on all the categories of specification listed in Appendix B3.

B6 MONITORING PERFORMANCE

Performance monitoring measures are also an essential feature for successful management. In addition to the financial performance measures, other monitoring measures include:

Specific targets to be achieved.
Checks on compliance to specifications.
Qualifications and training.
Quality Assurance (BS 5750)
Meetings
* daily (for ongoing liaison)
* weekly (for programme checks;
  and to review last week, next week)
* monthly (targets)
* quarterly (financial)
* user groups; clubs etc.
Complaints.
Customer Surveys.
Defaults.

Again these can all be written in a specification format.

Appendix C: Government directives

A book of this nature cannot be complete without a brief resume of the principal aspects of the legislation and government requirements in relation to competitive tendering. That then is the intention of this appendix. It should be emphasized however, that the appendix is but a brief resume, and does not attempt to interpret the legislation. The law is continually changing, being amended and updated. Professional legal advice should always be sought in respect of any contract situation.

However, for those involved in public sector leisure provision, it is important to be aware of the more important issues. It is essential that tender procedures and the operation of contracts are in accordance with these directives. The element of compulsion on local authorities is quite clear in the directives.

The list in this appendix only summarizes the more important instructions. It is provided for background information only. For guidance in specific issues it is essential to refer to the actual government document stated together with any amendments which have been made.

THE LOCAL GOVERNMENT ACT 1988

The Act clearly states its objectives at the outset. The very first sentence reads:

"An Act to ensure that local and other public authorities undertake certain activities only if they can do so competitively."

The Act refers to services like refuse collection, grounds maintenance, catering, building cleaning and other similar maintenance services, (sport and leisure management being added later).

Part I Competition

Section 1. Defined Authorities.
This first section of the Act states all the authorities covered by the Act.

Section 2. Defined Activities.
This section defines all the activities subjected to compulsory competitive tendering eg. cleaning of buildings, catering, maintenance of grounds although detailed definitions are left to Schedule 1 of the Act.

The Statutory Instrument (1989: No. 2488) added sports and leisure management into the Act, in this section – as detailed in the addendum to chapter 1.

Section 3. Other Definitions.
Other terms are defined here.

Section 4. Works Contracts: Restrictions.
A defined authority may not enter into a contract unless:

* an invitation to tender has been extended to at least three persons who are willing to carry out the contract and who are not defined authorities.
* the intention to let a contract must be advertized in at least one local newspaper and at least one specialist national publication (ie. one which circulates among leisure contractors).
* an authority cannot do anything which may have the effect of restricting or distorting or preventing competition.

Section 5. Works Contracts: Transitional.

Section 6. Functional Work: Restrictions.

Section 7. The Conditions.
This section states the manner in which contractors are to be invited to tender. The key features are:

* advertisements must include brief descriptions of the work and a statement that interested contractors may freely inspect, or buy a copy of the detailed specification; and that interested contractors should notify the authority of their interest, by the time stated in the advertisement.
* between three and six months following the advertisement, authorities are to invite tenders from at least three applicants who are not defined authorities (or less than three, if less than three apply).
* an authority's in house contractor is to prepare and submit a written bid indicating their wish to carry out the work (in the same manner as external contractors).

Section 8. The Conditions: Further Provisions.

Section 9.   Accounts to be kept.
Detailed accounts are to be kept (separately) for each defined activity.

Section 10.   Financial Objectives to be met.

Section 11.   Report for the Financial Year.

Section 12.   Information.
Where an authority awards a contract for a defined service, then the authority is to provide a statement of the decision and the financial details of all tenders received, including that of the in-house bid, to anyone who requests such information.

Section 13.   Notice for purpose of getting information.
This section requires an authority to provide information to the Secretary of State where it appears that a contract has been awarded in contravention of the legislation.

Section 14.   Power to give Directions.
This section allows the Secretary of State to direct an authority to limit or cease in-house work (invariably after an investigation, following a section 13 notice).

Section 15.   Orders, Regulations, Specifications and Directions.
This section allows amendments and additions to the Act by means of Statutory Instruments (following approval by both Houses of Parliament).

Section 16.   Supplementary.

Part II Public Supply or Works Contracts

Section 17.   Local and other public authority contracts: exclusion of non–commercial considerations.
This section states a number of non–commercial considerations (eg. political affiliations), which cannot be considered when awarding a contract.

Section 18.   Race Relations matters.

Section 19.   Provisions supplementary to, or consequential on, Section 17.

Section 20.   Duty of public authorities to give reasons for certain decisions within section 17.

Section 21.   Transitional duty of public authorities as regards existing lists.

Section 22.   Exclusion of charges for inclusion in approved list.

Section 23.   Commencement.

The Act then covers other matters.

Part III   Privately Let Housing Accommodation
Part IV   Miscellaneous and General

Schedules
The Schedules to Acts of Parliament are always important. For example, Schedule 1 of this Act contains the detailed definitions of activities subject to compulsory competitive tendering.
It is important to note that the Act is an 'enabling Act'. Thus additions and changes are easily possible (by Statutory Instrument – see Section 15 above).

STATUTORY INSTRUMENTS

The Secretary of State for the Environment may take regulations (and in effect, amend the Act) via the powers contained in Section 15 of the Act. For example: Statutory Instrument 1988: No. 1371 provided for a phasing of all contracts, across all defined authorities, so as to allow the gradual introduction of competitive tendering. For ground maintenance, work had to be let to tender in tranches of not less than 20% per year, over a maximum period of five years.

Other Statutory Instruments are issued from time to time. One of the most important, as regards sports and leisure management, is summarized in the addendum to chapter 1.

GOVERNMENT CIRCULARS

Some of the principal government advice and guidance is contained within circulars issued from relevant ministries from time to time (eg. the Department of the Environment, the Welsh Office).

The aim of circulars is to draw to the attention of authorities certain aspects of the legislation to which the Secretary of State attaches particular importance, and where clarification is needed on certain issues.

One circular issued by the Department of the Environment (No. 8/88) and the Welsh Office (No. 12/88) detailed a number of non commercial matters.

The circular builds on Part II of the Act and is designed to prevent authorities discriminating against particular contractors due to political matters which are irrelevant to the contract process.

Some of the non commercial matters which the authorities are not allowed to consider include:

* rates of pay
* the area of residence of the workforce
* the number or proportion of apprentices or women employed
* and other matters

The circular does however state that authorities may make reasonable enquiries about the contractor's health and safety records, and may ask questions about the qualifications of a contractor's workforce.

a specific race relations questionnaire is included with the circular (reproduced in this book within the addendum to chapter 2).

On the 8 August 1988, a further circular was issued from the Department of the Environment. Some matters of specific interest in relation to leisure management include the following:

* licensed bars were seen as being incorporated within the Act;
* this circular contained the first formal announcement that sports and leisure management would be brought into the provisions of the Act from 1 January 1992.
* the £100 000 'de minimis' threshold was clarified. If the estimated gross cost to an authority of carrying out a defined activity, exceeds £100 000 in any one financial year, then the whole of that activity has to be exposed to competition. Conversely, if the gross cost is less than £100 000 (for the activity as a whole), then the activity is considered 'de minimis' and need not be subject to competition.
* detailed specifications are to be available three to six months before the formal tender invitations.
* anti-competitive behaviour can include:
  contracts being packaged into large amounts;
  allowing too little time for a contractor to respond to a tender;
  seeking detailed and sensitive information about companies which goes beyond that needed to assess their ability to carry out work properly;
  seeking excessive performance bonds;
* it is accepted within the circular that the cost of redundancy to an authority may be taken into account when assessing the total value of tender bids, once.
* the minimum and maximum lengths of the contracts are stated (e.g. 4–6 years) before an authority has to retender (where the authorities in house contractor is operating the contract).
* a 5% rate of return on capital employed is specified for most of the CCT defined activities.

So, although this appendix provides a brief overview of the legislation, it can be seen that it is continually changing in the light of experience. The law is rarely static.

Appendix D: Customer satisfaction surveys

INTRODUCTION

The importance of satisfying the customer means the difference between profit and loss. For the client, customer satisfaction is a clear indication of the success or otherwise of the contract.

The success of the contract of course, relies as much on the client as on the contractor or client responsibilities. The customer will not differentiate between contractor or client responsibilities nor distinguish between an element of service which is, or is not, detailed in the contract.

All the customer will perceive is the service as it affects his or her use of the facility. There is no better indicator available to contractor or client.

Regular customer perception surveys should therefore be an integral feature of every contract. The results will help the contractor sharpen service delivery in areas which are seen by customers to be poor, or less than adequate. The results will also prompt the client to change the contract to more closely reflect the needs of leisure facility users.

A customer perception survey should not be confused with a market research survey. A market research survey will critically analyse, in depth, all aspects of the market place and clearly indicate how to change a leisure facility to accomodate the desires and demands of the catchment area.

This appendix is provided as an illustration of a possible customer perception survey. Regular use will benefit everyone. The results will provide hard factual information which cannot be disputed. For accuracy, every tenth customer leaving the facility should complete a form. A member of staff will be needed to encourage and assist.

Spare copies of the form may be made available for anyone to complete. However, it is absolutely essential that these returns are analysed separately from the 'every tenth' customer survey. The head Receptionist could undertake the delegated responsibility for analysing all returns.

LITTLE LONDON SWIMMING POOL

YOUR VIEWS PLEASE

We would like to know your views about the Little London Swimming Pool. This will help us plan changes and improve – for your benefit.

Please place completed forms in the red box at reception. Each completed form will be entered in

A FREE PRIZE DRAW

Place one tick in each section or add in the information requested. First, a few details about your visit.

Have you been: Using the:

   1. Swimming   2. The health suite
      Spectating   Sauna/Solarium
      Neither   Neither

Other (please state) _____

Are you:

   3. In a group   4. A regular
      Family   At least weekly
      Friends   At least monthly
      On own   6–12 visits per year
      None of these   Less often

   5. Taking lessons   6. A club member
      Beginners   Amateur Swimming
      Improvers   Sub Aqua
      Competitive   Synchronized
      None of these   None of these

Now a few details about yourself.

   7. Male   Female

   8. Age   9. Working or not
      under 10   Full time
      11–18   Part time
      19–24   Student
      25–34   Unemployed
      35–44   Retired
      45–54   Not working
      55–64   and not seeking work
      65+   None of these

If working, please state

10. Your job _____
    (title or type)

How good do you think we are?

	Very Good	Good	Fair	Poor
11. Value for money				
12. Reception area				
13. Changing rooms				
14. Toilets				
15. Helpfulness of staff				
16. Cleanliness				
17. Water temperature				
18. Air temperature				
19. Signs				
20. Catering				
21. Your visit overall				

22. What was the worst aspect of your visit?
    _____

23. What was the best aspect of your visit?
    _____

24. State any (minor) improvements you wish to see.
    _____
    _____

25. Are you prepared to pay slightly more if these improve-
    ments are implemented?   Yes/No

Finally a few general questions.

26. How did you get here?
    Walked
    On a bicycle
    By car
    By bus
    None of these

27. Where do you see or
    hear of us?
    Noticeboards
    Leaflets
    Local radio
    Local papers

28. Would you like details of our special promotions mailed to
    your home (£1.00 per year)?   Yes/No

29. What papers, if any, do you read regularly?
    National _____
    Local _____

30. How would you describe your ethnic group?
    Black/Afro–Caribbean/African
    Asian   White   Other

THANK YOU FOR YOUR HELP AND ASSISTANCE.

To be entered into the free prize draw, please leave your name and address:

Name: _____

Address: _____

Postcode: _____

Appendix E: Acknowledgements and references

This appendix provides a comprehensive list of the various specialist sources of information used, or referred to, in the book.

The Audit Commission for Local Authorities
in England and Wales
1 Vincent Square,
London SW1P 2PN

Acknowledgement is given to The Audit Commission, and to the Controller of Her Majesty's Stationery Office, for various extracts contained within the book; and especially from the publications entitled *Sport for Whom* 1989, and Management Paper No. 6 *Management Buy-Outs: Public Interest or Private Gain?'* 1990. These publications may be purchased from Her Majesty's Stationery Office, at the address given below.

The British Quality Association.
10 Grosvenor Gardens,
London SW1W 0DQ

Thanks are due for permission to reproduce part of their document *Quality Assurance, Cleansing Services, Grounds Maintenance and Leisure Facilities* as an addendum to chapter 11.

The BQA Leisure Services Quality Committee,
c/o The Sports Council,
16 Upper Woburn Place,
London WC1H 0QP

This Committee has produced a valuable publication: 'Quality Assurance for Leisure Services', which includes leisure management case studies where a Quality Assurance system has been introduced.

Circa Leisure plc.
Clements Hall Leisure Centre,
Clements Hall Way,
Hawkwell,
Essex SS5 4LN

Grateful acknowledgement is given to Peter Johnson for agreeing to the case studies in relation to Circa Leisure plc contained in chapters 5 and 10.

City Centre Leisure,
35 Shouldham Street,
London W1H 5FP

Grateful acknowledgement is also due to Phil Reid and Roger Bottomley of City Centre Leisure. Their experiences in relation to tendering and buyouts is detailed in chapters 5 and 10.

Civic Leisure Ltd,
New Malden House,
1 Blagdon Road,
New Malden,
Surry KT3 4TB

Many thanks are due to Chris Lightfoot for providing details about the origins and development of Civic Leisure Ltd, in chapter 13.

The Cornell H.R.A. Quarterly
School of Hotel Administration,
20 Thornwood Drive,
Suite 106,
Ithaca,
NY 14850
USA

Acknowledgement is due to the Editor for allowing reference to the Quality Circle given in chapter 11.

Crossland Leisure,
Playground, Westfield Lido,
West Ham Park,
Basingstoke,
Hampshire RG22 6PG.

Acknowledgement is given to the information made available by John Staniland of Crossland Leisure.

Great Western Royal Hotel,
Praed Street,
London W2 1HE

Gratitude is expressed to Mr. Kneer, who gave a most useful insight into hotel management in London. The case study in chapter 7, provides details.

Harperley Hotel,
Harperley Country Park,
Stanley,
Co. Durham DH9 9TY

Acknowledgement is given to Mr. Morris, for sharing his own business skills which helped transform a local authority hotel in County Durham, detailed in chapter 7.

Her Majesty's Stationery Office
(Publications Division – Copyright).

Material from the Audit Commission (listed above); extracts from the Local Government Act 1988, the Statutory Instrument detailed in the addendum to the first chapter and the resume of government directives in Appendix C are reproduced by permission of the Controller of Her Majesty's Stationery Office.

Publications are available by post or telephone:

HMSO Publications Centre,
PO Box 276,
London SW8 5DT
Tel. 071 873 9090
general enquiries: 071 873 0011
or through HMSO Bookshops or accredited agents (see Yellow Pages) and through good booksellers.

Innsite Hotel Services Limited,
Innsite House,
Park Lane,
Cranford,
Hounslow,
Middlesex TW5 9RW

Acknowledgement is given to Innsite Hotel Services Ltd for the use of their details in the addendum to chapter 8.

The Institute of Baths and Recreation Management,
Giffard House,
36–38 Sherrard Street,
Melton Mowbray,
Leicestershire LE13 1XJ

The Institute of Leisure and Amenity Management,
Lower Basildon,
Reading,
Berkshire RG8 9NE

Grateful acknowledgement is due to ILAM/IBRM and their working party members for the production of the definitive guide to leisure management contract documentation *ILAM Competitive Tendering: Management of Sports and Leisure Facilities 1990*.

Longman Industry and Public Service Management,
6th Floor,
Westgate House,
The High,
Harlow,
Essex CM20 1YR

Acknowledgement is due for the reproduction of the extracts from *ILAM Competitive Tendering: Management of Sports and Leisure Facilities 1990*, contained in the addendum to chapters 2 and 5.

Quota Computer Associates Ltd,
Ivy House,
High Street,
Shrivenham,
Swindon SN6 8AW

Acknowledgement is given to Quota Computer Associates Ltd., for the reproduction of their information in the addendum to chapter 4. The company has provided a number of specialist applications for leisure management purposes.

Alex Sayer Project Services
Arcade Chambers
Bognor Regis
West Sussex
PO21 1LL
Also of London

Thanks are due to Alex Sayer Project services. Their experienced qualified building surveyors, available on a consultancy basis, provide advice on all aspects of leisure centre building – not just the project management and design of new centres but also the ongoing maintenance and refurbishment of existing centres. They are always pleased to advise and to carry out necessary surveys, negotiations etc.

The Sports Council,
see 'The BQA Committee' above

The Sports Council,
Greater London and South East Region,
PO Box 480,
Crystal Palace National Sports Centre,
Ledrington Road,
London SE19 2BQ

Acknowledgement is given to the Greater London and South East Region Sports Council for permission to reproduce their Management Paper Measuring Performance, contained in the addendum to chapter 9. A debt of gratitude is owed to the joint authors, Chris Hespe, Alan Sillitoe and John Thorpe for collating this information into one single source.

The Target Group Index,
British Market Research Bureau Ltd,
Saunders House,
53 The Mall,
London W5 3TE

Grateful acknowledgement is given for the permission to reproduce the information supplied in the addendum to chapter 12 and the time and trouble taken by Philip Mitchell.

Thamesdown Borough Council,
Oasis Leisure Centre,
North Star Avenue,
Swindon,
Wilts SN2 1EP

The Oasis has the proud record of being the first local authority leisure centre to achieve registration to BS 5750: Quality Assurance. For the brief reference made possible in chapter 11, I am indebted to Graham Swatton and Martin Sheppard.

I should also like to place on record my appreciation to everyone who has helped in the production of this book, whether listed above or not. The book was only made possible through the widespread and generous support given by so many. Finally, and of particular importance to a book of this nature, I would like to place on record my personal appreciation to Rose – the graphic artist who provided the illustrations to the text.

Index